COMMUNITY RENEWAL
THROUGH MUNICIPAL INVESTMENT

COMMUNITY RENEWAL THROUGH MUNICIPAL INVESTMENT

A Handbook for Citizens and Public Officials

Edited by Roger L. Kemp

McFarland & Company, Inc., Publishers
Jefferson, North Carolina, and London

The present work is a reprint of the library bound edition of
Community Renewal Through Municipal Investment: A
Handbook for Citizens and Public Officials, *first published*
in 2003 by McFarland.

LIBRARY OF CONGRESS CATALOGUING-IN-PUBLICATION DATA

Community renewal through municipal investment : a handbook
for citizens and public officials / edited by Roger L. Kemp
p.   cm.
Includes bibliographical references and index.

ISBN-13: 978-0-7864-3156-4
(softcover : 50# alkaline paper) ∞

1. Urban renewal — United States — Case studies.
2. Municipal budgets — United States — Case studies.
3. Community development — United States — Case studies.
I. Kemp, Rober L.
HT175.C627   2007   307.3'416'0973—dc21   2003003656

British Library cataloguing data are available

Cover photograph ©2007 PhotoSpin

Manufactured in the United States of America

McFarland & Company, Inc., Publishers
Box 611, Jefferson, North Carolina 28640
www.mcfarlandpub.com

Jonathan and Wendy,
may you always reach for the stars

ACKNOWLEDGMENTS

Grateful acknowledgment is made to the following organizations and publishers for granting permission to reprint the material contained in this volume.

American Planning Association
Congressional Quarterly, Inc.
Government Finance Officers Association
Nolan Media LLC

PRIMEDIA Business Magazines & Media
  Inc.
Urban Land Institute

CONTENTS

PREFACE

Local public officials, in increasing numbers, are making public investment decisions in their own communities to both enhance the quality of life, as well as to improve economic development conditions. Public officials are beginning to realize that they can plant the seeds of revitalization, renew their downtowns and neighborhoods, as well as attract private investment.

These new programs are not municipal give-away programs, or what some conservatives would call corporate welfare programs. Rather, they represent the efforts of public officials to invest wisely in their downtowns and neighborhoods with the goal of revitalizing them, and to bring citizens downtown in record numbers. They hope that business and commerce will follow.

The case studies contained in this volume are highlighted below showing the name of each city and state represented in these case studies, as well as the states and regions that these cities and towns represent. The types of municipal investments and their major groupings are also shown, along with a brief description of the appendices contained in this volume.

- *Case Studies*— Atlanta, Baltimore, Baton Rouge, Berkeley, Boulder, Cambridge, Mass., Charleston, S.C., Chattanooga, Chesterfield County, Va., Chicago, Cleveland, Denver, DuPont, Wash., Grand Forks, N.D., Hampton, Va., Hartford, Hayward, Calif., Houston, Kansas City, Mo., Lake Worth, Fla., Little Rock, Madi-

son, Wis., Minneapolis, Nashville, New Bedford, Mass., Newark, N.J., Oakland, Calif., Orlando, Petaluma, Calif., Portland, Ore., Saint Paul, Minn., Santa Monica, Calif., Seattle, Toronto, and Washington, D.C.

- *States Represented*— Arkansas, California, Colorado, Connecticut, Florida, Georgia, Illinois, Louisiana, Maryland, Massachusetts, Minnesota, Missouri, New Jersey, North Dakota, Ohio, Oregon, South Carolina, Texas, Tennessee, Ontario, Virginia, Washington, Wisconsin.

- *Regions Represented*— Central Canada (1), Four Corners (2), Grant Lakes (3), New England (3), Middle Atlantic (5), North Central (4), Northwestern (3), South Central (3), Southeastern (6), and Southwestern (5).

- *Types of Municipal Investment*— Arts centers, arts districts, business improvements districts, libraries and museums, master planning, new land uses, parks and open spaces, streetscape and walkways, transportation systems and options, revised street patterns, revisions to zoning codes, train stations, waterways, riverfronts and shoreline areas.

- *Major Investment Groups*— Business Improvement Districts, Cultural and Historical Amenities, Protection and Restoration of Nature, Parks and Open Spaces, Planning Process and Codes, General Public Improvements, Revised Street Patterns, Streetscapes and Walkways, and Public Transit Systems.

- *Appendices*— A *Regional Resource Directory*,

1

a *National Resource Directory*, and a *Bibliography*. The *Regional Resource Directory* includes a listing of those local government organizations and special district agencies included in the case studies in this volume. The *National Resource Directory* lists those major professional associations and research organizations serving municipal governments in the field of development and redevelopment. The *Bibliography* provides a comprehensive list of books, monographs, articles, and other sources in the evolving field.

These case studies reflect state-of-the-art practices in the area of municipal investment. Only the best case studies available are examined in this volume. The munici-

pal investment strategies and options examined are typically applied in a piecemeal and incremental manner. For the most part, public officials are doing their own thing within their own political jurisdiction.

For this reason, the case studies on municipal self-investment contained in this volume represent an important codification of knowledge in this field. The volume collects, for the first time, materials based on a national literature search, and makes it available to citizens and public officials throughout the United States.

Roger L. Kemp
Meriden, CT
April 2003

CHAPTER 1

MUNICIPAL SELF-INVESTMENT FOR COMMUNITY RENEWAL

Roger L. Kemp

Our nation's downtown areas and their surrounding neighborhoods, located in the very heart of our communities, flourished in their early years. They were well-known places that attracted commerce and industry, manufactured those goods and services needed by area residents, and created the jobs and economy necessary to make the surrounding neighborhoods survive, if not thrive. Families, young people, and children alike flocked to these downtowns for shopping and entertainment. While many citizens worked there, everyone went there. These downtowns were the center of community life.

As America's network of roadways expanded geographically, both in number and size, the jobs and houses slowly relocated to the suburbs, and millions of people followed. Even when jobs remained in our downtown areas, the distances to reach them from outlying suburban areas seemed to shrink because of the increased speed allowed by these automobile expressways. As the flight from the downtown areas of our communities continued throughout the years, it left functionally obsolete buildings and antiquated streets in its path. This gradual deterioration continued for decades. Life in our downtowns, and their surrounding neighborhoods, gradually declined to the point where many were like ghost-towns.

As our nation enters the 21st century, the condition of our downtowns and their contiguous neighborhoods are undergoing a renaissance. Our public leaders in the communities impacted by these negative trends have learned to cope, even make considerable progress, in the rebuilding of these downtown areas and their neighborhoods. In the decades ahead, the state of our downtowns and their neighborhoods, and the quality of life they provide to citizens, will improve dramatically. Traditional economic development tools are now giving way to community-renewal programs, whereby cities and towns can attract private investment through investing in new municipal cultural amenities as well as traditional civic infrastructure improvements.

While we cannot change our roadway networks, many smaller companies and younger citizens are relocating to our downtowns and their neighborhoods in record numbers. While the number and size of our suburban shopping malls will not diminish, selected commercial establishments and residential neighborhoods not only exist but are starting to flourish. Many of our downtowns have been retrofitted with large municipal parking garages to accommodate our main mode of transportation, the automobile. In some cases aging streets have been closed to vehicular traffic and remade as attractive pedestrian walkways. Public officials in our downtown areas are focusing their attention on restoring an outdated public infrastructure, and creating more civic open space for citizens and their families to enjoy. New civic improvements are being built that serve to revitalize a community's development patterns.

Some of these areas are undergoing a renaissance in the types of civic improvements, as well as the level of municipal investment. Public officials are beginning to realize that they can plant the seeds of revitalization, renew their downtowns and neighborhoods, as well as attract private investment. These new programs are not give-away programs, or what some conservatives would call corporate welfare programs. Rather, they represent the efforts of public officials to invest in their downtowns and neighborhoods with the goal of revitalizing them, and bringing citizens back downtown in great numbers. As citizens return to downtowns, so do businesses. This cyclical pattern is the essence of evolving efforts as community renewal through municipal self-investment.

The traditional methods of community revitalization included an assortment of financial and land-based economic development incentives, and several different types of municipal delivery systems to implement them. Financial incentives included everything from business assistance programs, to low-cost financing, to tax increment financing. Land-based incentives included an assortment of tools from enhanced building density bonuses, to allowing mixed land uses, to revising aging city zoning codes. Typical municipal delivery systems included the use of community development corporations, to the use of enterprise and empowerment zones, to providing old-style redevelopment areas. A complete listing of these traditional economic development incentives as well as their delivery systems is provided in Figure 1.

In recent years, particularly during the past decade or so, citizens have demanded that their downtowns be brought back to life not only for their own sake, but also for the sake of future generations of citizens to enjoy. Our municipal officials have responded to this challenge in a number of different and creative ways. Numerous community self-investment options and strategies have evolved in recent years to revitalize these aging center city areas, as well as those neighborhoods that adjoin them. In many cases, where the original downtown was located on a natural amenity, such as a beach, river, or other waterway, steps are being made to restore previously damaged areas of such natural amenities. While America's downtowns were founded next to waterways for transportation purposes, these old transportation methods are now obsolete, permitting the restoration of many of these areas to their natural beauty.

While municipal public officials can ensure the public's safety by hiring more police officers and fire fighters, and they can rebuild the public infrastructure, other measures are needed to attract merchants and professionals to fill up vacant space in our downtown areas. Over the past decade, the municipal self-investment options to rebuild our downtown areas and neighborhoods have evolved from a loose assortment of investments to the use of many diverse, yet highly focused, investment programs. In many cases these municipal investments can be targeted to achieve specific objectives. Investment decisions may be made to attract citizens downtown, to create a critical mass of people to entice shop owners, and to attract sufficient numbers of people and small businesses to create a market for other related businesses, such as an assortment of professional services and eating establishments.

There are now virtually dozens of types and forms of municipal investment options available to help public officials revitalize their community. The case studies examined in this volume describe over 30 types

---

FIGURE 1
Traditional Economic Development Incentives
(Financial, Land-Based, and Delivery Systems)
Listed in Alphabetical Order Within Each Category

Financial

Business Assistance Programs
Business Retention Programs
Community-Based Assistance
Leveraging Private Investment
Low-Cost Financing
Personal Property Tax Incentives/Rebates
Pooled-Income Financing
Real Property Tax Incentives/Rebates
Small Business Development Loans
Tax Increment Financing

Land-Based

Building Density Bonuses
Cleaning Contaminated Sites
Development Standards
Height and Bulk Bonuses
Land Subsidies
Mixed Land Uses
Off-Site Improvements
On-Site Improvements
Parking Improvements
Transfer of Development Rights
Zoning Regulations

Delivery Systems

Community Development Corporations
Development Disposition Agreements
Economic Development Corporations
Economic Development Departments
Empowerment Zones
Enterprise Zones
One-Stop Permit Processes
Planning Departments
Redevelopment Project Areas

---

of municipal investment options. These self-investment programs range from restoring natural amenities and nature areas, to building massive civic improvement projects. Case studies involving improvements to natural conditions include restoring beachfront property, providing linear trails, creating open spaces, providing public parks, restoring riverfronts, and providing public walkways next to downtown waterways. Those case studies involving civic improvements include such public projects as municipal libraries, museums, arts centers, rapid transit routes, public housing, and the restoration of old train stations. A complete listing of the types of municipal investments contained in the case studies in this volume are shown in Figure 2.

The case study examples contained in this volume examine 31 tools for community renewal. These tools are examined in detail in each of these case studies. All of these tools are readily available to local public officials. Each of these tools, or methods of municipal self-investment, is designed to achieve a specific purpose or goal. To assist the reader, a separate figure is presented that shows the specific purpose that each type of municipal investment is designed to achieve. Figure 3 shows the type of municipal investment, its intended purpose, as well as the city and state where it was applied. One county is included, Chesterfield County, because the actions of county officials were designed to preserve the quality of life in communities within their county's jurisdiction.

FIGURE 2
Case Studies in Municipal Investment
(Shown by Type of Investment)
Listed in Alphabetical Order

Type of Investment

Arts Center	Public Library
Arts District	Residential Streets
Beachfront Property	Revenues
Business Improvement District	Riverfront
Bus Rapid Transit	Street Patterns
Community Spaces	Streetscape Project
Downtown Streetscape Projects	Subsidy for Public Transit
Land-Use/Transportation Planning	Town Center
Linear Trails	Train Station
Master Plan	Transit Options
Open Spaces	Transit System
Parks	Transportation/Land-Use Planning
Planning Group	Walkways
Planning Process	Waterfront
Public Housing	Zoning Codes and Laws
Public Improvements by Transit	

Toronto, Ontario, Canada is included because of its closeness to the U.S., and because of the similarity that exists between Canadian and U.S. municipal governments. The District of Columbia was included because it is as large as many communities, and it serves as an excellent example of the use of light-rail public transit systems on both urban and suburban community development and redevelopment.

The 35 community case studies examined in this volume represent 22 states, the District of Columbia, and one municipality in Canada. Those cities selected represent all major geographic areas of the U.S. These geographic areas include the Four Corners (two cities in one state), Great Lakes (three cities in three states), New England (three cities in two states), Middle Atlantic (five cities in three states, plus the District of Columbia), North Central (four cities in three states), Northeastern (one city in one state), Northwestern (two cities in two states),

South Central (three cities in three states), Southeastern (six cities in four states), and Southwestern (five cities in one state) regions of our nation. These regional divisions of the U.S. represent those used in the *National Geographic Atlas of the World* (6th Edition, 1996). Figure 4 sets forth each of these regions of the U.S., as well as a listing of each city, and its state, used in these case studies.

The communities selected for these case studies represent all population sizes, forms and types of government, personal and family income levels, and political persuasions. Smaller communities include Petaluma, California; Lake Worth, Florida; Hampton, Virginia; and DuPont, Washington, to name a few. Larger cities, with populations in the hundreds of thousands, or even more, include Chicago, Illinois; Denver, Colorado; Minneapolis and Saint Paul, Minnesota; Newark, New Jersey; Cleveland, Ohio; Houston, Texas; and the District of Columbia. These communities all have one

FIGURE 3
Case Studies in Municipal Investment
(Shown by Type of Investment, Purpose, City, and State)
Listed in Alphabetical Order by Type of Investment

Type of Investment	*Purpose*	*City/State*
Arts Center, Creation of	Redeveloping an Aging Downtown Area	Newark, NJ
Arts District, Creation of	Revitalize Old Downtown	Berkeley, CA
Beachfront Property, Restoration of	Create Landmark and Civic Improvement Amenity	Lake Worth, FL
Business Improvement District, Creation of	Share Management of Commercial Areas	Hampton, VA
Bus Rapid Transit, Creation of	Improve Downtown Transportation	Orlando, FL
Community Spaces, Creation of	Foster Quality Residential Development	Chesterfield Co., VA
Downtown Streetscape Project, Use of	Improve Traffic and Transit Patterns, Pedestrian and Transit Linkages, and Landscaping	Santa Monica, CA
Land-Use and Transportation Planning, Integration of	Fight Sprawl and Preserve a Lifestyle	Madison, WI
Linear Trails, Building	Link Neighborhoods to Inner-City Harbor Districts	Baltimore, MD
Master Plan, Development of	Revitalize Historic Downtown	Baton Rouge, LA
Municipal Investment, Multiple Types of	Redevelopment of an Aging Downtown Capitol Area	Little Rock, AR
Open Spaces, Creation of	Improve Public Access to Town Square on River in Old Downtown Area	Grand Forks, ND
Open Spaces, Creation of	Stimulate Private-Sector Development in Inner-City Neighborhood Area	Houston, TX
Open Spaces, Designing	Improve the Quality of Life for Downtown Residents	Cambridge, MA

Type of Investment	*Purpose*	*City/State*
Parks, Inner-City	Revitalize Downtown	Atlanta, GA
Planning Group, Use of Private	Improve Downtown and Lakefront Areas	Cleveland, OH
Planning Process, Creation of	Civic Leaders Plan for the Future of their Downtown	Chicago, IL
Planning Process, Public and Private	Preserve History, Integrate Neighborhoods, and Restore Urban Ecology on an Existing River	Saint Paul, MN
Public Housing, Replacement	Stabilize Inner-City Neighborhoods	Atlanta, GA
Public Improvements, by Transit System	Facilitate Inner-City Development	Oakland, CA
Public Library, Building a New	Stimulate Community Revitalization	Charleston, SC
Residential Streets, Redesigning of	Restore Quality of Life to Residential Neighborhoods	Boulder, CO
Revenues, Raising	Finance Science and Cultural Facilities	Denver, CO
Riverfront, Redevelopment of	Enhance Downtown Redevelopment and Stimulate Inner-City Tourism	Hartford, CT
Riverfront Area, Investment in	Stimulate Downtown Redevelopment in Aging Inner-City Area	Nashville, TN
Street Patterns, Changing	Allow More Transit-Sensitive Development	DuPont, WA
Streetscape Project, Development of	Stimulate Private-Sector Development in Inner-City Downtown Area	Houston, TX
Subsidy, Bus Transit System	Improve Downtown Transportation	Orlando, FL
Town Center, Creating New	Revitalize Inner-City Shopping District	Chattanooga, TN
Train Station, Renovation of	Creating Science Center for Downtown Redevelopment Purposes	Kansas City, MO

Type of Investment	Purpose	City/State
Transit Options, User Friendly	Reorganizing a Downtown Around an Existing River	Petaluma, CA
Transit System, Use of	Improve Downtown Access for Residents and Tourists	Denver, CO
Transit System, Use of	Stimulate Downtown Redevelopment	Hayward, CA
Transit System, Use of	Stimulate Private-Sector Development in Inner-City Downtown Area	Houston, TX
Transit System, Use of	Guide Urban Growth and Reduce Automobile Congestion and Pollution	Portland, OR
Transit System, Use of	Link the Inner-City to the Suburbs to Stimulate Development	Washington, DC
Transportation and Land-Use Planning, Integration of	Fight Sprawl and Preserve a Lifestyle	Madison, WI
Walkways, Creation of	Improve Public Access to Town Square on River in Old Downtown Area	Grand Forks, ND
Waterfront, Redevelopment of	Revitalize Original Waterfront Port and Whaling Area	New Medford, MA
Zoning Codes, Revision of Old	Permit More Flexible Development Standards	Minneapolis, MN
Zoning Laws, Undoing of Old	Stimulate Waterfront Development on an Existing River	Toronto, ON, Canada

thing in common. They have used one or more types of municipal self-investment strategies to help revitalize their downtown and its surrounding neighborhoods. Figure 5 shows these cities, for ease of reference, by the state in which they are located, followed by the name of the city(ies) in each state.

When the previous information provided on the case studies contained in this volume is juxtaposed, the results provide the reader with an easy reference guide to all case studies. This information includes the name of each city, the state in which it is located, the type of municipal investment made by its public officials, the region of the U.S. where it is located, and the chapter where the case study can be located in the following pages of this book. Figure 6 sets forth this information in alphabetical order by name of city. This information will enable the reader to reference individual communities, states, geographic regions of the

FIGURE 4
Case Studies in Municipal Investment
(Shown by Region of U.S., and by City and State)
Listed in Alphabetical Order by Region of U.S.

Region of U.S.*	City	State
Central Canada	Toronto	Ontario
Four Corners	Boulder	Colorado
	Denver	Colorado
Great Lakes	Chicago	Illinois
	Cleveland	Ohio
	Madison	Wisconsin
New England	Cambridge	Massachusetts
	Hartford	Connecticut
	New Bedford	Massachusetts
Middle Atlantic	Baltimore	Maryland
	Chesterfield County	Virginia
	Hampton	Virginia
	Newark	New Jersey
	Washington	District of Columbia
North Central	Grand Forks	North Dakota
	Kansas City	Missouri
	Minneapolis	Minnesota
	Saint Paul	Minnesota
Northwestern	DuPont	Washington
	Portland	Oregon
	Seattle	Washington
South Central	Baton Rouge	Louisiana
	Houston	Texas
	Little Rock	Arkansas
Southeastern	Atlanta	Georgia
	Charleston	South Carolina
	Chattanooga	Tennessee
	Lake Worth	Florida
	Nashville	Tennessee
	Orlando	Florida
Southwestern	Berkeley	California
	Hayward	California
	Oakland	California
	Petaluma	California
	Santa Monica	California

*This figure uses the division of the U.S. as set forth in William L. Allen, Editor, National Geographic Atlas of the World (6th Edition, 1996), published by the National Geographic Society, Washington, D.C.

FIGURE 5
Case Studies in
Municipal Investment
(Shown by State and City)

Listed in Alphabetical Order by State

State	City
Arkansas	Little Rock
California	Berkeley
	Hayward
	Oakland
	Petaluma
	Santa Monica
Colorado	Boulder
	Denver
Connecticut	Hartford
District of Columbia	Washington
Florida	Lake Worth
	Orlando
Georgia	Atlanta
Illinois	Chicago
Louisiana	Baton Rouge
Maryland	Baltimore
Massachusetts	Cambridge
	New Bedford
Minnesota	Minneapolis
	Saint Paul
Missouri	Kansas City
New Jersey	Newark
North Dakota	Grand Forks
Ohio	Cleveland
Ontario	Toronto
Oregon	Portland
South Carolina	Charleston
Texas	Houston
Tennessee	Chattanooga
	Nashville
Virginia	Chesterfield
	Hampton
Washington	DuPont
	Seattle
Wisconsin	Madison

of all reference information provided for each of these case studies.

The final chapter, *The Future of Municipal Self-Investment*, examines the future of this evolving form of community economic development. This section is intended to provide critical thinking about how local public officials should make investment decisions for community renewal. It is important that public officials work closely together to improve the quality of life for the citizens they serve as our nation enters the 21st century. A model of community investment is set forth that stresses the importance for public officials at the local level to invest wisely in their own downtowns, before seeking financial assistance from higher levels of government. Once the pride of self-renewal is shown by the investments made by municipal officials, it will be easier to solicit public officials at higher levels of government to make similar investments in their communities. The editor believes that public investment is a forerunner to private investment, and that public officials must first show their financial commitment before asking the executives in the private sector to invest in their downtowns.

A listing of regional and national resource organizations concerning the case studies in this book, as well as written materials about economic development in general, is included at the end of this volume. The *Regional Resource Directory* includes the names and addresses, and other contact information, for each of the case studies referred to above. Readers may wish to contact these organizations for further information about the types of municipal investments made, the purpose for making these investments, and how these decisions resulted in community renewal. The *National Resource Directory* includes the names and addresses, and related information, for major national professional associations and research organizations in the U.S. relating to municipal economic development and community

U.S., types of municipal investment, and chapters where this information can be found. This figure represents a compilation

FIGURE 6
Case Studies in Municipal Investment
(Shown by City, State, Type of Municipal Investment, Region of U.S., and Chapter)
List in Alphabetical Order by Name of City

City	State	Type of Municipal Investment	Region of U.S.*	Chapter
Atlanta	GA	Building Inner-City Parks	Southeastern	2
Atlanta	GA	Replacing Aging Public Housing with New Public Housing to Stabilize Inner-City Neighborhoods	Southeastern	3
Baltimore	MD	Using Linear Trails to Link Neighborhoods to City's Redeveloped Harbor District	Middle Atlantic	4
Baton Rouge	LA	Using Citizens to Develop a Master Plan to Revitalize a Historic Downtown	South Central	5
Berkeley	CA	Revitalizing an Old Downtown through the Creation of an Inner-City Arts District	Southwestern	6
Boulder	CO	Redesigning Residential Streets to Restore Quality of Life to Residential Neighborhoods	Four Corners	7
Cambridge	MA	Designing Civic Spaces to Improve the Quality of Life for Downtown Residents	New England	8
Charleston	SC	Building a New Public Library to Stimulate Community Revitalization	Southeastern	9
Chattanooga	TN	Creating a New Town Center Out of an Aging Inner-City Mall	Southeastern	10
Chesterfield County	VA	Preserving and Creating Community Spaces to Foster Quality Residential Developments	Middle Atlantic	11
Chicago	IL	Government Planners Use Civic Leaders to Plan for the Future of their Downtown	Great Lakes	12
Cleveland	OH	City Uses Private Planning Group to Improve its Downtown and Lakefront Areas	Great Lakes	13
Denver	CO	Using Light-Rail Transportation to Stimulate Downtown Access for Residents and Tourists	Four Corners	14

City	State	Type of Municipal Investment	Region of U.S.*	Chapter
Denver Metro Area	CO	Raising Revenues for Science and Cultural Facilities	Four Corners	15
DuPont	WA	Changing Traditional Street Patterns to Allow for More Transit-Sensitive Development	Northwestern	16
Grand Forks	ND	Creating Open Space and Walkways to Town Square on River in Old Downtown Area	North Central	17
Hampton	VA	City Approves Business Improvement District to Share Management of Commercial Area	Middle Atlantic	18
Hartford	CT	Redeveloping Riverfront Spaces to Enhance Downtown Redevelopment and Stimulate Inner-City Tourism	New England	19
Hayward	CA	Targeting Light-Rail Mass Transit to Stimulate Downtown Redevelopment	Southwestern	20
Houston	TX	Using Streetscape, Open Space, and Transit Access to Stimulate Private-Sector Development in Inner-City Downtown Area	South Central	21
Kansas City	MO	Renovating Old Train Station into Science Center for Downtown Redevelopment Purposes	North Central	22
Lake Worth	FL	Restoring Municipal Beachfront Property as a Landmark and Civic Improvement Amenity	Southeastern	23
Little Rock	AR	Multiple Municipal Investments for the Redevelopment of an Aging Downtown Capitol Area	South Central	24
Madison	WI	Integrating Transportation Planning and Land-Use Planning to Fight Sprawl and Preserve a Lifestyle	Great Lakes	25
Minneapolis	MN	Revising Antiquated Zoning Codes to Permit More Flexible Development Standards	North Central	26
Nashville	TN	Investment in Riverfront Area to Stimulate Downtown Redevelopment in Aging Inner-City Area	Southeastern	27
New Bedford	MA	Using Waterfront Redevelopment to Revitalize Original Waterfront Port and Whaling Area	New England	28

City	State	Type of Municipal Investment	Region of U.S.*	Chapter
Newark	NJ	How an Arts Center Can Be Used to Redevelop an Aging Downtown Area	Middle Atlantic	29
Oakland	CA	How Light-Rail Transit Can Facilitate Inner-City Development through Public Improvements	Southwestern	30
Orlando	FL	Using Innovative and Free Bus Rapid Transit to Improve Downtown Transportation	Southeastern	31
Petaluma	CA	Reorganizing a Downtown Around an Existing River with Pedestrian-Friendly Transit Options	Southwestern	32
Portland	OR	Guiding Urban Growth, Reducing Automobile Congestion and Pollution, with the Use of Light-Rail Public Transit Systems	Northwestern	33
Saint Paul	MN	Using Public Planning to Preserve History, Integrate Neighborhoods, and Restore Urban Ecology, Focusing on an Existing River	North Central	34
Santa Monica	CA	Improving Traffic and Transit Patterns, Pedestrian and Transit Linkages, and Landscaping Using a Downtown Streetscape Project	Southwestern	35
Seattle	WA	Using a New Public Library as a Tool for Economic Development and Community Revival	Northwestern	36
Toronto	ON	Undoing Old Zoning Laws to Stimulate Waterfront Development on an Existing River	Central Canada	37
Washington	DC	Using Public Light-Rail Transit System to Link the Inner-City to the Suburbs to Stimulate Development	Middle Atlantic	38
Washington	DC	Promoting Development Near Light-Rail Public Transit Stations Improves Neighborhood Development	Middle Atlantic	39

*This figure uses the division of the U.S. as set forth in William L. Allen, Editor, National Geographic Atlas of the World (6th Edition, 1996), published by the National Geographic Society, Washington, D.C.

renewal. All of these organizations have a wealth of material and information available from their respective internet websites.

A comprehensive *Bibliography* on municipal economic development and investment for community renewal is included at the end of this volume. This bibliography provides a listing of books, monographs, articles, and other written sources on municipal development and redevelopment. Reference to the authors, titles, and publishers are provided for over five dozen books, over 50 monographs, nearly 150 articles, and ten other sources that do not neatly fall into the above bibliographic categories.

The use of municipal investment tools and strategies has evolved primarily over the past few decades. They are typically applied in a piecemeal and incremental fashion by public officials from city to city. Since the efforts of public officials are limited to the confines of their own communities, the need exists to codify the available information concerning the best practices for downtown renewal and neighborhood revitalization. This information must be made available to our local elected leaders, our appointed municipal public officials, and, most importantly, to the citizens they represent and serve. It is the goal of this volume to provide the best available literature, featuring the best practices that can be used in other urban and suburban communities as citizens and their public officials grapple with the issues and problems relating to this evolving field.

CHAPTER 2

ATLANTA BUILDS INNER-CITY PARKS TO REVITALIZE DOWNTOWN

Barbara Faga

Big downtown parks are back. Atlanta's Centennial Olympic Park — the largest new inner-city park built in the last quarter of the 20th century — and San Francisco's Yerba Buena Gardens soon will be followed by a major urban central park at Denver's Stapleton airport redevelopment, and comparable public spaces in Pittsburgh and Chicago. Projects in such cities as Chattanooga, Tennessee, and Modesto, California, are more limited in scale, but equally keyed to an urban core. Meanwhile, historic spaces like New York's Bryant Park and Washington, D.C.'s Franklin Square have been rescued from decay and revamped as lively urban focal points.

There have been a number of changes over the years in the revitalization of downtown parks, including more private and public/private funding, and an emphasis on activity and a sense of place rather than a focus on pastoral escape. The ability of a well-timed, well-conceived park to generate both short- and long-term value is in keeping with the experience of more than 200 years.

While American cities have never stopped building parks, between World War II and the 1990s parkland was often treated as a utilitarian recreational amenity and often begrudgingly maintained. New parks typically involved preserved watersheds and woodlands left by suburban development, or narrow riverfronts abandoned by industry and not fit for much else. Older city parks, including the great "icon" parks designed by the Olmsteds and others between about 1870 and 1920, often seemed lost to decay and crime. Mid-century modern architects rarely considered parks interesting in themselves. By 1961, even the humanist critic Lewis Mumford could publish the 650-page *The City in History* with barely one mention of "park" in the index.

It took another generation — excited by preserving and exploring urban history, and revitalizing rather than reforming cities — to see parks once more as centers of urban design and urban life. William H. "Holly" Whyte, like Central Park codesigner Frederick Law Olmsted, a prolific journalist, led the way by observing and recording how people actually use urban open space. The neighborhood meetings and workshops that exist today reveal similar specific wish lists of both active and passive uses for parks. These days, parks seldom serve as escape valves for overcrowded industrial cities;

Originally published as "Parks Downtown," *Urban Land*, Vol. 60, No. 7, July, 2001. Published by the Urban Land Institute, Washington, D.C. Reprinted with permission of the publisher.

more often, they help inject life into low-density cores, as in the pioneering culture parks at Yerba Buena and Paris's La Villette.

Amid renewed interest in cities, public life, and public places, urban parks are in. Architect/writer Witold Rybczynski made parks a major topic of his recent book *City Life*, depicting their openness and mobility — and decay and rebirth — as keys to understanding North American cities. In the Urban Land Institute's recently published *Inside City Parks*, author Peter Harnik surveys 25 representative U.S. cities and finds that they spend more than $500 million a year on capital building and rebuilding.

The new attitude toward downtown open space has plenty to do with the renewed competitive energy of inner cities as places for knowledge and service professionals to live and work, and as destinations for entertainment and tourism. At the same time, this renewed energy goes back 200 years or more to English designer/developers like John Wood (Bath's Royal Crescent), John Nash (Regent's Park in London), and their successors.

How much value parks add always is hard to quantify, admits Atlanta's Dan Graveline, whose Georgia World Congress Center Authority (GWCC), a state agency, created and now owns and manages Centennial Olympic Park. Employing an ad hoc 501(c)3 catalyst group named Centennial Olympic Park Area, Inc. (COPA) and using no public money, Graveline and his team assembled 60 acres of parking lots and other semibrownfield downtown land fronting the GWCC's key sports and convention locations at pre-Olympic prices no higher than $2 a square foot.

Partly developed as the six-acre, $18 million centerpiece for the 1996 Olympics, the 21-acre park was finished the next year for an added $12 million, with the remaining land made available for private, mixed-use development. With about half the park frontage now committed to projects ranging from super-luxury condominiums and a hotel to new facilities for CNN and the Coca-Cola Company, the value of that development today is near $1 billion. Property values are now $200 a foot and climbing.

As good as that is, however, there are added direct and indirect economic benefits to the owners and to Atlanta — less quantifiable and taking longer to mature, but also less dependent on the national economic boom. In fact, the most successful such projects have long been a multifaceted overlay of art, social purpose, and commerce, as the granddaddy of big U.S. city parks still reminds us.

Central Park, which (with the Brooklyn Bridge) *New York Times* design critic Paul Goldberger calls New York's greatest work of architecture, may also be its greatest real estate investment. Considering only land, the city's purchase of 843 acres of distinctly suburban land for $5.8 million, a gamble in 1856, in effect generated the incremental land values and rents of Fifth Avenue and Central Park West, where today apartments with park views alone sell for $5.8 million. But how can the value of Central Park be quantified as a tourist attraction — enhanced after two decades of restoration of architect Calvert Vaux's buildings and enforcement of higher standards of cleanliness and safety? Or its value as a photographer's favorite — consider the advertising value to the Plaza hotel alone? Or as a venue for public celebrations and events, a place for free Shakespeare and free rock concerts? Or as a site for such profitable restaurants as Tavern on the Green? Or — as Olmsted predicted — a social safety valve. Large and small, these and other benefits from Central Park have contributed for decades to New York's real estate and business economy, and its intangible leadership among world cities. Yet, none of this was preordained or permanent.

Although clearly in the path of development, in the 1850s the site of Central Park was a semirural brownfield of shacks and tanneries. More than a little vision was required. Far from simply preserving nature, Olmsted, as both superintendent and codesigner, and Vaux took the land apart and reworked it with a thoroughness, and artifice, rivaling modern theme parks. The project's instant success helped Olmsted launch what became the country's first national-scale design firm, preceding the first large architecture and engineering firms by decades, and create vast, sophisticated park systems throughout North America at a time when few cities employed a trained planner.

To be sure, not all parks have proved to be real estate bonanzas. Beyond design lies maintenance, and beyond that, real stewardship. From the beginning, Olmsted fought encroachments on Central Park as well as mismanagement and neglect, and it has weathered many crises since, as both patterns of use and the city's commitment to the public realm have changed.

More than a century later, and on a far different scale, Centennial Olympic Park is still recognizable as a revival of the Central Park idea, with its own mix of short- and long-term, and tangible and intangible rewards and challenges. As a prototype for the current downtown park revival, its key ingredients include:

- The initial opportunity to acquire underused, semibrownfield property near the core — an ingredient of many low- and medium-density U.S. cities. (In current projects in Dayton, Ohio, and in Pittsburgh, the sites involve a riverfront, but the locations are still closer to the center of town than the edge.);
- The need to provide a better setting and better access for existing properties, in this case the Georgia Dome, the convention center, and Phillips Arena; as Graveline points out, this need alone justified replacing derelict blocks with a park;
- The challenge and the opportunity of pre-

senting the 1996 Centennial Olympics, which was a galvanizing force that accelerated and focused the effort;
- The attraction of a "pure" real estate venture, allowing an imaginative leap from a wasteland to a prime parkside address that can, and here did, succeed handsomely;
- The chance to create a public amenity with 100 percent private funding through the quasi-public COPA as development agency and broker, and the quasi-private Georgia World Congress Center as park owner/manager;
- The unusual status of the property as a Georgia state park, which enabled special tax and zoning tools, and the possible use of eminent domain;
- The existence of well-funded, interested neighbors like CNN and Coca-Cola;
- The unfulfilled market for downtown luxury housing, quality hotel rooms (always logically located next to the convention center, but previously scared off by the setting), and other upscale mixed uses;
- The market for revenue-generating activities in the park itself, from one-time outdoor fairs and corporate receptions to daily vendors, with natural synergy created by the adjacent sports and convention facilities — an example of what Whyte disciple Fred Kent, president of the nonprofit Project for Public Spaces, would call "triangulation"; and
- The city government, tourism/hospitality industry; business community, and general public all eager to boost Atlanta's image — and promote their own interests — with a new, photogenic urban setting.

Additional aspects of the project might be thought of as post-Olmsted design. Most fundamental, perhaps, is the shift from the idea of park as refuge from the city's bustle, to parks that — at least in some places — actually add bustle, although in fairness,

Olmsted designs often provide lively open areas like Central Park's Bethesda Terrace where people can see and be seen. This comes in part from today's more active tastes in recreation, and in part from the need to prime the pump of downtown revival with visible urban excitement.

In cities where lack of density and isolation have replaced crowding and noise as major problems, new parks like Atlanta's must often double as plazas, making physical and visual connections among previously separated streets and neighborhoods, and providing a variety of magnet stages for daily activities and special events. Centennial Park's design device of a quilt is a metaphor for community and a symbol of regional history — part of today's interest in narrative urban landscapes that celebrate a city's particularity, rather than support a rural fantasy. But it also is a fairly direct expression of the pedestrian routes that now cross and meet at the park.

Connection and visibility also serve the need for security, an ever-changing but constant concern for America's open, democratic parks, as it was in Olmsted's time. Today's park designs not only omit the shadowy bosques and crags of Victorian landscapes, they also avoid all sharply elevated or sunken areas to increase both real and perceived safety. Bright, even theatrical lighting where appropriate, as with Atlanta's light towers, can also make places feel both more secure and more engaging.

Centennial Olympic Park is still a place in progress, already evolving from its Olympic fame toward becoming the center of a downtown residential and commercial neighborhood. As for its economic value, the evidence can be seen in more than mere statistics. CNN, for example, has in effect moved the front of its building around to face the park.

As for the next evolution of the Central Park model, the new urban neighborhood on the site of Denver's former Stapleton International Airport provides an example. At 4,700 acres, the project is less a neighborhood than a town (12,000 housing units, three million square feet of retail, 10 million square feet of office and tech space) about to be attached to adjacent downtown Denver. An 1,100-acre open-space plan, which includes a 250-acre first phase of neighborhood squares, playing fields, and connecting greenways, will feed into a true central park — in fact, "Central Park" is its working name — roughly 1,000 feet wide and nearly a mile long. While built on the almost blank slate of Stapleton's former runways, the park and its design will grow out of several influences. One is a streambed, long hidden under the airstrip, which will be restored. Another is Denver's tradition of fine old Olmsted-designed city parks, which this added "central park" will explicitly recall. Overall, this Stapleton park will expand the city's park system by 25 percent. A third influence is the expansive view of plains and distant mountains from the large open site, which has led to the design of both rolling mounds and a flat, prairielike meadow.

And yet, with all these influences, the park still will clearly be the result of design, rather than pure forces of nature. A bold diagonal connector, a central gathering space, a music bowl, and a clearly human-planted "urban forest" that will act as a "stroll garden" for adjacent office workers suggest a purpose-created space targeting active, sports-minded families — clearly an artifact of the 21st century.

"A great object of all that is done in a park, of all the art of a park, is to influence the minds of men through their imaginations," Frederick Law Olmsted wrote back in the 1800s. After 150 years, Olmsted's insight that parks could define the city, increase the value of property within it, and enhance the quality of life of its citizens still holds true.

Chapter 3

Atlanta Stabilizes Inner-City Neighborhoods with New Public Housing

Christopher Swope

It is hard to believe that the Villages of East Lake, Atlanta's newest golf course community, was once a dangerous public housing project. From the wicker rocking chairs behind the leasing office, the view is one of country club elegance: an enticing swimming pool, a pair of gleaming new tennis courts, golf carts buzzing to the next tee. Gone are the infamous old housing blocks of East Lake Meadows, a place that was so violent people called it "Little Vietnam." In their stead are hundreds of three-story townhouses done in beige with red-brick accents and white picket balconies. The main public hazard is no longer flying bullets. It's flying golf balls.

It does not take much of an eye for architecture or urban planning to see that the transformation at East Lake is truly astounding. There are still public housing residents here, yet the homes are trim and the streets are clean. Crime in the neighborhood is way down, and property values are way up. Come here on a weekday afternoon and there aren't people idly hanging around as there used to be. That's because everyone is working.

Come here on a weekend afternoon, however, when the residents are out golfing or dipping in the pool, and there is another, more subtle transformation to see. The people enjoying this community, by and large, are not the same people who lived here before. This is a "mixed income" development now. Half of the residents are middle-class folks paying market rents. The other half are public housing tenants who have been screened and who have agreed to abide by stringent rules. Of the 428 families who lived here in the Little Vietnam days, only 79 moved back when it came to resemble a resort.

A similar makeover is happening in projects all over Atlanta. One by one, the city is tearing down its old public housing projects, places such as Carver Homes and Kimberly Courts, whose very names evoke a failed era in which society's poorest people were warehoused in enclaves of despair. Rising from the dust is the new face of public housing: quaint neighborhoods of townhomes where the working poor live next door to the middle class. By every measure, these new communities are better places to live.

Originally published as "Ghosts of Public Housing," *Governing*, Vol. 14, No. 8, May, 2001. Published by Congressional Quarterly Inc., Washington, D.C. Reprinted with permission of the publisher.

But there's a nagging issue that's often overlooked in the enthusiasm for renewal. If most of the previous tenants don't live here, where did they all go?

It's a surprisingly difficult question to answer. It's an increasingly important one, though, as cities nationwide continue a drive to demolish their worst public housing projects. The infamous housing towers of Chicago, Philadelphia and Newark are coming down; Baltimore blew up the last of its high-rises in February. Meanwhile, equally decrepit low-rise units, more like barracks than apartments, are disappearing in Seattle, Nashville and San Antonio. Nearly everywhere, the demolished projects are being replaced with traditional looking, mixed-income neighborhoods.

It is all very encouraging. But there is a simple math tied to this revitalization, one that poses both short-term and long-term consequences. Cities are building fewer housing units for poor people than they are tearing down. Nationally, around 100,000 units came down in the 1990s, and about 60,000 were scheduled to be replaced. In the short-term, housing authorities are legally obligated to relocate residents whose homes are demolished. In the long-term, the question is: With the stock of affordable housing shrinking, where will poor people live?

Only now, a decade after the wrecking ball began to swing, are researchers and policy makers finally starting to look at these issues. Several national think-tank studies are currently under way. Meanwhile, the U.S. Department of Housing and Urban Development, which has funded revitalization work in 130 cities through its "Hope VI" public housing reform program, is asking cities to assess the local impact on people and neighborhoods.

The single best place to ask the question may be Atlanta. This is the city that pioneered the whole mixed-income concept when it leveled and began rebuilding the Techwood/Clark Howell projects in 1995. Since then, it has begun turning 10 additional projects into mixed-income townhouse developments and planning three more, making it a virtual poster-city for Hope VI. Yet, when you ask the awkward questions about tenant displacement, you get wildly inconsistent answers. Depending on whom you ask, the Hope VI policies have either liberated hundreds of families with a new range of housing choices, or dumped some of Atlanta's poorest people out on the street.

Officials at the Atlanta Housing Authority, whose job it was to relocate residents, say they know exactly where families ended up. A small percentage returned to the new developments, but most received Section 8 vouchers and are living in apartments in the private rental market. Some residents moved into other public housing units in Atlanta, and a few even bought homes. "For some people, this is the first time they've had housing choices in their lives," says executive director Renee Lewis Glover. "They can move to where they like the schools or have more job opportunities."

Others, however, say that Hope VI reminds them of the urban renewal policies of the 1950s and '60s, when cities bulldozed low-income neighborhoods and forgot about the people who lived there. According to lawyers representing Atlanta tenants, hundreds of families were emptied out of the projects before any choices were offered to them, and nobody has any idea where they are sleeping at night. Meanwhile, as Atlanta loses one-third of its public housing stock to demolition, more people who need housing are turned away. "Where have the poorest gone?" asks Frank Alexander, an Emory University law professor who represented East Lake's tenants. "They are on the streets, under overpasses and in shelters. There's a direct correlation between the bulldozing of public housing and the increased demand for homeless shelters."

If you had lived at Little Vietnam before it was demolished, you had to meet certain criteria in order to return to the new Villages of East Lake. If able-bodied, you needed to be working, or receiving job training or enrolled in school. You couldn't have a history of skipping out on your rent payment. You and any family members on your lease could not have a violent criminal history or recent conviction. And finally, you had to agree to regular housekeeping checks.

The screening represents a new philosophy for Atlanta, one that is being echoed around the country. Public housing shouldn't be a semi-permanent holding pen for homeless people and welfare mothers. It should be a safe place for people to work their way to self-sufficiency. "We don't apologize for high standards," Glover says. "We believe every able-bodied person can be successful."

Few would disagree with that goal. But one impact of the screening has been to impose a drastic limit on the number of people who can come back to redeveloped housing sites. In Atlanta, the average return rate is less than 15 percent. The vast majority of people whose suffering justified tearing down the projects in the first place aren't coming back. In a national audit of Hope VI two years ago, HUD's inspector general noted that "some housing authorities ... have accomplished impressive physical revitalizations at their Hope VI sites. However, improvements to the lives of the residents who lived there are much less obvious."

It's not just Atlanta that has seen relatively few original residents return. According to the inspector general's report, eight percent returned to a revitalized Hope VI site in San Antonio, and 16 percent returned in Charlotte, North Carolina. Columbus, Ohio, managed 35 percent.

Housing advocates have pounced on the low return rates in making the case that this is 1950s urban renewal all over again. Georgia Tech planning professor Larry

Keating has watched the redevelopment process unfold in Atlanta since 1990. He argues that the housing authority's policies have essentially abandoned the poorest and toughest-to-help residents, in favor of the less desperate. "If you're sincere about a policy meant to improve the lives of poor people, then work with the existing folks," Keating argues. "Don't just throw away the first bunch and get a better class of poor people."

Atlanta officials argue it is misleading to judge its policies by the number of residents who return after renovation. Not everybody wanted to return, they say. And nobody was cast out into the street. Instead, residents received extensive relocation counseling and had several housing options available to them. When offered a Section 8 voucher, most residents jumped at the chance to move out of public housing and into a private rental. Housing officials even drove them around to look for apartments and paid their moving costs, security deposits and utility hookup fees. "Not all of the families wanted to come back," Glover says. "The fact that they decide to stay in Section 8 is a success."

Keating admits that those residents who stayed long enough to receive relocation assistance were treated fairly. But he alleges that while some left by choice, others left because of deliberate efforts of the housing authority to step up evictions or cut back on building maintenance. (The authority denies this.) In any case, by the time relocation began at Techwood, half of the 1,115 original families had already left, forfeiting their right to relocation benefits. "The housing authority offered relocation assistance to 545 families," Keating says, "it should have been 1,115 families, not 545."

Another relocation debate has sprung up around the reliance on Section 8 vouchers. Section 8 is already squeezed in tight rental markets such as Atlanta's and it can be difficult for public housing tenants to find apartments in decent neighborhoods. In good times, landlords can afford to be choosy, and given the choice, most of them prefer non-subsidized tenants over tenants using Section 8. The result, housing advocates argue, is that residents are moving from one ghetto to another.

The Atlanta Housing Authority has taken steps to try to avoid that fate. It has had some success recruiting landlords into the program, and its policies prohibit more than 40 percent of any one apartment complex from becoming occupied with Section 8 tenants. Tenants have relocated across a wide geographic area and in every county in the Atlanta metropolitan region. The 2000 Census, somewhat surprisingly, showed that the inner-suburban counties of DeKalb and Clayton both had non-white majorities. Some attribute this in part to Section 8 dispersals under the Atlanta revitalization program.

On a national level, HUD is encouraging cities to use its databases to analyze how Hope VI is affecting local concentrations of poverty. Urban institute researcher Tom Kingsley recently picked through data from 48 cities to look for patterns. "The results were all over the place," Kingsley says. "It doesn't confirm either side's arguments. It's not like everybody moved out to the suburbs, but it's also not the case that everybody is just moving into the building across the street."

The impact, it seems, depends a lot on the particular city and the strength of the real estate market. In Philadelphia, the flood of Section 8 tenants out of five demolished projects has substantially changed the character of certain neighborhoods. Investors have been buying up early 20th-century rowhouses in deteriorating parts of North and South Philly in order to cash in on above-market Section 8 rents. Neighborhoods that were historically high in home-ownership are now turning substantially over to renters, and the influx has caused a Section 8 backlash.

The Philadelphia Housing Authority has had to step up anti-crime efforts and beef up its outreach in order to quell unrest from neighbors who are upset about seeing so many poor people moving in. "Section 8 doesn't create housing," says executive director Carl Greene. "In older cities like Philadelphia, it's changing the makeup of some neighborhoods from blue-collar working class to public housing. It's caused a different community dynamic that's forced some longtime neighborhood residents out to the suburbs."

It may be, as Renee Glover and other Hope VI advocates contend, that Section 8 is the primary answer to the question of where the displaced tenants are winding up. But judging by the evidence from Philadelphia, it may also be that the dispersal of Section 8 tenants and their destabilizing effect on fragile neighborhoods will create the next serious crisis in public housing.

Of the many mixed lessons coming out of the revitalization efforts, one seems relatively clear: It is easier to tear down housing for the poor than to rebuild it.

The sheer geography of mixed-income townhouse communities generally requires that fewer public housing units be rebuilt than were there previously. It is virtually impossible, after all, to replace a vertical tower that has 300 apartments with a comparable number of townhouses. The amount of land is insufficient. Even at more spread-out communities such as East Lake, the density is declining. The old community had 650 units. The new one will have 542. Half of those are reserved for market-rate rentals, leaving only 271 units for public housing.

Until recently, housing authorities that tore down units were required to replace them one-for-one. Congress lifted that requirement in 1995, setting the stage for a significant decline in the amount of "hard units" in the nation's public housing stock. Atlanta, for example, had 15,000 public housing units in 1994, although some of them sat vacant. Today, the number is closer to 10,000.

While some of the slack has been taken up with additional Section 8 vouchers, housing activists decry the loss of these hard units. They see Section 8, which Congress must reauthorize every year, as a tenuous commitment that is vulnerable to the political winds in Washington.

Hope VI advocates, however, argue that public housing as we came to know it was so irreconcilably broken that it had to be fundamentally changed. In Atlanta, Glover says that the loss of units is a concern, but that it shouldn't stop revitalization. With vouchers, Atlanta is serving more families now than it did before, she says, and the idea that Congress would suddenly cancel Section 8 and toss millions of people into the street is ludicrous. "It was fundamentally wrong to warehouse the poor," Glover says. "Why would you ever want to sustain a Little Vietnam?"

The issue of replacement units for the poorest residents has been at the heart of the revitalization debate in Seattle. The federal one-for-one requirement was still in place when planning began for Seattle's first big redevelopment, renovation of a World War II-era project called Holly Park. But when the numerical requirement was dropped, planners scaled back the number of units targeted for public housing. The old project had 871 units of public housing. The new one called for only 530 units to replace them.

An activist outcry led the city to reverse itself and adopt a one-for-one replacement plan. Affordable housing in Seattle is already in a tight crunch, they said, and losing these units would only make things worse. "In an era of rapidly rising rents, of gentrification, and increasing numbers of homeless people on the street, we should be preserving our low-income housing stock, not tearing it down," says John McLaren, an activist with the Seattle Dis-

placement Coalition, which pushed for the change.

Meeting the one-for-one commitment, however, is proving tricky. The Seattle Housing Authority is building some off-site units itself, but it is relying on local non-profits to build 221 of the replacement units. The work is coming along more slowly than expected. While 40 replacement units are built and occupied, the others have yet to get off the ground.

A similar one-for-one requirement in Baltimore has been even more problematic. The city blew up the last of its public housing high-rises in February, and construction of replacement homes on the old sites is well under way. But a consent decree that calls for 814 units for home ownership or rentals outside the inner city, as well as 40 public-housing rentals in mostly white, middle-class neighborhoods, remains unfulfilled. Last fall, when plans to buy the first scattered-site replacement units came to a hearing, hundreds of neighbors turned out to protest. Baltimore dropped the plans.

Advocates on both sides of these issues will be eagerly watching for results from two forthcoming studies. The studies, both being done by the Urban Institute, are the first academic efforts to try and answer the question of where all the public housing residents have gone, and whether their lives have improved.

In the first study, researchers are looking at eight cities that received Hope VI grants between 1993 and 1998. Using lists of names from HUD and the housing authorities, they are trying to track down 100 people who lived at each site before it was torn down. The researchers are hoping to get a read on whether people ended up better off than they were before, in terms of their housing quality and employment, and find out what services they received along the way. Results should be in by the fall, although Sue Popkin, who is overseeing it, cautions that there are limitations to this kind of a retrospective study. For one thing, people's memories fade. For another, the only tenants studied are those whom researchers are able to find, not the ones who have, for better or for worse, disappeared.

The other Urban Institute study holds out the greatest promise for a reasonably complete answer. Researchers will take a prospective look at five Hope VI grantees from last year: Atlantic City; Chicago; Durham; Richmond, California; and Washington, D.C. Over the course of four years, they will track a baseline sample of 200 residents. This study will look at a more detailed set of outcomes, including the mental and physical health of residents.

Residents will be tracked over time, whether they stay in public housing or leave it. "Hope VI is a really ambitious effort and is really transforming communities," Popkin says. "But we know very little about how it's affecting the people who lived there the day redevelopment began."

So it seems we will have to wait until 2005 to find out which view is correct — the housing authorities' rosy outlook, or the housing advocates' bleak one. Most likely it is a little of both. For some residents, demolition was probably the gentle kick in the butt they needed to move up and out of public housing. For others, no doubt, it was more like a kick in the stomach.

CHAPTER 4

BALTIMORE USES LINEAR TRAILS TO LINK NEIGHBORHOODS TO HARBOR DISTRICT

Martin J. Rosen

Until several years ago, the meandering stream corridor in the Gwynns Falls Valley, in Baltimore, Maryland, was scoured by floods, piled with trash, and all but abandoned by the residents of the middle- and low-income neighborhoods through which it passed. Back in the early 1900s, the sons of Frederick Law Olmsted had envisioned the 14-mile-long stream corridor as a linear urban park to be anchored by the existing 1,400-acre Gwynns Falls/Leakin Park. But the vision was never realized and the downward spiral of the stream corridor escalated over the last 30 years.

Now, thanks to funding from local philanthropies, state and municipal government, and the federal Intermodal Surface Transportation Efficiency Act (ISTEA) for the park's construction — along with the acquisition of an additional 35 acres — the Gwynns Falls Trail soon will link Baltimore's neighborhoods to the city's redeveloped harbor district — and, just as important, to a new spirit of urban possibility.

This park project and other similar projects reveal a major shift in the way parks and open space are being created and revitalized in U.S. cities. Since the early 1980s, federal government support for local parks and open space — through the Land and Water Conservation Fund state grant program — has been slashed, even in the face of rising need. A 1994 study by the National Recreation and Park Association showed that $30.7 billion of state and local recreational investment would be needed between 1995 and 1999 in order to meet public demand. With the decline in federal support and the tendency of cities to cut park budgets when money is tight, many of our urban parks are in dire need of repair and rejuvenation, and money is simply not available.

Recognizing that the need for parks does not go away, cash-strapped states and cities are scrambling to raise local money and take advantage of private funds. At the same time, there is a growing belief that the most successful parks emerge from broad community participation and contribute bankable value to nearby residential and commercial districts. This confluence of forces is leading to new public/private partnerships to create, rejuvenate, and sometimes manage urban parks and open space.

Originally published as "Reviving Urban Parks," *Urban Land*, Vol. 56, No. 11, November, 1997. Published by the Urban Land Institute, Washington, D.C. Reprinted with permission of the publisher.

In 1994, The Trust for Public Land (TPL) created the Green Cities Initiative to help cities meet the need for more parks by providing assistance in real estate acquisition, finance, and negotiations, and by exploring new ways of involving communities in public finance strategies and park management. While every park is different, successful park efforts share two or more of the following characteristics:

• A formal planning and "visioning" process involving a broad spectrum of public and private stakeholders;
• Catalytic leadership from the public and private sectors;
• A strong connection between parks and open space and broader goals such as economic development, community identity, neighborhood renewal, and provision of needed services;
• A mix of private and public funding, with public funds often coming from state or local sources;
• The advice and assistant of nonprofit partners such as academics; urban planning groups; local civic, community gardening, and "friends-of-parks" organizations; and conservation real estate specialists such as TPL.

Such stakeholder-driven, public/private partnerships will be a primary force in America's future urban park efforts. The challenge of the modern urban parks movement is to ensure that these partnerships develop productively and equitably. From what has been accomplished so far, successful parks will depend on visioning, team building, broad community support, and creative financing and real estate skills. Just as important, new public/private partnerships will have to be forged to maintain and manage parks, so that the great parks created today will remain great parks tomorrow.

If there is a single danger in the public/private approach, it is the risk of sending the wrong message about the need for public sector funds and leadership. Private money can no more bear the entire cost of park creation than public money can, and in a time of rising need, governments need to appropriate more funds for parks, not less. Similarly, the public sector must take the lead in creating change. It is the public sector that must call for community investment in parks, create the visioning process, and invest in the master plans and documents that will get private partners involved. Healthy partnerships cannot be sustained without a substantial public commitment.

Successful Parks/Successful Partnerships

A successful park is more than an island of green space marooned in the concrete of the city. Its success emerges from its relationship to surrounding development and from the special features that attract users and make the park central to a city's image and personality. Its success is also related to the value it provides to the community — be it economic or qualitative value. Success depends not only on good planning and sound execution of park design, but also on continued public/private support for and involvement in park programming and management. In most cities, the era when a simple purchase of land by the city would lead to the creation of a city-envisioned and -designed park is gone. Instead, park creation and redevelopment involve putting together a development team, assembling land (often from multiple and diverse owners and users), raising funds from sources outside the city budget, and ensuring participatory planning every step of the way.

Significant strides have been made toward building productive partnerships. In communities across the country, committed and visionary leaders are beginning to understand the power that parks have in knitting together the frayed urban fabric. But no matter where the impetus comes from, the most successful partnerships include the widest range of stakeholders. The most obvious of these are government, business, and charitable foundations, who may together provide the major financial support for a park project. One significant national foundation partner is the Lila Wallace-Reader's Digest Fund (LWRDF), which has invested $15 million to create and improve urban parks in 11 cities and to share lessons with public and nonprofit leaders about best practices in the field. The LWRDF supported TPL's research on urban park needs in the early 1990s. In 1994, with the foundation's continuing support, TPL launched its Green Cities Initiative to bring its deal-making, fundraising, and park-planning skills to a wide range of public and private urban partners.

But the most important partners in any park plan may be nearby residents and neighborhood groups. The time should be long past when political leaders and professional park designers create parks for — instead of with — neighborhoods. The success of any park depends on how it is used; to ensure neighborhood involvement and support, professional designers and facilitators can use community meetings, written surveys, and individual interviews to lead local residents — the ultimate users — through the visioning process.

What is sometimes not understood about the park visioning and planning process is the extent to which it can transcend creation of a specific park or open space and deal with larger questions about community identity and purpose: What kind of city do we want to become? What role will parks play in our community? How do we want open space resources to be distributed in our city? What social and economic benefits do we want parks to provide? How will park programs serve city residents? And how will residents resolve conflicts over these issues?

There are success stories worthy of examination across the country. For example, the creation of Cedar Lake Park and Trail in Minneapolis, Minnesota, reveals a city that prizes nature, bicycle transportation, active recreation, and citizen initiative. Similarly, the process that created Downtown Park in Bellevue, Washington, suggests a city that has used a park to create a sense of place and encourage a pedestrian-friendly, densely populated center. Mill Race Park, in Columbus, Indiana, shows that the city prizes volunteerism and cooperative effort. And in Spartanburg, South Carolina, Flagstar Corporate Plaza and Jerome Richardson Park are examples of a city committed to downtown revival.

In some instances, a major park project simply cannot get off the ground until a community answers larger questions about how the park might shape and confirm its future. In Seattle, voters have twice rejected efforts to create an 86-acre "commons" in a lower-income, light-industrial neighborhood north of downtown. Seattle Commons has been supported by the mayor and city council, generous contributions from corporations and philanthropies, and enthusiastic volunteers and professional staff. But other Seattle residents have worried about gentrification, rising rents and land prices, and the diversion of city resources from smaller neighborhood parks. If and when this park is created, it will be stronger and more successful because the process has addressed these issues to the satisfaction of most residents.

Whether Baltimore would become the kind of city that links its neighborhoods to larger community resources is a question to be answered, in part, by the creation of the Gwynns Falls Trail. For two decades, Baltimore had been working to rejuvenate its downtown harbor district as a cultural, recreational, and retail showplace. In this context, Baltimore officials and residents began looking toward the western neighborhoods, which are joined to the harbor by the lush — though trash-strewn — ribbon of Gwynns Falls. Plans for the prime open space began taking shape in 1988, when the late Ralph Jones, Baltimore's park director, challenged the Yale School of Forestry and Environmental Studies to help create a new vision for Baltimore parks. Inspired by this work, the city soon forged a partnership with two organizations — TPL and Parks and People, a local nonprofit — to link that vision to a revival of Baltimore's neighborhoods. The visioning process to revitalize the Gwynns Falls corridor, which took more than four years, included contributions from 16 community groups, 11 nonprofit organizations, and eight city agencies. Residents were polled on their open-space needs, properties were studied, and a master plan was created. Since then, trash has been cleared, boardwalks have been built, and a schedule for major trail construction has been set — all to answer the larger question about what kind of a city Baltimore would become.

Assembling Urban Parkland

Assembling land for today's urban parks is complicated by the involvement of various stakeholders and multiple jurisdictions, complex ownership patterns, and the frequent need for extensive environmental assessment and cleanup. Razing abandoned buildings and cleaning up contaminated "brownfield" sites can turn economic sinks into economic engines for a city, but such projects are also complicated by myriad federal, state, and local regulations that can make the politics of a project as complicated as the economics. Rarely do city park departments have the staff or financial resources to take on assemblages and cleanups. Completion of these new parks often requires interdepartmental teams within a public agency and the support of nonprofit and for-profit development partners.

In Winston-Salem, North Carolina, for example, civic leaders have long despaired of salvaging the city's southeast gateway district, a blighted patch of abandoned warehouses adjacent to the Old Salem historic park — Winston-Salem's major tourist attraction. An eyesore at the very doorway of a bustling downtown, for years the southeast district has offered no shopping, lunch spots, or gathering place for Old Salem visitors — or for students from the four surrounding prep schools and colleges. And easy access to a greenway along Salem Creek and a "strollway" along a former trolley line was blocked by a public road (which is now slated for closing).

In the early 1990s, local business leaders, educational institutions, and civic groups joined to forge the Southeast Gateway Council, a private nonprofit organization dedicated to renewal of the southeast district. In 1992, the American Institute of Architects sponsored a two-day design workshop to envision a plan for the area, which involved a land assemblage. But as a relatively small city, Winston-Salem lacked the staff and expertise to complete the ambitious project. At the request of the city, TPL researched the feasibility and costs of assembling almost nine acres of commercial properties west of Main Street for a proposed public plaza and retail village. The organization contracted for title searches, environmental audits, appraisals, and an economic feasibility study, and also negotiated with the eight area landowners to secure options to purchase their properties. Working together, TPL, the city, and a group of civic leaders came up with a financing package for the project: approximately $1 million will come from the site's developer, and several million more will come from the county, the city, and private donations from individuals, foundations, and corporations. Plans call for a new visitors' center for Old Salem, a pedestrian shopping plaza, and completion of the two greenways.

Creating parks from urban sites often requires such multiple and complex partnerships. Sometimes a development component is built in to support the park, and the developer becomes part of the partnership. Outside planning and design groups may donate their expertise; an example is the work undertaken by the American Society of Landscape Architects to help create a vision for a greenway along the Los Angeles River. Private funding for the planning stage may come from local philanthropic foundations that hope to leverage a public commitment in the form of a bond act or tax measure, as was the case in Los Angeles County, where a bond measure — the Los Angeles County Park, Beach, and Recreation Act — was passed in 1996 that will provide about $319 million for acquisition and capital improvement projects, including $9 million dedicated to improving and restoring the Los Angeles River with a greenway. This is at a cost of about $7 per year for an average household.

Other models are emerging, particularly in urban areas where vacant, underused, and often contaminated urban lands and buildings offer cities key resources for the revitalization of their waterfronts and neighborhoods.

TPL, with seed funding from the James Irvine Foundation, recently launched the California Center for Land Recycling (CCLR), whose mission is to foster land recycling as a way to redirect growth away from the fringes of metropolitan areas and to revitalize the urban core. To assist in the development of new policies and strategies for rejuvenating urban centers, CCLR supports and documents model projects that incorporate community participation, economic development efforts, and brownfield remediation.

Understanding the assets and roles of public and private partners is key to building successful and strategic partnerships. Nonprofits may bring short-term efficien-cies to a project, taking advantage of the dynamic real estate market on behalf of a public agency that cannot move quickly; flexible funding and financing from creative and entrepreneurial sources that can leverage public sources; organizational flexibility to build staff around projects, hire consultants, and track down the expertise needed; and community credibility, through their contacts with broad constituencies and their goal of working on behalf of the public's interest. The public sector can add stability and legitimacy to a project, grounding it with a stable base of funding, a long-term commitment to public use and management, and the ability to link the project to a broader city vision or plan, which can support and leverage the project.

Raising Money and Forging Transactions

Usually, the first question park advocates and public officials ask about any park or open space project is, how will we pay for it? An analysis of nearly 100 land acquisition cases that TPL has completed with local public agencies showed close to 20 different sources of acquisition and development funding, including sources at the state and federal levels. And these numbers showed few projects with single sources of support: 58 projects relied on at least two sources of funding.

Funding sources are as varied as the projects themselves. Sometimes private stakeholders bear all or most of the costs of park development, as was the case for the Park at Post Office Square in Boston and the Flagstar Corporate Plaza and Jerome Richardson Park in Spartanburg, South Carolina. More often, private stakeholders such as businesses and foundations provide capital grants, indirect capital (through fundraising campaigns), management assistance, and publicity — or, in the case of developers, an influx of residents or workers to use and support the park. In exchange for these private contributions, governments may contribute free or discounted land, tax and financing concessions, and city support services for the park or open space.

In 1995, officials and residents of Santa Fe, New Mexico, hoped to buy a 50-acre former railyard — the last major open parcel in the city's booming downtown. The Catellus Development Corporation — the successor of the Atchison, Topeka & Santa Fe Railroad — did not lack prospective buyers for the land, which was appraised at $29 million. The city of Santa Fe wanted at least a portion of the parcel for a park and other public use, and it wanted some control over how the balance of the property was developed, but it was not sure how it would pay for the land. At the city's request, TPL stepped in to bargain with Catellus. By offering a tax benefit to the corporation, TPL acquired the land at an $8 million discount. As part of the arrangement with TPL, the city agreed to dedicate at least ten acres of the property to a public park.

Funding and support for a single park project may come from many sources: federal, state, and local governments; foundation funds; corporate grants; developer concessions; and donations of land value by landowners. Often a nonprofit partner serves a coordinating and brokerage function — raising funds, combining funds, and structuring the final transaction. A nonprofit partner may also be able to maximize funds, reducing the cost of a property by offering a tax break to a landowner — as in Santa Fe — or accepting a donation of land for a city. In Boston, TPL accepted the donation of a 1.2-acre rail corridor from Consolidated Freight Corporation (Conrail) for a new greenway in East Boston, one of the city's most densely settled neighborhoods. To enable the city to accept the property, TPL agreed to have an environmental assessment and cleanup performed.

New Public Funds for Parks

Nonprofit partners can also help by building community support for open space protection. One of the most heartening developments in recent years has been the public's willingness to help fund new parks and open space acquisition. As is the case in all aspects of park creation, effective public fundraising is based on effective team building: when enough stakeholders show enthusiastic support for a project, a community will often commit new funds to parks and open space.

In the late 1980s, Austin, Texas, faced a serious open space crisis when development west of the city began to pollute Barton Springs, a downtown swimming hole that is one of the city's best-known natural and recreational features. Austin environmentalists had been trying to protect the creek corridor for decades, but the pollution of Barton Springs sparked wider community concern. In 1991, TPL began working with government and community groups to quantify Austin's open space needs. Questionnaires distributed to residents revealed that a majority would support new local taxes for recreation and park facilities. In 1992, in the wake of a TPL-organized campaign for the measure, voters approved a $20 million bond act to establish the Barton Creek Wilderness Park.

It is no accident that Austin's support for park facilities coalesced around a specific place. Citizen support for well-conceived financing measures with explicit goals for land acquisition continues to have good outcomes in cities. The "market share" of parks and recreation bonds in the municipal bond market increased in recent years from one to 1.5 percent. The municipal finance industry has noted the public's willingness to pay for parks. Voters are also more likely to approve new spending for parks if a property or properties have already been designated and optioned for acquisition. This not only protects a valuable park property while funds are being raised, but also provides a tangible focus for voters evaluating an open space tax or bond measure. While governments are usually prohibited from risking public funds to option properties in advance of voter approval, a nonprofit partner is not, and TPL has been asked to provide up-front financing in many communities.

Nonprofit partners can also help government and community groups by polling voters on open space needs and conducting funding and direct-mail advertising campaigns. Using such techniques, TPL has helped pass funding measures in Portland, Oregon; King County (Seattle), Washington; Dade County (Miami), Florida; Los Angeles County; Austin, Texas; and Pima County (Tucson), Arizona.

Even after a measure is approved, a public agency may ask a nonprofit partner to hold land until funds accumulate, structure a special lease-purchase agreement, or arrange for the land to be transferred in several phases to meet budgetary or legal requirements. A lease-purchase agreement can be particularly helpful if a city has decided to acquire land and does not have up-front funds. For a new park in Lakewood, Colorado, TPL structured a 30-year lease-purchase transaction. The lease is renewable year by year, and the city has reserved the right to purchase the property before the 30 years have passed.

In other instances, a public agency may ask a nonprofit partner to assemble properties for a planned unit development (PUD), so that park or conservation lands can be transferred to the public agency and the remaining land can be sold to private developers for cluster development. After voters in Austin, Texas, approved a $20 million bond initiative to acquire land along Barton Creek, TPL used a portion of those funds to purchase a 1,000-acre historic ranch for the Barton Creek Wilderness Park. The city's PUD ordinance allowed TPL to sell 240 acres to private developers for cluster development; the remaining acreage was sold to the city for the wilderness park. The subsidy provided by the development purchase allowed the city to acquire the conservation land for approximately a quarter of what city planners had expected.

Partnerships in Ongoing Management

Public/private partnerships have proven highly effective in generating vision, creating public support for new parks, raising and maximizing funds, and structuring workable land-acquisition transactions. The greatest need for the future is to enlarge the focus of partnerships to include park management. In uncertain budgetary times, some cities hesitate to create parks because of the ongoing obligation to manage and maintain them. But there is no reason to assume that the creativity and energy that partnerships bring to park creation cannot also be applied to park management and maintenance. The public sector, which can no longer run the nation's urban park systems alone, must call on the ideas, skills, and strengths of private partners, not only to create parks, but also to guarantee their long-term health and usefulness.

Many successful park projects continue to depend on private support. In some instances, this support is monetary. In Spartanburg, South Carolina, the Flagstar Corporation pays to maintain the plaza and park it largely created. Management of Manhattan's Bryant Park is funded mostly by proceeds from the park's restaurant and café and from assessments of a business improvement district — an increasingly popular way for businesses to return to the public some of the wealth generated by urban open space. And at the Park at Post Office Square in Boston, fees for private parking support park management.

But just as important as financial support are the energy and vision private partners bring to parks. In the most successful park processes, the same partners who help envision and build parks stay involved to help fund and manage them. Through continuous evaluation, planning, programming, and use, these committed private partners seek not only to create but also to sustain valuable parks.

At Cedar Lake Park in Minneapolis, park neighbors organized as the Cedar Lake Park Association have continued their involvement — not only by raising more than $1.2 million for the park's support, but in hands-on efforts to restore natural ecosystems absent for 100 years. In Pinellas County, Florida, groups and communities along the Pinellas Trail have raised money for plantings, benches, water fountains, and other amenities, and have also donated greenery and planted demonstration flower boxes. One community along the trail has created a bicycle and pedestrian plaza, organized musical performances where the trail passes through downtown, and is making it possible for its segment of the trail to be used at night. Such measures draw users to parks, who come to value them in a whole new way. Through such efforts, the real meaning of a park emerges, one user-day at a time.

The largest and most productive public/private park partnership in the nation is the partnership between the New York City Parks and Recreation Department and the Central Park Conservancy, which was established in 1980. In its first 15 years, the conservancy raised $110 million to restore and reclaim Central Park from decades of declining maintenance and increasing vandalism. In addition, the conservancy contracts with the city to help develop programs for the park. and the nonprofit's 175 staffers bear many responsibilities traditionally borne by city employees. Not only has Central Park been largely rejuvenated through the conservancy's ministrations, but the effort has freed the city parks department to devote funds and staff time to smaller neighborhood parks.

In Philadelphia, declining public monies and a venerable philanthropic tradition have led to a three-way partnership between the Philadelphia Recreation Department, the Fairmount Park Commission (manager of one of the nation's largest urban parks), and Philadelphia Green, the inner-city division of the Philadelphia Horticultural Society. The organization also assumes broad responsibilities often borne by a city parks department: it plants, prunes, and removes trees; beautifies boulevards and neighborhoods; fights graffiti; and organizes environmental education programs. Some of the more than $3 million the horticultural society spends on such projects each year is raised through its annual flower show; the balance is from traditional philanthropic sources. Although staffing remains half of what it was in the early 1980s, the city recently responded to this private energy by incrementally restoring staff to the Philadelphia Recreation Department.

The experiences in New York and Philadelphia bear important lessons for the urban parks movement. The first is that great parks are not created once, but are recreated over and over again, as is happening in New York City. The experience in Philadelphia teaches us that, despite the worries of some observers, private efforts can be solidly democratic, can forge strong community partnerships, and can create important open space resources in low-income neighborhoods.

The promise of the new public/private partnerships is that they will remain flexible and open to new approaches — constantly reinvigorated by their mix of governments, businesses, charitable and stakeholder groups, and nonprofit consultants. Such partnerships represent the greatest hope of the urban parks movement.

CHAPTER 5

BATON ROUGE USES MASTER PLAN TO REVITALIZE HISTORIC DOWNTOWN

Jeffrey C. Fluhr and *Denny St. Romain*

The movement to derive a new master plan for downtown Baton Rouge, Louisiana, was initiated as a result of a lecture series in 1997 sponsored by the Baton Rouge Area Foundation, which stressed less dependence on the automobile and the importance of designing and implementing neotraditional neighborhoods and creating a more vibrant city center. In the months that followed, public interest in exploring new urbanism principles for the city increased. People liked the idea of neighborhoods with integrated commercial centers, of neighborhood grocery or retail stores within walkable distance.

In response, the Baton Rouge Area Foundation formed a new urbanism committee made up of business and community leaders to gather additional information regarding new urbanism as well as information about the firms performing such planning throughout the United States. It was decided to initiate new urbanist planning principles in an area that was manageable and in which the entire city had ownership — the city's downtown. The plan — named PLAN Baton Rouge — would build on the redevelopment and development efforts already un-

derway by the city's Downtown Development District (DDD). Once the plan is implemented successfully, its principles will be applied to other areas of the city.

Involving the community is critical to the success of any plan. In the weeks leading up to the charrette, consultants presented lectures to the public as part of their respective pre-site visits, showing examples of how other cities such as West Palm Beach, Florida, and Chattanooga, Tennessee, through planning, had become attractive, livable places. The consultants met with downtown organizations such as the Downtown Merchants Association, neighborhood associations, and downtown property owners to hear their visions and concerns.

The recommendations presented and incorporated into the Baton Rouge plan included items that could be implemented in the short term with little or no expense, items that required governmental action, and proposals that would require private development. Many of the recommendations improved upon projects already underway downtown. For example, two parking garages soon will be built in conjunction

Originally published as "Baton Rouge Blueprint," *Urban Land*, Vol. 59, No. 10, October, 2000. Published by the Urban Land Institute, Washington, D.C. Reprinted with permission of the publisher.

with the State Capitol Complex building program — a program initiated by the DDD through state legislation to consolidate state government within downtown Baton Rouge. To ensure a positive reception of the new garages by the public, it was recommended that the bottom floor in one garage incorporate retail space, a YMCA health club (scheduled to open next month), and a daycare facility, and that the other garage's bottom floor house an expansion of Baton Rouge's already successful farmers' market.

Recommendations for private development included a multiscreen cinema across the street from one of the new parking garages. To encourage the private sector to consider this proposal, the state agreed to allow the cinema to have free use of the new garage for evening and weekend patrons. Two riverfront tracts of land also were singled out as potential development sites. The proposal included closing down the last block of the street that runs between these tracts and donating it to the developers; in return, the developers would agree to develop the areas for retail and entertainment uses and include a public plaza with a fountain.

Since many blocks of downtown Baton Rouge have lost one or more buildings and are now occupied by parking lots, a two-story "liner" building roughly 20 feet deep was proposed to be built throughout the central business district to create continuous street frontage while also allowing for parking in the rear. The building can house apartments, retail space, and offices on the second floor and parking on the first, which already has proven financially attractive to many nearby parking lot owners.

One recommendation that could alter the downtown market dramatically is the reintroduction of a light-rail transit system. It was suggested that passenger rail service, running along existing rail tracks, be reestablished, connecting downtown's civic center, museums, and federal, state, and city governments with Louisiana State University's 35,000 students and staff and Southern University's 10,000 students and staff.

A site plan already has been submitted for a 490,000-square-foot mixed-use development incorporating retail, office, and residential units. The project will be the first residential development within the central business district in more than 30 years, which in turn increases the probability of specialty retail and restaurants coming into the area.

The Baton Rouge plan also has encouraged redevelopment of downtown historic structures. One project will convert a prominent and currently vacant building along the Third Street corridor into office space with retail space at the street level. This project will complement a coffeehouse, a gallery, and an antique car museum currently under construction within a two-block radius.

The latest calculations indicate that more than $300 million in public and private investments will be made on downtown Baton Rouge for the year 2000–2001, compared with approximately $350 million during the entire previous decade.

Public Sector

More than $160 million in capital improvements will be commenced by the state of Louisiana for 2000–2001, funded through lease revenue bonds issued by a statutory nonprofit organization, the Office of Facility Corporation. The state of Louisiana will construct more than one million square feet of state offices encompassing over five city blocks within the city center. The bonds will be paid by state revenues normally appropriated to pay state leases. The new state buildings, which will save more than $500 million in lease payments during the next 30 years, include a 350,000-square-foot facility for the department of revenue and taxation; a 450,000-square-foot facility for the department of administration; and a 2,000-car parking garage. Planning for four new structures also will get underway this year: a 350,000-square-foot facility for the department of environmental quality and control; another 2,000-car parking garage; a facility for the department of insurance; and a new Baton Rouge visitor's center and museum. Once completed, the complex will consolidate more than 3,000 employees within the city center.

A joint project between the state of Louisiana and the city of Baton Rouge is the new planetarium and space theater, which will be constructed adjacent to the Louisiana Arts and Science Center located on the city's riverfront. The city will pay 50 percent of the costs of the $6 million facility and the state of Louisiana will pay 50 percent. The city will bond revenues obtained from state sales tax rebates, and the private sector has raised an additional $3 million for an operating endowment.

The city's convention center is planning a 100,000-square-foot addition to the existing 30,000 square feet of exhibition space that will involve a 50/50 joint venture between the city of Baton Rouge and the state of Louisiana. Site development is scheduled to commence during the fourth quarter of this year. The city will bond revenues derived from state sales tax rebates as well as an additional one percent increase in the hotel/motel bed tax as approved by the voters. The new tax will provide an additional $600,000 annually to be bonded and will remain in place until the bonds are paid.

Private Sector

Private sector development is comprised of hotels, renovations of existing buildings, and new office and residential construction. To assist developers in the per-

mitting process, the DDD serves as a liaison between the developer and the local and state regulatory agencies. The city of Baton Rouge is offering a number of financial programs to encourage private sector development within the city center.

Local financial institutions are offering loans of $25,000 to $250,000 to attract new businesses to the city center. The stipulations of the loans allow the capital to be applied to leased and owned properties and may be used for working capital, improvements, interim financing, furniture and fixtures, and inventory financing. Applicants receiving loans also receive $1,000 from the DDD for closing costs. The loans have been successful in assisting art galleries, offices, renovations, and interim financing. They typically require 15 to 20 percent equity investment and are based on a 15-year term.

Popular with existing and new businesses is the economic development zone program, a state and local initiative that provides a $2,500 tax credit for jobs created within the city center; a minimum of two jobs must be created within five years. A rebate of state sales tax on materials to construct or expand a business as well as on machinery and equipment is also available. A five-year property tax abatement on improvements to structures also is being offered, in addition to a 20 percent credit on improvements made to a historic structure within the city center. The DDD currently is working with other Louisiana downtown development districts to adopt state legislation that will allow for an additional 25 percent state tax credit for eligible costs and expenses of the rehabilitation of an approved historic structure. The legislation is modeled after legislation adopted by the state of Missouri.

Currently, there are three hotel projects underway downtown: one new construction project and two renovation projects. Each is securing funding through private resources. Driving hotel development is the expansion of the city's convention center, which will require a minimum of 500 full-service rooms in the adjacent area. Downtown Baton Rouge currently has only 200 rooms in an economy-style hotel.

Baton Rouge-based Dean Classic Properties has renovated more than six structures downtown for office and residential use and has purchased the grand hotel of the city, the Heidelberg Hotel, a circa 1920s 300-room hotel that has been closed since the mid–1980s. Dean is finalizing public and private funding for the interior and exterior renovation. The renovation may utilize HUD section 108 funding.

Golden Opportunities, Inc., of Utah, owner of the only operating downtown hotel — General Lafayette — is embarking on a $4 million-plus renovation of the structure. The company is exploring funding and a national hotel chain marquee.

Argosy Gaming, one of two riverboat gaming operators within the city of Baton Rouge, is moving forward with the construction of a 305-room, full-service convention hotel. The project is a component of a contractual agreement with the city of Baton Rouge for the city's endorsement of Argosy Gaming's riverboat gaming license. The hotel is being constructed within one block of the expanded convention center and will be under the Sheraton national hotel chain marquee. The hotel is scheduled to open in December.

Numerous renovations also are underway transforming older downtown structures into prime office space. Approximately 22,000 people work in downtown Baton Rouge, and more than 100,000 individuals travel daily to the district to conduct business. The major employers downtown are federal, state, and local governments. On average, Class A office space is commanding $18 to $22 per square foot, with a tenant base of attorneys, financial services, and private enterprise. The occupancy rate of Class A office space exceeds 90 percent. Class B office space is attracting $13 to $18 per square foot with the same tenant base as noted above but with the addition of limited retail. The occupancy rate for Class B space exceeds 80 percent.

The first new private office building in 15 years has received preliminary site approval. A Hartley/Vey Development, the project is comprised of approximately 220,000 square feet of Class A office space, 180,000 square feet of condominiums, and 77,000 square feet of office and retail space. The project also encompasses 262,000 square feet of parking. By offering sweeping views of the Mississippi River and the latest in corporate design, the developers plan to attract tenants who have been in office markets outside of the downtown area. The residential component should strengthen the market base for specialty retail interests and restaurants in the area.

Furthering the development of the arts is crucial to ensuring activity downtown after 5:00 p.m. Several galleries and artist co-ops have opened downtown during the previous months, using the low-interest loan program and assistance from the Greater Baton Rouge Arts Council. One concept being proposed is to use an old architecturally significant parking garage, owned by the state of Louisiana, as a community cultural center. The garage overlooks the Mississippi River and is adjacent to the Old State Capitol building, which was renovated and reopened in 1994 and now serves as the State of Louisiana Center for Political History.

Plans call for the renovation of the circa 1920s garage into a center for visiting artists and space for the private sector to open restaurants, a coffeehouse, and specialty art retail. Property adjacent to the building has been acquired to allow for the future development of a performing arts center. The state has made available an additional $3.5 million of matching funds, through the state capital outlay for the performing arts center, to be used for construction. The Baton Rouge Area Foundation is serving as the fiscal agent, with the Arts Council of Greater Baton Rouge responsible for raising the required match.

The opportunity given to city and state officials to work with town planners, retail specialists, and implementation strategists has been an experience that not only captured a vision for the city of Baton Rouge, but also provided increased understanding of the multiple components critical to the redevelopment and development of a vibrant city center.

CHAPTER 6

BERKELEY REVIVES ITS OLD DOWNTOWN THROUGH CREATION OF AN ARTS DISTRICT

Judith Rubin

Next month, the Berkeley Repertory Theatre, in Berkeley, California, opens its much-awaited second stage, the Theatre Next Door, but the opening ushers in much more than a new performance space. The Theatre Next Door has become the nucleus of Berkeley's new Addison Street Arts District, which in turn is the standard-bearer of the city's burgeoning downtown revitalization movement — and a testament to the power of the arts to rally development forces and to foster common-cause partnerships in a politically and socially diverse area.

The locally and nationally acclaimed Berkeley Repertory Theatre (known as the Rep) received a Tony Award in 1997 for outstanding regional theater. In 1990, the Rep found it was outgrowing its 400-seat space in its building at 2025 Addison Street, in the middle of a block given mostly to automotive uses but otherwise well located and only a short walk from the downtown Berkeley BART (Bay Area Rapid Transit) station. "We were surrounded by body shops and couldn't get control of the property," comments Susie Medak, the Rep's managing director, "so we were considering relocating to Oakland."

Downtown Berkeley was beginning to emerge from a slump marked by empty storefronts, seedy nighttime denizens, and a decline in restaurant patronage. The downtown plan that the city adopted in 1990 hinted at increased cultural uses. At the same time, then-mayor Loni Hancock helped the Rep sort out some of the real estate issues, so the theater was able to purchase land on both sides of its property. Next, the Rep needed the money to expand.

Two years later, the city of Berkeley and the Downtown Berkeley Association (DBA) jointly sponsored a study to determine how to position the downtown economically. "From that emerged the notion of starting with our strengths — that we had a unique, existing identity to build on, featuring arts, entertainment, and specialty retail," relates Michael Caplan, assistant to the city manager, who throughout the past decade has been a major force behind the arts district. In his previous post as downtown coordinator for Berkeley's Office of Economic Development (OED), Caplan was OED staff liaison to DBA. Caplan and Medak started talking to property owners,

Originally published as "Arts as Economic Catalyst," *Urban Land*, Vol. 60, No. 2, February, 2001. Published by the Urban Land Institute, Washington, D.C. Reprinted with permission of the publisher.

promoting their vision of downtown as an arts and entertainment center for the city and the region. "I was like Bob Preston in *The Music Man*," he laughs.

Medak met with Shirley Dean, who, in the midst of launching her run for mayor, embraced the concept of creating a full-fledged arts district anchored by an expanded Rep, making it a major plank of her campaign platform. "She was dogged in her support," says Medak. "She is still holding monthly meetings to make sure that the coalition of arts groups and developers hold together."

The year Dean became mayor, 1994, also was the year that the city approved the Downtown Berkeley Public Improvements plan, drawn up by Donlyn Lyndon and Allan Jacobs, both well-known urban designers associated with UC (University of California) Berkeley. "It was the first time the arts district became codified and approved," notes Caplan. "One of the things it did was specify identities for discreet subregions in the downtown, including Addison Street as the focus for the arts." The city eventually demonstrated its commitment by granting $4 million for the Berkeley Rep Campaign for Expansion through certificates of participation and by providing $1 million for related projects in the form of loans and grants. "Normally, we get $1,000 or $2,000 a year from the city," remarks Medak. "Across the country, the average an institution like ours gets is six percent of its city's operating budget; we get less than two percent. "The $4 million was a huge issue."

Berkeley residents showed their support for downtown when they approved the 1996 earthquake retrofit bond measure, Measure S, which green-lighted another $4 million for downtown streetscaping. Intended to secure $49 million primarily for seismic work downtown at Berkeley's Civic Center and main library, plus a library expansion, Measure S needed a two-thirds ma-

jority, and it initially was expected to fail. An article in the October 27, 1996, *San Francisco Chronicle* stated that "regardless of the need, Berkeley voters may indeed have reached their tax saturation point." According to Caplan, "Targeting $4 million [of the $49 million] for streetscape improvements made Measure S more appealing to voters." A stroll through downtown today shows Measure S funds at work: both the library and city hall are under construction, and new sidewalks, trees, tree grates, lighting, and public art installations on Addison Street are nearly complete.

"For Dean and the members of the city council, the arts district is a legacy project," says Caplan. "There was some political opposition, but it turned around because of the diversity of uses and the overall success of the project. Everyone now understands the vision." The resulting cultural synergy is expected to multiply the number of visitors far beyond the number that the Rep alone could bring in. "We couldn't sustain the desired level of activity on our own," says Medak, a founding board member of DBA. "The more the merrier. It's in our best interest, and the city's," she adds.

The Rep's new 600-seat, three-story auditorium with a proscenium stage is being rapidly completed to adjoin the west side of the original building; they will have a common courtyard and lobby. It was designed by local architect Donn Logan during his last years with ELS/Elbasani and Logan Architects, which is serendipitously located on Addison Street across from the theater. Logan, who co-founded ELS in 1967 and now practices independently in West Berkeley, is a specialist in projects involving urban retail, the arts, and downtown development. He says that he welcomed the opportunity to apply his expertise in his own backyard. "This was a more personal thing — my town," explains Logan, who served five years on the DBA board as head of its design committee. "The arts district is one of those things that bubbled up in a lot of minds simultaneously." He worked closely with Berkeley-based landscape architect John Northmore Roberts to design the new Addison streetscape, which helps to proclaim the block the center of the new arts district.

The city's $5 million in seed money has helped draw more than $30 million in private money to the Addison Street block alone. The Rep was able to attract millions more for its expansion from such donors as the Ask Jeeves Foundation and the Kresge Foundation. Next door to the Rep at 2071 Addison, the historic Golden Sheaf Bakery is being restored by local developer Avi Nevo and will reopen this summer as the Nevo Education Center. The building, erected in 1905 and designed by architect Clinton Day, was placed on the National Register of Historic Places in 1978. Nevo purchased it from the Rep and will lease it back at $1 per year.

Probably the most significant new resident coming to this block of Addison is the nonprofit Freight & Salvage Coffee House, since 1968 a local icon of folk music, presently housed several blocks west. The Freight bought two buildings across the street from the Rep (one is leased to the Capoeira Arts Café, a combination martial arts school and coffee shop) and is raising money to design and build a new 400-seat venue with the goal of creating a strong co-anchor for the Rep. The Aurora Theatre Company also is expected to join the district shortly with a 160-seat theater in the round, its first permanent home.

Relocating to the arts district in 2003 will be the Judah L. Magnes Museum. Founded in 1962, the Magnes is said to be the third-largest Jewish museum in the United States; it currently is located in the north of the city. The museum has purchased a building on nearby Allston Way that is temporarily housing the public library while the library's permanent building on Kittredge undergoes seismic retrofit.

When the library returns home, the Magnes will renovate the building.

Tying in with the new facilities are 22 existing cinema screens in six locations within a few blocks of Addison Street, including the historic, single-screen, 1,500-seat UC Theatre, built in 1917, as well as several bookstores and numerous restaurants and bars. About a year ago, a block of nearby Center Street was redeveloped with several new restaurants, boutiques, and sidewalk cafés. Because it enhanced a pedestrian gateway between nearby transit hubs and the university, this joint project of the city and the University of California received funds from the state department of transportation under the federal Intermodal Surface Transportation and Enhancement Act.

Civic arts coordinator Mary Ann Merker-Benton is responsible for administering $300,000 in Measure S money for public art in downtown Berkeley; $100,000 has been allocated for the Rep block of Addison Street. The money has been devoted mostly to the sidewalks, which are being inset with more than 100 poetry squares edited by Robert Hass, Berkeley professor and former U.S. poet laureate, and 12 wedge-shaped panels created by eight Berkeley artists. All surfaces must be nonslip and comply with ADA (Americans with Disabilities Act) regulations, and some new technologies are being developed in the process under the auspices of the project's technical director, Scott Donahue, working with the local Fireform Foundry.

The remaining $200,000 has been distributed among new gates for the public library, two outdoor sculptures on Shattuck Avenue (the downtown's main artery), and a street median project on University Avenue to mark the Shattuck-University gateway to downtown. A special effort was made to open the project to artists who were new to public art, and two workshops were held to instruct artists in the process. Merker-Benton admits that the project's scope is ambitious and that money is spread thin, but she notes that local support continues to rise to the occasion — as demonstrated by the pro bono work of landscape architect Roberts, the fundraising efforts of Hass, and the willingness of the artists involved to find ways to supplement their budgets.

Merker-Benton stresses the constant involvement of the community. "We did a lot of listening to focus groups, and we received vital support from the Berkeley Cultural Trust of 21 nonprofit arts organizations. A lot of public art projects get in trouble for not including the community," she observes. "All of a sudden something goes up somewhere, and people hate it. And the National Artists Rights Act prevents you from just taking it down again, unless it is a public hazard. You don't want that to happen."

In activist Berkeley, Merker-Benton has had to juggle numerous political groups as well. "There are almost 40 commissions in the city," she points out. "They have to be part of your process. This city doesn't have a long history of working with arts administrators," Merker-Benton adds. "The challenge for me was educating the city about what good arts policy is." To help, she mounted "an interior public art program," installing artworks around the OED building. The local Kala Institute agreed to loan the city some 50 works by Berkeley artists; Merker-Benton organized a staff group to select them, and the city paid to have them framed. Daily exposure to art in its own workplace fostered an understanding within OED of the value of public art. "After that, everything changed," says Merker-Benton. "City staff started coming here for their meetings. We put art in the city hall. Now we have staff who will not let you take a cer-

tain piece of art away from them. It opened things up and changed people's minds."

Berkeley's new gateway to the arts also is opening the gate to other kinds of development essential to meeting the goal of creating an active, 24-hour downtown. These include housing, mixed-use and infill projects, and hotels, some already on the drawing boards. Linking them to the arts makes them more likely to survive what can be a tough review process in a city of many political factions concerned with issues such as land use, preservation, chainstore propagation, density, parking, and transit corridors. "There are properties that have sat undeveloped for years," points out Medak. "Now things are starting to happen."

"Right now, downtown's clout is mostly in entertainment: nightlife, movies, music," observed Logan. "There are lots of restaurants — probably too many at the low end of the scale. What has been lost over the decades is downtown as a shopping place," he adds. "Berkeley politics makes it hard to get a coherent vision that represents most groups. The arts was a breakthrough. Nobody could be against it; everybody could get behind it," says Logan.

"One of the most remarkable things about the way this unfolded financially," notes Caplan, "is that we had no standard redevelopment agency assistance. Downtown Berkeley is not a designated redevelopment district. We created an incremental process, using certificates of participation, bond funds, end-of-year capital monies, federal transportation dollars, and other sources as they became available," he adds. "'Arts and theater district' sounds better than 'urban revitalization' or 'urban redevelopment' to most people anyway. I like to call it 'arts-led revitalization.'"

CHAPTER 7

BOULDER REDESIGNS RESIDENTIAL STREETS TO RESTORE QUALITY OF LIFE TO ITS NEIGHBORHOODS

John Fernandez

Boulder, Colorado, has a problem shared by cities across the country. Too many of its streets divide rather than integrate. They are single-purpose arteries, emphasizing cars over people. They despoil the environment with their expansive impervious surfaces. They encourage speeding. And they support faceless suburban development patterns guaranteed to worsen traffic congestion.

Residential streets are key determinants of neighborhood quality. They offer a place to walk, to play — and of course to park. Yet ever since the start of the post–World War II housing boom, residential streets have become increasingly devoted to traffic movement. The wide lanes required by today's codes lead to higher speeds, more accidents, and greater urban fragmentation.

In recent years, many planners — and even some traffic engineers — have begun to question whether wider streets are as functional as their advocates claim. Increasingly, designers, public officials, and developers — often spurred by neighborhood activists — are considering the virtues of a hierarchical street classification that would provide for a variety of residential street types, each reflecting different traffic conditions.

Local History

Like many western cities, Boulder was laid out, in 1859, on a grid based on a 400-foot block and 25-foot lots, a pattern admirably suited to speculation. It should be noted, however, that the Boulder City Town Company set high rates for town lots, up to $1,000 for a 50-by-140-foot building site. Even then, it appears, Boulder favored slower growth.

The post–World War II subdivisions disrupted the grid pattern, with larger lots and blocks set along curvilinear streets, and no alleys. In the 1960s and 1970s, more cul-de-sacs appeared, with fewer connections to adjacent development. Today, the city is characterized by a high rate of car ownership (two vehicles for every three people) and a significant jobs-to-housing imbalance. Boulder's employment-to-population ratio

Originally published as "Boulder Brings Back the Neighborhood Street," *Planning*, Vol. 60, No. 6, June, 1994. Published by the American Planning Association, 122 South Michigan Avenue, Suite 1600, Chicago, Illinois 60603-6107. Reprinted with permission of the publisher.

is 0.83, more than 40 percent higher than the figure for the eight-county Denver metropolitan region. If current trends continue, total employment will exceed population by 2010.

Boulder also has several recent examples of more sensitive residential planning. In 1983, a local developer built the Cottages, a 37-unit affordable housing project, on a woonerf-style street. The 5.3-acre site abuts city-owned open space on the north side. And in 1990, another local developer, William Coburn, built Walnut Hollow, a high-end infill project consisting of nine Victorian-style houses — with detached garages — arrayed along an 18-foot-wide street just east of downtown.

But these projects, both planned unit developments, resulted largely from individual initiatives and not from a communitywide vision of what constitutes better urban development. Moreover, neither would be allowed under the current regulations. In the past, the city's planning department used the PUD ordinance to vary street standards. But as concerns grew over liability, policy makers were unwilling to grant individual waivers in the absence of new citywide street standards.

For the most part, recent new subdivisions have complied absolutely with the letter of the Boulder rules, laid down in the zoning code and subdivision regulations adopted in 1971. The result: three-car garagescape uniformity, the "loops and lollipops" pattern exhibited so well in the city's expanding northeast quadrant.

In 1992, the planning department, aware of the community's growing unhappiness with the look and operation of the new subdivisions, decided to take a more aggressive role in neighborhood design. The staff noted that the city's 1989 transportation master plan called for new residential street guidelines to enhance neighborhood safety and livability.

As it happened, a large new project had just been proposed for the northeast edge of the city — the 140-acre Four Mile Creek. The planning department hired Peter Brown, AICP, an urban designer in Houston, to conduct a design charette before the project entered the development review phase. Brown toured the site and interviewed the developers, a consortium of local builders. Then, working with other team members, he compared construction costs for both a conventional subdivision and a neotraditional design, complete with narrow streets and pedestrian paths, and drew sketch plan alternatives.

The plan that resulted was then presented to the developers, and they used many of the neotraditional design elements in their annexation application. (The annexation ordinance was the legal device used to vary the city's street standards.) The 309-unit project is now under construction. Its gridded street plan includes both boulevards and narrow streets. It also features short blocks; motor courts (oblong cul-de-sacs with central landscaping and parking); a raised intersection (road surface matches elevation of crosswalk); traffic circles; and an alley. There is also an extensive bicycle and pedestrian path network.

The Four Mile Creek exercise was considered a success in that it convinced the city to move beyond simply responding to proposals to assuming a leadership role in defining a vision for development. Under the leadership of its new planning director, Will Fleissig, Boulder is now attempting to relate its street design standards to an overall community planning and urban design program.

Complete Overhaul

The vehicle for this new approach is the Residential Access Project (RAP), which was initiated jointly in the spring of 1992 by the city's planning and public works departments. The impetus was the increasing restiveness of neighborhood residents concerned about traffic congestion. At that point, the planning staff proposed to broaden the residential street guidelines to include the entire movement network in residential areas and to create urban design guidelines.

The entire project is being carried out in house, with no special funding except for a small graphics budget. Both the public works staff member — a transportation planner — and I devote about a fifth of our time to RAP. We report to an inter-departmental steering committee.

The first part of the two-phase project was aimed at devising a statement of purpose and a richer menu of street standards. The project staff has spent the last two years researching standards in other cities and involving residents in a collaborative planning process. A spinoff effort, the neighborhood traffic mitigation program, will encourage the use of traffic calming measures.

In March of this year, the planning board endorsed the staff's recommendation that the city's one-size-fits-all street standard be replaced. The current standard requires 12-foot travel lanes, six-foot parking lanes, curb, gutter, and sidewalk in a 48-foot right-of-way. The new standards would offer four classifications, all of them narrower than the current requirement.

The two lowest classifications would be low-speed (15–20 m.p.h.) "queuing" streets. They could be as narrow as 20 feet, and they would allow on-street parking. To mollify fire officials, the standards provide for fire set-up areas (pads long and wide enough to accommodate fire trucks and close enough together so fire hoses can reach the back of all dwellings).

The standards would also allow alleys, which are officially discouraged in the current subdivision regulations. The planners noted that Boulder residents consistently rate traditional neighborhoods with alleys as most livable.

The planning board also endorsed the staff's recommended street purposes statement. A clear definition of intent is expected to guide all those involved in administering the new regulations.

The final proposal for phase one is to be presented to the planning board this month. The next step is to translate the proposal into an ordinance for consideration by the city council. That's expected to be done this summer.

Phase two of RAP will address the broader topic of residential-area design, including the building-street relationship, network standards, and "shared" streets (such as the Dutch woonerf). A set of performance-based standards will parallel the new prescriptive standards.

The planning department is putting the draft standards to the test in a subcommunity plan now being prepared for north Boulder. With 9,200 residents spread over 2,300 acres, "NoBo" is the least developed of the city's nine subcommunities. It was annexed four years ago, and its many vacant and underutilized parcels are considered ripe for redevelopment.

At a five-day public charette held the first week of May in the National Guard Armory, more than 300 citizens suggested ways of intensifying the movement grid and reconnecting streets. Their recommendations included both boulevards and skinny streets. A Miami-based urban design consulting firm, Dover, Kohl & Partners, is incorporating their recommendations and many of the RAP concepts into the plan being prepared for city council consideration in July.

Searching Out Models

There seemed to be few models when Boulder started this project two summers ago. Most jurisdictions still use some variation of the highway-oriented street standards that arose in the late 1930s with the creation of the Federal Highway Administration and the "Green Book" published by AASHTO, the American Association of State Highway and Transportation Officials.

Recently, designers associated with the movement coming to be known as "the new urbanism"—Andres Duany, Anton Nelessen, AICP, Peter Calthorpe, and others—have received considerable media attention. But most of their work has been on large tracts of raw land, not the infill projects that are typical of places like Boulder.

There are other models with broader applicability to the situations in which most planners find themselves: infill, redevelopment, and fringe-area development.

One such example is an early one, the "performance streets" standard adopted by Bucks County, Pennsylvania, in 1980. It provides a model ordinance that includes a rich hierarchy of street types, although its use as a model is limited by the emphasis on cul-de-sacs and loop streets, and its lack of attention to alternative modes of travel.

The performance streets concept is also the basis of a new set of supplemental standards for residential neighborhoods now being considered by the city of Houston and surrounding Harris County. The city currently has only two types of residential streets: a 28-foot pavement section with a 50-foot or 60-foot right-of-way. The new standards would create eight street types and allow narrower streets in new subdivisions, with such design elements as "chicanes" (jogs to slow traffic) and flare-outs. The standards were prepared by Peter Brown in collaboration with Patricia D. Knudson & Associates and Terra Associates, both of Houston.

Portland, Oregon's 1991 "skinny streets" ordinance applies to residential blocks where lots are over 5,000 square feet. It allows 20-foot-wide streets with parking on one side, or 26-foot-wide streets with parking on both sides—thus overturning the long-entrenched idea that all streets must provide at least two through lanes of traffic. City engineer Terry Bray reports that 30 blocks of skinny streets were built in the first two construction seasons.

Olympia, Washington's state capital, has approved transportation policies that prohibit new cul-de-sacs. The policies, adopted in 1992, are an outgrowth of a visual preference survey and urban design plan undertaken with the help of New Jersey consultant Anton Nelessen.

Nelessen also prepared the urban design guidelines now being reviewed in Santa Fe, New Mexico. The guidelines offer 16 distinct land-use and circulation prototypes. Widths range downward to 18 feet, sometimes with no building setback requirement, and curb radiuses as tight as four feet. Frank Diluzio, the city's newly appointed fire chief, says he supports the standards provided that new streets "pretty much keep a 20-foot clear zone," meaning that no parking rules must be strictly enforced.

In Squim, Washington, a retirement community on the Olympic Peninsula, a "block standard" includes a 12-foot alley in a 20-foot easement. Public works director Richard Parker says the alleys work well for utility placement and the city's automated garbage collection system.

Another model is the west end of Vancouver, British Columbia, where traffic calming measures have proven to be an important adjunct to street standards. Street closures and diverters have created a pleasant walking environment in a high-rise district flanked by busy shopping streets.

But the most promising model is an Australian one: the code for residential development prepared in 1992 by the planning and housing department in the state of Victoria. This exemplary document covers the entire residential environment, from lot orientation to regional street networks, and it defines a broad hierarchy of local streets.

The Victoria code includes both performance-based and prescriptive standards, and is specific about details like deflection angles (for speed control). It also requires that all dwellings be located no more than 700 meters (about 2,300 feet) and three "junctions," or intersections, from a major street to balance the amount of time motorists are forced to spend in low-speed environments.

Most important, the code requires development planners to plot out pedestrian and bicycle lanes as well as the usual environmental constraints and opportunities — before the street system is laid out. In this, the Australian planners echo the advice of California architect Christopher Alexander, who says that in urban design, pedestrian spaces should be designed first, then the buildings, then the roads.

Wendy Morris, the senior urban designer in the department's Melbourne offices, described the code in Alexandria, Virginia, last October at the first Congress on the New Urbanism. She said a key to making it effective has been inter-disciplinary workshops: "We found that to make real change in building patterns, those who make design, permitting, and development decisions must be involved and retrained."

Ready for Change

Back in the U.S., the Florida Department of Community Affairs has undertaken an ambitious project to develop "community design guidelines" for everything from energy conservation to affordable housing to streets. The project's principal researcher, Reid Ewing, of the Joint Center for Environmental and Urban Problems at Florida Atlantic University/Florida International University in Fort Lauderdale, says the "overriding rationale is to make the street more livable, less energy-consumptive, and environmentally sound." His team has proposed a 20-foot-wide standard for all local streets.

Ben Starrett, the director of strategic planning and policy coordination for the community affairs department, says he expects the guidelines to be published soon.

Even the Institute for Transportation Engineers, long a holdout against alternative street standards, is becoming part of the solution. In February, the institute's technical committee on neotraditional town design issued an "informational report" entitled *Traffic Engineering for Neotraditional Neighborhoods.* Frank Spielberg, a traffic engineering consultant in Annandale, Virginia, who chairs the committee, says members hope that ITE will endorse the "recommended practices," which include narrower streets in some cases, within the next year.

As to liability, the bugaboo of city officials, one member of the ITE committee, Walter Kulash — a traffic engineer in Orlando — contends that "legal obstacles to narrow streets are a red herring." He notes that a 1993 study he co-authored for the National Conference on Tort Liability and Risk Management for Surface Transportation concluded that tort cases "invariably have to do with high speed," not street width.

Finally, for those ready to change, a few basic reminders:

The public interest requires safe, livable, and attractive streets that contribute to the urban fabric.

Streets should be designed to suit their function. Many streets, especially local ones, have purposes other than vehicular traffic. Some local residential streets should be designed for speeds of less than 20 m.p.h. Remember that the general population is aging, with the cohort over 85 growing fastest of all.

A hierarchical street network should have a rich variety of types, including bicycle, pedestrian, and transit routes.

Reid Ewing believes the "overall system design has fallen into the cracks between the planning and engineering professions." The entire movement network should be considered, with connectivity given prominence.

Standards should be developed to enhance local streets' contributions to urban design. That means paying attention to "sense of enclosure" ratios (on residential streets, the distance between houses should be no more than 80 to 100 feet), landscaping, parking, setbacks, lot width to depth ratios, block length and perimeter maximums, materials, street furniture, and signs.

A useful guide might be the "performance street" concept, which matches street types with adjacent land uses. Creating a street plan based on this model might seem a daunting task, but be assured that controlling scale (what's called "morphological zoning") can go a long way to ensuring the proper mix of urban elements.

Make the new standards available for infill and redevelopment, not just for new development. Where densification is a concern, maintain existing rights-of-way but narrow roadway width.

Streets should be designed in a collaborative, interdisciplinary process. Do a visual preference survey. Try workshops and charettes. Include your legal counsel. After construction, set up what Kulash calls a "robust, simple, and executable monitoring system."

Don't let cost stop you. We estimate that it will take $1.3 million to reconfigure Norwood Avenue, a 6,000-foot-long residential subcollector in north Boulder, as a 20-foot-wide street incorporating such traffic-calming measures as raised intersections, berms, a multipurpose path, and neckdowns (flared curbs constricting a street entrance). It would take $2.3 million to build a typical 32-foot-wide street. The reconfiguration design has been approved by the city council and is now going through the capital improvements programming process.

Ideally, putting these ideas into effect will lead to a revival of street-centered small communities. Vaclav Havel, president of the Czech Republic, put it best in his 1992 book, *Summer Meditations*. "Villages and towns," he wrote, "will once again begin to have their own distinctive appearance, ... and the environment will become a source of quiet everyday pleasure for us all."

By planning our residential areas at a human scale, considering the needs of the most vulnerable among us, and relegating the automobile to its proper role, we can regain what we have lost.

CHAPTER 8

CAMBRIDGE DESIGNS CIVIC SPACES TO IMPROVE LIVING FOR DOWNTOWN RESIDENTS

Terry J. Lassar

In 1634, Boston created what would become the nation's first large-scale urban civic space, the Boston Common. Now 365 years later, another grand civic space, the Common at University Park, has been added to the cityscape. A common ground for neighborhood residents, university scientists, and office workers, the 1.3-acre park is the centerpiece of a new, mixed-use neighborhood developing next to the Massachusetts Institute of Technology (MIT) in Cambridge.

More than 25 years ago, MIT began acquiring land adjacent to its campus for the development of a corporate office research and development (R&D) park that would help accelerate the transfer of technology into the commercial marketplace. In 1983, MIT selected Cleveland-based Forest City Enterprises to develop University Park at MIT. Forest City also owns and operates the development under a long-term lease.

Unlike some suburban-style, corporate research facilities affiliated with universities, such as those at Stanford and Princeton, University Park at MIT is decidedly urban and urbane. The 27-acre corporate campus,

located in the heart of Cambridge, is a lively, integrated community of offices, laboratories, restaurants, shops, a hotel, residences, and parks. The first office/R&D space opened in 1987 in a rehabilitated shoe factory. Two office buildings followed in 1989 and 1990, together with 142 loft-style residences in a renovated cookie bakery. Subsequent development was put on hold for nearly a decade until the economy strengthened. In 1998, an additional phase opened, including an office building, hotel, and retail services. A full-service supermarket, which had not been contemplated in the original master plan, also was included in this phase in response to community demand. Located on the second level of the hotel, the supermarket has its own street-level entry as well as direct access from the adjacent parking garage.

The latest development phase — 270,000 square feet of office/R&D space in twin buildings, a parking facility, and the landscaped 1.3-acre University Park Common — opened this past spring. The primary occupant is Millennium Pharmaceuticals Inc., a biotech company that relocated its

Originally published as "On Common Ground," *Urban Land*, Vol. 58, No. 10, October, 1999. Published by the Urban Land Institute, Washington, D.C. Reprinted with permission of the publisher.

headquarters to the research park. Cereon Genomics, LLC, a collaboration between Millennium and the Monsanto Company, also has established its headquarters there.

The Cambridge market has long been propelled by technology companies that are attracted to the area because of the presence of MIT and Harvard. Forest City's strategy for University Park was to develop buildings that would be sufficiently flexible to address the evolving needs of high-tech companies as they matured, while responding to fundamental shifts in the high-tech industry over time.

The first University Park buildings targeted the high-tech industries that had populated Cambridge for the past 30 years, such as defense, computer, and software firms. In the late 1980s, however, just as the park's buildings were delivered, the region's high-tech market sector, along with New England's overall real estate market, entered an economic tailspin. At the same time, though, a new technology-based industry — biotechnology — was emerging from university research laboratories and beginning to establish itself in the commercial sector. Many early-stage biotech companies require a decade to achieve significant revenues, let alone a profit, and the cost of tenant improvements, which typically ranges between $75 to $100 per square foot, is significantly higher than for traditional office space. Moreover, the city's supply of research laboratory space was severely constrained and unable to meet the needs of emerging biotech firms. Initially, the economic downturn left few developers and lenders favorably disposed to risking their capital to build for the biotech industry. It was in this uncertain environment that Forest City recognized an opportunity to serve a developing market niche.

The flexibility built into the structures at University Park — high floor-to-ceiling heights, large ventilation shafts, and higher-than-average power capacity — was originally geared for high-tech users but also met the functional needs of the growing biotech sector. MIT scientists were involved in many of the startup companies and were attracted to University Park because of its proximity to the institute. The MIT "halo effect" helped draw other Cambridge-based biotech startup firms. As the number of firms grew over the years, some expanded into additional space at University Park.

By the late 1990s, the industry was beginning to mature, and some larger firms, such as Millennium Pharmaceuticals, which leased space in several buildings throughout the Cambridge area, were looking to consolidate. University Park was the logical choice for two reasons. First, Eric Lander, one of Millennium's founders, runs the genomics center at MIT's Whitehead Institute, and other company scientists also have close ties to MIT. Second, Millennium selected University Park for its new headquarters because no comparable facilities were located nearby. Although other universities in Boston have started developing biotech-related facilities, none is as extensive as University Park and none offers a similar academic campus environment.

Although Forest City did not start out to develop a biotech park, biotech firms now occupy 90 percent of the 700,000 square feet of the park's existing R&D space. "It was a marriage of need and opportunity," explains Peter Calkins, vice president for planning and project development with Forest City. "With an expanding biotech industry competing for a limited supply of suitable space, these value-added buildings generate attractive returns. At full build-out — within the next four to five years, according to Calkins — University Park will encompass 1.3 million square feet of office/R&D space, a 212-room hotel and executive center, 150,000 square feet of retail space and restaurants, 650 housing units, structured parking for more than 3,000 cars, and seven acres of parkland. The development is currently 50 percent completed.

University Park is built largely on blighted, unused industrial land in the Cambridge neighborhood. Located across the Charles River from Boston, Cambridge was once a thriving manufacturing district. As with many other communities in the northeastern United States, Cambridge's economy flagged after World War II when most of the city's blue-collar industrial base moved to the suburbs, leaving behind a jumble of derelict warehouses and neglected parking lots.

The city of Cambridge, after working for several years to spark developer interest in the vacant site, welcomed Forest City's mixed-use concept. In 1988, the city approved the master plan and passed the requisite zoning and design guidelines. In addition to the planned commercial space, the developers agreed to provide a minimum of 400 residential units, including a significant affordable housing component. Some of the affordable residences are located in the renovated F. A. Kennedy Steam Bakery, original home of the Fig Newton cookie. Additional affordable housing is included at Auburn Court, a family-style development on the neighborhood edge of University Park. A community-based nonprofit developer is building this residential phase under rights sublet from Forest City.

In addition to the special zoning district created for the development, the developer, the city of Cambridge, and MIT entered into a series of development agreements governing specific issues — including traffic generation and mitigation, housing obligations, and roadway improvements — that may be changed only by mutual consent of all three parties. University Park represented the first use of development agreements to augment the city's zoning process. The city's community development department views University Park as the new paradigm for large-scale development and will likely employ similar agreements for future projects.

Like many dense neighborhoods in mature urban centers, Cambridge has a scarcity of parks. The public voiced strong concern that large-scale developments such as University Park should provide plenty of green open spaces for the neighborhood. "Because we're in a dense, urban location," says Calkins, "our intent was to create a research park with its own identity that, over time, would knit into the adjacent neighborhood structure." In the master plan for University Park, Koetter Kim & Associates, a Boston-based architecture firm, used a framework of street edges and axially related parks and open spaces to integrate the development into the surrounding community. The centerpiece of the interconnecting open-space system — and the heart and soul of the master plan — is the University Park Common. Located alongside Sidney Street, the main north/south thoroughfare, the common will eventually take the form of an outdoor room defined by eight different buildings.

As designated in the master plan, the central open space has always been envisioned as a common ground for both Cambridge residents and University Park office and scientific workers rather than as a corporate enclave, isolated from the neighborhood. The developers hired a Boston landscape architecture firm, the Halvorson Company, Inc., best known for its design of Post Office Square, a park built above a parking garage in Boston's financial district. Halvorson's office worked closely with community representatives on the common design. The community was concerned that the initial concept designs were overly formal, with too much paving and not enough lawn areas to support passive recreational uses. They also felt that the common appeared to be a frontyard to the private office buildings.

In response, the designers reconfigured the plan, minimizing the building entries and making room for a larger green open space at the park's center. To encourage active use of the common as a destination park, the landscape architects integrated attractions — including a ministage area that turns the central green space into an amphitheater — as well as enclosed nodes for picnicking and reading and, most important, an abundance of seating. Its large open spaces make the common an ideal setting for neighborhood festivals. A system of meandering pathways runs diagonally through the common, inviting residents in the adjacent Brookline Street neighborhood to stroll through the park on their way to work at MIT or to pick up groceries at the supermarket.

The Brookline Street community actively participated in developing the art program for the common. The first art phase, Traces of History — a series of plaques and three-dimensional sculptures — depicts the history of the University Park site. Once part of the Charles River, the site was filled to expand Cambridge's land area. A variety of industries operated on and around the area, including Simplex Wire and Cable, shoe factories, a book publishing firm, a bakery, candy makers, audio products, and a telescope manufacturer. The new industry at University Park focuses instead on producing various pharmaceuticals and biotech products such as replacement material for bone and cartilage.

Also featured in the public art program and placed throughout the park are 18-inch square granite blocks with sand-blasted letters and symbols of hydrogen, lithium, and other elements of the periodic table. Some are freestanding on the lawn; others are laid out in a row near the main entryways to the buildings.

As a focus of the second art phase, neighborhood representatives encouraged the landscape architects to design a fountain for the common. Because Boston's frigid winters make it difficult to operate a fountain year round, the team came up with the concept of a fog fountain, designed not to freeze. The system is powered by a compressor pump that boosts water through a hydraulic line under high pressure and forces water out of nozzles to produce fog.

A major challenge for Boston architects Tsoi/Kobus & Associates was to create a building design for the Millennium Pharmaceuticals buildings that was compatible with the adjacent residential neighborhood, located due west of the 45/75 Sidney Street buildings. Since each building is 70 feet high and 200 feet long, scale was an important issue. On the service side facing the residences, the architects articulated the building facade into smaller components to reduce the scale and visually minimize the large plane of the wall. Likewise, the loading bays were buried inside the building and designed to reduce the number of external overhead doors. Residential bay-style windows on the west ends of the buildings — facing the residential neighborhood — frame the courtyard between the two structures that lead into the common. Ornamental street lights, trees, and planters along the west street edge also helped humanize the scale.

Several traffic-calming devices protect the residential neighborhood from the increased flow of cars and trucks to the Millennium buildings. For example, a Woonerf-style road near the exit from the parking garage discourages vehicles from cutting through the Brookline Street neighborhood and instead channels traffic to Sidney Street. This curvilinear road, which resembles an oversized walkway, is large enough to accommodate emergency vehicles in compliance with the city's access requirement.

The skybridge connecting the two Millennium buildings was controversial. Initially, some members of the planning board maintained that the bridge disrupted an important cross axis in the master plan. They were also philosophically opposed to the idea of taking people off the street. The architects responded by designing the bridge as a ceremonial gateway that reinforces rather than disrupts connections to the adjacent residential neighborhood. In addition, the mullions and ornamental curved arch design strengthen the gateway concept.

Unlike the self-conscious presence of many corporate headquarters, the Millennium buildings are deliberately unassuming. "They were intended as background buildings to the common," says Carol Chiles, who headed the design team for Tsoi/Kobus. For this reason, the entry facades facing onto the common were designed asymmetrically with the entryways shifted to the side streets. The entryways — curved glass and metal atriums — project into the park to welcome employees and visitors arriving from the garage or side streets.

"In this business, where change is a constant," says Chiles, "flexibility is critical. Research projects change over time; funding expands and contracts. Labs must be designed with ultimate flexibility to respond to these changes." In particular, modular planning and standardization accommodate changing needs. "You don't want a lab bench that is designed so specifically for one research group that it can't be adapted later for a different group," she adds. The architects created a template for each floor and designated general zones for office or laboratory space. As Millennium's space needs change, "it will be more cost effective to convert office to lab space, rather than the other way around, to avoid wasting expensive lab infrastructure," notes Chiles. In fact, some completed laboratories were substantially modified even before the first scientists moved into the buildings.

In addition to flexibility, Millennium wanted its new facilities "to encourage communication between the different research groups," comments Janet Bush, Millennium's vice president of finance. So the architects designed a number of informal break-out spaces that permit employees to meet for spontaneous brain-storming sessions. On every floor, 20-foot-long white writing boards are strategically placed near the coffee and snack kitchens. The ground-floor cafeteria, which features large glass windows facing the common, also serves as an off-hours meeting space.

The mixed-use development concept has been an important draw for many anchor tenants, including Millennium. "The central location and proximity of the hotel makes University Park attractive for recruiting purposes," say Bush. In addition, nearby public transit and on-site housing, along with such conveniences as the supermarket, daycare facilities, and restaurants, appeal to prospective employees, she adds.

In the next development phase, a market-rate apartment building rather than the originally planned R&D space will be constructed on the south end of the common. Forest City concluded that a residential building would better enhance the development's open space and encourage greater use of the park after business hours. Furthermore, the area's robust housing market, along with Cambridge's repeal of rent control three years ago, is prompting Forest City to build 246 additional residences beyond its original obligation of 400 units. Besides offering employees nearby living accommodations, a number of University Park companies lease apartments for use by out-of-town employees, consultants, and customers.

"It's rare that designers have the opportunity to work on such a large vacant site in a dense, older city like Cambridge," notes Boston landscape architect Robert Krieg of the Halvorson Company. "University Park, with its mix of residences, offices, laboratories, restaurants, shops, hotels, and parks, challenged us to create a whole new integrated community — a mini-village — within an existing city."

CHAPTER 9

CHARLESTON BUILDS NEW PUBLIC LIBRARY TO STIMULATE COMMUNITY REVITALIZATION

William Fulton and *Chris Jackson*

The years had not been kind to Calhoun Street. Charleston's main thoroughfare cuts across the peninsula separating the Cooper and Ashley rivers, the focal point of this historic South Carolina port city. But by the 1980s, much of the street had lost its colonial charm. Long stretches were dotted by vacant lots and rundown buildings.

It was on just such a bedraggled stretch of Calhoun Street that Mayor Joseph Riley announced a decade ago that he wanted to build the new main branch of the Charleston County Public Library. Since 1931, the main branch had been located a few blocks away on Marion Square, a small park surrounded by a cluster of landmark churches and the original home of the Citadel military academy. But that building was too small to support a growing collection and newer services like Internet work stations.

Despite pressure to move the library to the suburbs, Riley fought to keep it downtown as an anchor of the city's revitalization effort. "Libraries see the comings and goings of all people in the neighborhood, and because of that they nourish the street on which they are located more than any other public facility," Riley says. At his urging, the city bought the two-acre parcel and donated it to the county.

Give It Credit

It is now a year since the opening of the $11 million main branch, and Calhoun Street is on the mend, with residential and retail projects under way nearby. Suburbanites regularly visit the new library, lured by the expanded collection and state-of-the-art computer facilities. Local residents hold neighborhood association meetings there, and teens gather to plan school projects.

The new library can't take all the credit for turning Calhoun Street around. But in Charleston, as in cities across the nation, both librarians and urban planners are recognizing that a library can be a strong contributor to revitalization efforts, whether downtown or in the neighborhoods.

"Libraries are, in many ways, neigh-

Originally published as "Let's Meet at the Library," *Planning*, Vol. 65, No. 5, May, 1999. Published by the American Planning Association, 122 South Michigan Avenue, Suite 1600, Chicago, Illinois 60603-6107. Reprinted with permission of the publisher.

borhood living rooms," says Norman Holman, a senior vice-president of the New York Public Library. "Communities change, but the library stays there."

Ever since Andrew Carnegie's philanthropy made them a common feature of American community life a century ago, libraries have well understood their role as community centers. Some Carnegie libraries originally had boxing rings and lecture halls.

But in the last decade or so, American libraries have been rediscovered as place-based assets. Searching for strong anchors for downtowns and neighborhoods, urban revitalization experts have rediscovered libraries and other cultural institutions as "attractions."

At the same time, however, libraries are becoming more active as community centers, often including day care centers and homework centers. Internet access has become a draw for patrons without home computers. "The library as a place is as critically important as the resources in the library," says Susan Goldberg Kent, director of the Los Angeles Public Library.

"Libraries can do anything," says Robert McNulty, president of the Washington-based Partners for Livable Communities, one of those who supports this broadening of the library mission. Others are concerned that the new emphasis on aggressive programming goes too far. Libraries risk becoming "just another custodial facility," says Glen Holt, executive director of the St. Louis Public Library.

Whom Do They Serve?

Controversy over the mission of the public library is nothing new. According to historian Abigail Van Slyck, author of *Free to All*, the definitive history of Carnegie libraries, civic leaders often disagreed with Andrew Carnegie on just this point.

Carnegie, whose impoverished Scottish family came to the U.S. in the late 1840s and who made a fortune in the steel industry, viewed public libraries primarily as a bootstrap for immigrants and working-class families. His building program — which resulted in the construction of 1,679 public libraries between 1886 and 1917 — emphasized neighborhood libraries. Civic leaders, in contrast, envisioned monumental downtown libraries that would become "elite preserves."

As a compromise, Van Slyck writes, most big city library boards "embraced a two-tiered system of library facilities: a grand central library (built with or without Carnegie's financial help) in a City Beautiful setting, and more modest branches erected in working-class neighborhoods."

By the middle of this century, the urban public library had become a staple of upward mobility — well described by Philip Roth in his 1959 novel, *Goodbye Columbus*. In the 1960s and '70s, however, the flight of the middle class to the suburbs took its toll, and city libraries had to struggle to maintain patronage — and funding.

Ports of Entry

Quite apart from their place-based role, public libraries have changed dramatically in the past decade. In many cities, libraries have become ports of entry to new immigrants, providing them with a variety of services.

"We have partnered with Catholic Charities to help people in finding temporary housing," says Ramiro Salazar, director of the Dallas Public Library. "People use the library to teach English as a second language, literacy, and citizenship classes."

Many librarians are eagerly plunging into the social service arena, but Glen Holt, the director of the St. Louis Public Library and a former urban studies professor, is more cautious. "That's like a mouse getting into bed with an elephant," he says. "Libraries can't be everything." While acknowledging the library's role in the community, Holt adds, "I don't want the public library to become the public housing of the 2010s or the welfare system of the 2030s."

Partly as a result of such fears, some cities are focusing on the library buildings themselves, rather than on community service. The Seattle Public Library recently passed a multimillion-dollar bond measure to revamp its branches. At the same time, the system has reaffirmed traditional library pursuits by dubbing 1999 "The Year of the Collection."

To bolster their facilities, many financially pressed public libraries are learning the language of economic development. Holt's St. Louis system is an example. A recent survey of library users estimated that the library, which costs taxpayers $15 million a year to operate, provides the community with $67 million a year in benefits.

Crossroads

Today's libraries face two major challenges: the Internet and sophisticated retailing. On the one hand, the Internet has eliminated the reason for using the library — the need to find certain information. Meanwhile, the big retailers (especially bookstore chains) have used a casual atmosphere and comfortable seating to attract students and others who once hung out in the local library.

"Why this is coming to the forefront now is that libraries are at a crossroads," says Joseph Keenan, director of the public library system in Elizabeth, New Jersey. "People no longer need to go to the library to get a piece of information or research a paper." Nor do they need the library for intellectual stimulation or entertainment. "Barnes & Noble has lectures and readings. Even Burger King has story time," he says.

These challenges have forced libraries to reposition themselves as place-based assets in a way that dovetails nicely with urban revitalization efforts. The Internet, for example, has not eliminated the need for libraries, as many librarians feared it would. In many cases, it has reinforced the library's role as a place to go for information. Many public libraries now have large banks of Internet computers available to the public, thus increasing patronage and interest in the libraries.

"A lot of business people use the library for the Internet because they have access to human help, financial research, and genealogy," says Joseph Rizzo, an architect with the Hillier Group in Princeton, New Jersey, who has worked on many library projects.

Libraries have also begun to fight back by returning to their Carnegie roots as social centers — a trend that also reinforces their place-based role in the community. A decade ago, many libraries were converting their meeting rooms into storage areas to house expanding collections. Now they are reopening these meeting rooms — or as is the case of the new downtown Denver library, building so many new meeting rooms that they create a kind of mini-conference center.

Elsewhere, public libraries are promoting homework centers, bookshops, and other compatible retail uses, and they've made space for cultural activities such as art exhibits and museum shows. Chicago's Harold Washington Library, which opened in 1991 on a prime downtown block, has all these features and a white tablecloth restaurant to boot.

Librarians have changed, too. "My training in the 1980s focused only on the discipline," says Keenan. "It did not provide an understanding of how we make our libraries network with our community." Today, he notes, librarians have become entrepreneurs.

Bricks and Mortar

The effect of these changes on America's cities is striking. Downtown libraries rank with retail and entertainment complexes as redevelopment anchors in cities like San Francisco, Seattle, Nashville, and Memphis. Ironically, many — originally sited outside the commercial core — are today well positioned to anchor new development projects because the downtown has expanded around them in the intervening decades.

Nor is the library phenomenon limited to big cities or cities with established historic districts like Charleston. Muncie, Indiana, is about to begin a major expansion of its downtown library as part of a broader renewal effort. The city's original Carnegie library was built more than 90 years ago and is now far too small. A generation ago it might have been razed, but now it will be expanded to serve as a downtown anchor, along with a convention center and children's museum. "A lot of synergy can take place at the library if it works with the community that surrounds it," says library director Virginia Nilles.

Crucial though libraries may be downtown, they may be even more important in urban neighborhoods. Once overshadowed by their downtown counterparts, neighborhood branch libraries can now offer a much wider range of services because of the Internet, CD-ROMs, and other electronic forms of information. "What you can do now in a small branch library with limited space is unbelievable because of information technology," says Los Angeles librarian Susan Kent.

Nor are branches confined to library buildings. In Elizabeth, New Jersey, a new branch library shares space in a city-owned neighborhood center with a senior center, a clinic, and a preschool program. "The beauty of this arrangement is that I don't pay any overhead," says library director Keenan. "We just provide the collection and a small staff and the branch is used by most everyone who comes into the center."

In Ventura, California, a renewal program in a low-income neighborhood has combined a new library with affordable housing. Using federal community development block grant funds, the city last year renovated a 1920s retail and apartment building, putting affordable units on the upper floors and a branch library below. The new library has the highest walk-in traffic of any of Ventura County's 15 libraries, underscoring the synergy between library and neighborhood.

In Portland, Oregon, the smallest branch library is located in a mostly vacant strip mall. When the health food chain Natures Fresh bought one of the vacant storefronts for a new store, the company was adamant about keeping the adjoining library in place.

There's no mystery about that, says Eleanor Jo Rodger, president of the Urban Library Council, a national association of large public libraries. When a library goes in, "foot traffic goes up," and the area "becomes livelier and a more interesting place to be."

In the end, there may be disagreement about the exact role a library should play in the community, but there is little question that both downtown and neighborhood libraries are potential catalysts for urban revitalization. "Libraries have always known they are community assets," says Los Angeles's Susan Kent. And especially today, she adds, "there are very few public places that are welcoming to everybody."

CHAPTER 10

CHATTANOOGA CREATES TOWN CENTER OUT OF AGING INNER-CITY MALL

Richard Bailey

The city of Chattanooga's most recent urban revitalization project is not urban at all. After years of successful downtown redevelopment along the city's 200-acre riverfront and more recently in the 640-acre southern end of the central business district, Chattanooga has broadened its focus with a project to revitalize four square miles in the inner suburban ring anchored by the city's oldest suburban mall, long in decline.

When Eastgate Mall opened 35 years ago, it drew shoppers, stores, and economic vitality from downtown Chattanooga to the developing suburbs. Ten years ago, the cycle continued as the larger Hamilton Place mall opened several miles further out, drawing economic vitality away from Eastgate and the surrounding area. But last year, with a new mayor and a new mall owner, the fortunes of Eastgate's declining mall and surrounding suburb began to change. Now "urban" redevelopment is following in the aftermath of suburban sprawl.

Chattanooga's Mayor Jon Kinsey, a real estate developer before his election last March, described Brainerd, the area surrounding the declining Eastgate Mall, as "an

older suburb with the same concerns as most downtowns. We need to make sure that we do something about our core city," he stressed, "and Brainerd is clearly part of our core city." After taking office last April, Mayor Kinsey requested that the Chattanooga-Hamilton County Regional Planning Agency develop a plan to revitalize Brainerd. The following summer, the idea acquired reality and momentum when AT&T leased one of the mall's former anchor store sites for a call center and a new owner purchased the southern half of the mall where AT&T would be located.

By fall, a consulting team had been selected for a planning study to be managed by the regional planning agency but funded primarily by the stakeholder group the agency assembled. The winning proposal was submitted by Miami-based Dover, Kohl & Partners Town Planning. The new urbanist firm proposed creating a multidisciplinary team that included Walter Kulash, a principal of Glatting Jackson Kercher Anglin Lopez Reinhart in Orlando, to oversee traffic planning and economic planner Robert Gibbs of the Gibbs Planning Group,

Originally published as "Mall Over," *Urban Land*, Vol. 57, No. 7, July, 1998. Published by the Urban Land Institute, Washington, D.C. Reprinted with permission of the publisher.

based in Birmingham, Michigan, to handle retail planning. Private sector stakeholders funding 80 percent of the study included 40-percent-leased Eastgate Mall, fully leased Brainerd Village strip center next door, Osborne Office Park adjacent to the mall, and other businesses and banks in the area.

Designing in Public

In January, after preliminary field evaluation and market research, a public design charrette was held by the regional planning agency that drew 300 residents and business owners to help create a new vision for the mall and the surrounding area. The heart of the week-long process was a six-hour "designing in public" event in which 150 community members gathered in an empty storefront inside the mall and broke into groups to create separate plans for the area. Over the next few days, elements of these plans were evaluated and combined to form a composite draft plan that was presented at the end of the week to an audience of about 250. The high level of participation in the charrette and participants' positive emotions surrounding the failed mall surprised planners, local officials, and mall owners. The charrette also was unusual in other ways.

Victor Dover, of Dover, Kohl & Partners, noted that the plans created by 11 groups of "citizen planners" all had a prodevelopment theme. "They envisioned more development, building their way out of the problem instead of downsizing. That was interesting, because in some communities the reaction to development is much cooler. In many other places, folks have given up on the idea that development can make things better and have adopted a not-in-my-backyard (NIMBY) attitude," he said. "We really didn't see any of that here, which says that folks realize this place has to be more like a town, rather than less like a town, to be successful."

Even more unusual was that expectations for what could be accomplished rose dramatically during the charrette, particularly for the new mall owner. According to Gibbs, "something very interesting happened at the charrette. The plan kept getting better and better and better in terms of design standards," he said. "I've never seen that before — when the planners started showing sketches, the developer got motivated and said things that made the planners raise the bar. The mayor said some things, and the standard kept rising higher and higher. It ended at a very sophisticated level."

Norie Harrower, who leads Eastgate Mall, LLC, the Hartford, Connecticut-based investment group that purchased half of the mall at the same time that AT&T became a tenant, approached the charrette process with considerable skepticism. "I tend to believe a lot of those things are exercises in futility," he said. "Everybody gets all excited, and the visionaries come into town and spin the wheel and then leave. Nothing happens — and it costs a lot of money."

Owning a mall was not on his mind when, acting as a real estate consultant, Harrower suggested Eastgate as a location for AT&T's new 65,000-square-foot call center. New York Life owned the southern half of the mall, which included the space he recommended to AT&T. But when Harrower proposed that, in return for a ten-year lease, New York Life pay for a $2 million renovation of the empty anchor store in which AT&T would be located, the insurance company would not consider investing in the property. Harrower ultimately assembled a group of investors and bought New York Life's share of the mall, primarily to help AT&T get the space it wanted but also because the price was so low that he could break even without bringing any new tenants other than AT&T to the mall.

When the mayor told the new mall

owner that he was integral to the kind of comprehensive revitalization of Eastgate that the city had accomplished earlier downtown, Harrower was not enthusiastic. He had expected only to improve the mall property and sell it for a modest profit. But, at the urging of the mayor and other local officials, Harrower agreed to host the charrette in the mall.

"That was when I got hooked because all of a sudden I saw hundreds of people. I thought 20 or 30 irate citizens would show up and say, 'Tear the damn place down.' I saw some real articulate people coming in who cared. What I picked up on first was the emotion," he recalled. "And the mayor was there. I began to see that the city was really behind this process. It is important to a developer to have a city behind you," adds Harrower. "The citizens were behind it. They didn't want to tear it down. They actually wanted us to revive it. Of course, that was what we wanted to do."

A draft plan was presented in public at the end of the week-long charrette. Harrower had worked extensively with the consultants as they created the composite plan from designs proposed by the citizens. What he asked for in exchange, he says, was that "whatever we came up with had to be doable. It had to be achievable."

Over the next few weeks, the plan was polished and the realities of funding, traffic engineering, and the real estate market were considered. The plan did not change substantially from the January draft, but it gathered so much support from the city, the mall, and prospective tenants that the final public presentation in April—made soon after Harrower's group acquired the rest of the mall in a second transaction—included not only the finalized plan but also announcements of the first projects to implement the plan.

Connecting the Pieces

The new plan calls for creating a town center by turning the mall literally inside out and embedding it in a street grid with new office, retail, and residential construction. The mall's exterior will be refaced with new outward-facing storefronts in one- and two-story urbanistic designs. Much of the 50 acres of parking will be used for new housing, parks, civic buildings, and a town square. The plan also reshapes Brainerd Road, the pedestrian-hostile arterial street on which the mall fronts, which currently has seven lanes and no sidewalks.

One of the plan's most dramatic and symbolic recommendations will be the first to be implemented. Brainerd Town Square is intended to create a signature space for the revitalized district, what planner Dover calls "a center for the town center." The traditional town square will replace the main entrance to the mall—now simply a right turn past a small sign that is difficult to see from the road—with one acre of grass and trees in an unused parking area. Two- and three-story mixed-use retail and commercial buildings will surround the square on three sides.

Before the ink was dry on the new plan—indeed, before the consulting team had provided a final, written plan—construction on Brainerd Town Square was announced. At the final public presentation of the plan in April, Mayor Kinsey announced that the mall owners would donate one acre of parking for the town square and that he would ask the city council to provide $250,000 to build the public park. Mall owners revealed at the same time that construction would begin on three buildings along one side of the square. Retail space in two of the buildings already had been leased by a delicatessen and a dry cleaners.

Urbanism and Economics

Gibbs sees the planned conversion of Eastgate from a mall to part of a mixed-use town center as an example of a new category of shopping center — a hybrid of a main street and a mall — that is beginning to be built in significant numbers. "There is a huge movement right now in retailing to go back to main street. Today all the national chains are looking for space on main street. The shopping centers are learning from the cities."

For now, because these hybrid main streets or village shopping developments remain less common, they command trade areas two to two and a half times the norm, said Gibbs. "We're at the very tip of that wave. Tenants are demanding that developers do it, and brokers are saying that it's not doable, that no one will shop there. But tenants and developers are ignoring them and they're being leased out." Under Gibb's influence, rather than simply defining the highly visible and symbolic Brainerd Town Square as a green space surrounded by mixed-use buildings, the plan calls for five to seven stores totaling 15,000 to 20,000 square feet. This level of detail emerges from Gibbs's "void analysis" of potential retail development in and near the mall. Based on the number of households in the trade area, typical expenditure per household based on demographics, and current spending in stores within the trade area, Gibbs develops an estimate by retail category of spending that can be captured by new stores.

Gibbs notes that preliminary interviews with local brokers and developers were consistently negative about the area's ability to support any new development but that his research strongly contradicted those views. "We found a very viable market area. There is a solid neighborhood, a mature residential community, a lot of office space, excellent visibility, and vehicular access. All the elements you need for a good stew were

there. The region had developed a bias against the area that was not true."

Even before redevelopment, there were bright spots. Although the mall had few tenants, some were very successful. A Gap Outlet store that predated the new owners is one of the chain's top performers, and a Goody's discount clothing store has been successful. Both stores face outward. Within several blocks of the mall, Chili's and Bennigan's restaurants, a Lexus dealership, Staples, and other businesses are doing well. According to Gibbs, "The money is here. The potential is here. A lot of businesses are doing well here. It just doesn't look like it."

The plan's overall retail mix recommends a "town center commercial" area around the new Brainerd Town Square and designates most of the northern half of the mall and some new buildings in the eastern parking lots as a "core retail" area, while most of the southern end of the mall is devoted to office, hotel, and recreational uses. Neighborhood retail and services will occupy most of the refaced western edge of the mall, on both north and south ends, as well as an area of new construction between the mall and Brainerd Road.

Connections Within the Town Center

The boldness of building a traditional town square next to a stereotypical suburban strip-commercial street is matched by another dramatic feature of the plan: a new road that cuts the mall in half and connects it with existing residential and office development on either side and with a proposed greenway.

As it cuts through the mall, the new road will pass new outward-facing, neighborhood-oriented retail stores and a new hotel with an attached conference center built in a former anchor store. At the mall's western edge, the plan envisions a second green square surrounded on three sides by new residential development built in a former mall parking area next to existing postwar single-family housing. Immediately east of the mall building, in what is now parking, the road will pass through new office buildings that will include a proposed transit transfer center, then enter the existing Osborne Office Park. The plan proposes infill office buildings close to the new road to define a boulevard-like passage, encouraging pedestrian and vehicular traffic between the mall and office areas. Similar connections are proposed between the office park and adjacent strip commercial development along Brainerd Road. While the 100-percent-leased Brainerd Village currently turns its back to the Osborne Office Park, the town center plan proposes new pedestrian connections and a new road to pass through the back of the strip center and into the office park.

In addition to humanizing the pedestrian-hostile Brainerd Road arterial street, the plan is notable for what it does not do in terms of transportation planning. The study calls for no new highway access for the mall, despite local conventional wisdom about the necessity for new interstate access from nearby I-75 and I-24. "Eastgate is an example of the departure from allowing infrastructure, in this case a major interstate, to determine how a community grows and regrows," said Ann Coulter, executive director of the regional planning agency. "The community said, and the market and transportation analysis confirmed, that access to I-75 was neither necessary nor desirable for the success of the project."

What Happens Next?

With strong public input, a visionary plan has been created for the future town center that guides its physical design and economic development. Partnerships and working relationships have been established among local government officials, planners, and business owners. The first projects to implement the vision have been announced. If all the pieces fall into place, what happens now and over the next few years?

According to Kulash, "With real success it would look like a true town, no longer auto-dominated. The overriding impression would no longer be that of moving and storing automobiles, which it is now."

In five years "the mall will be a very profitable, highly active center with many strong national and local tenants" and potentially a complementary shopping destination for out-of-town visitors to Warehouse Row, believes Gibbs. This designer label outlet mall built downtown in 1989 in renovated turn-of-the-century warehouses attracts shoppers from as far away as Atlanta.

Harrower envisions "a mall that no one will really recognize here in another 12 months. In five years you'll see a vastly different terrain." He describes a scene with outdoor cafés, streets that have sidewalks and grassy medians, and acres of asphalt broken up with plantings and water features — a place built to human scale, "where people could spend the day and not be in a car."

Dover sees 100 years of sustained economic development and a beautiful, livable community, but he cautions that the vision is just the first step in a long transformation. "We can't predict everything that will happen. The vision should allow you to do anything at any size and know that your piece of it will fit the greater whole that we're attempting to build over time. A single property owner, a mall developer, or a subdivision developer can do that with great confidence because they control all of the land. But here, with a variety of property owners, small and large, the only common manager of the whole process is the community, the city. That's why the city is involved in the planning, because no one else is responsible for the big picture."

The task in this suburban area is the same one Chattanooga is addressing successfully in its downtown: restoring a lost center for the community. The pieces are there — community services, stores, offices, homes, and walking trails. Under the guidance of the new plan and its stakeholders, those pieces will be pulled together to create a vital town center.

CHAPTER 11

CHESTERFIELD COUNTY PROTECTS NATURE TO FOSTER QUALITY RESIDENTIAL AREAS

Thomas Jacobson

There's still enough of the rural South left in Chesterfield County, Virginia, to attract new residents and corporate offices. Newcomers are drawn by the county's tall forests, its rivers, its historic houses, and its laid-back life style.

But Chesterfield County, which stretches south and west from Richmond, has many of the same characteristics as growing suburban counties all over the U.S., including standardized subdivisions and ungainly commercial strips. Already up to 250,000 residents, the county is expected to add another 100,000 people within the next 20 years.

Moreover, surveys of prospective home buyers indicate a strong preference for large lots in a country setting — with urban conveniences readily accessible. New buyers want to be close to shopping centers, office parks, and cultural and recreational facilities while still living in the countryside.

Resolving this dichotomy between rural dreams and urban needs is the focus of our planning efforts. Our approach is based on a synthesis of urban form and rural char-

acter, with particular attention to the preservation and creation of special community places.

Our design program has evolved from an appreciation and understanding of our suburban "customers" — a diverse group that includes people who prefer urban-type settings and people who seek rural home sites.

Basic Beliefs

We've based our program on these principles:

- Land-use relationships will be improved by integrating land use and infrastructure development, locating mixed-use centers in central locations, and discouraging development outside planned urban development areas.
- The suburban land-use pattern should provide for a variety of development densities, with some areas designated very low density.
- Rural visual characteristics should be pre-

Originally published as "Suburban Design: One Step at a Time," *Planning*, Vol. 64, No. 5, May, 1998. Published by the American Planning Association, 122 South Michigan Avenue, Suite 1600, Chicago, Illinois 60603-6107. Reprinted with permission of the publisher.

served. Forests, stream valleys, and scattered farmsteads should provide the design foundation for new suburban development.

- Special places deserve particular design attention. Renewed towns and villages, and new, well-designed mixed-use centers can provide a focus for nearby residents.

Setting Standards

Throughout the 1980s, Chesterfield County grew in a typical sprawl pattern with subdivisions scattered randomly throughout the countryside. Within the last few years, however, several amendments to the comprehensive plan have steered development to designated planned growth areas.

The plan identifies appropriate areas for continuing development (infill and redevelopment areas), for new fringe development, and for deferred future development.

A key feature is the flexible urban service boundary. The plan sets restrictive standards for exurban residential development (five-acre minimum lot size, 300-foot frontage on existing rural roads, no subdivision) beyond the boundary.

Within subdivisions, the plan's standards for developer-financed public water and sewer lines foster a more compact and orderly development form. All development within the planned growth areas must connect to public water and sewer lines. The plan also calls for a modified grid arterial road network and interconnecting pedestrian paths.

A key element of our planning is to steer new office, retail, light industrial, and multi-family residential development into mixed-use activity centers. Our aim is to shift from the traditional suburban commercial strip to a nodal pattern.

Our zoning ordinance establishes a hierarchy of activity centers based on market area (regional, community, neighborhood, sub-neighborhood). Design standards focus on pedestrian and vehicular circulation, and the integration of building and site design.

Rural Flavor

Maintaining the county's rural character is a key goal of our planning efforts.

We started by identifying some of the hilltop views, tree-lined corridors, and idyllic ponds that we hope to save. In 1993, we adopted zoning and subdivision ordinance amendments that specifically require presentation of such visual resources to "the maximum extent practicable." We have encouraged the preservation of historic plantations and farmhouses, which ideally provide the architectural theme for surrounding new development.

An extensive area has been designated for large lot development (generally two acres or more). This area has many rural amenities and its soils and hydrology are suitable for septic tank drainfields. No future sewer extensions will be built here. Our hope is that we will avoid the pressure for increased development density that often occurs in unplanned exurban development.

Throughout the county, we are encouraging the use of landscaping features, such as wood fences and gates, that add to the rural flavor of suburban development.

Keeping Green

Hardwood and pine forests cover much of the county's rural area, and the tree-lined roads are a major aesthetic asset.

Protecting this asset has been a key goal of county planning efforts. Tree preservation has been relatively easy to accomplish in residential and office areas. Forested residential lots and office parks have proved to have strong market appeal. The job is harder in commercial areas where merchants insist on visibility from public roads.

In 1989, after considerable debate, the county adopted a zoning ordinance provision that requires preservation of the mature tree canopy along major public roads. The ordinance allows low-growing vegetation to be cleared to provide visibility to adjacent commercial developments. A 50-foot setback along arterial roads is required to preserve large trees and ensure that view corridors will be maintained.

Special Places

We have designated a series of activity centers as community focal points. These "places of special design character" include the county's historic courthouse area, five village centers, and several new shopping centers.

Unlike other parts of Virginia, Chesterfield County has few intact historic villages. In most cases, the 18th and 19th century buildings within the village's commercial core are scattered among more recent buildings.

Nevertheless, the five existing villages — Bon Air, Chester, Ettrick, Matoaca, and Midlothian — have a special place in the hearts of county residents and thus are worthy of special design consideration.

Our design standards specify that the form and texture of new structures in the villages should be compatible with their older neighbors, and that the traditional street pattern and setbacks should be maintained.

Chester is an example. The village was established in the mid–19th century at the intersection of two railroads. In recent years, subdivision and shopping centers have grown up along Route 10 at the edge of the village.

The village plan adopted by the county in 1989 proposed that a new village center be created adjacent to the commercial core.

Now under construction is the first phase of the 85-acre Chester Village Green project, an outgrowth of that plan and the work of local developers. Eventually, the development will include 300 units designed in a neotraditional fashion, with shops, offices, and restaurants. A new public library will anchor the new commercial core, which will be oriented around a village green. An art center has also been proposed, along with a new post office.

Heads Up

There's no shortage in planning journals of recommendations for rehabbing typical suburban areas like those in Chesterfield County. I think it's important to realize, however, that no single design philosophy — neotraditionalism, for instance — will do the trick.

Each suburban jurisdiction should guide its building form in a way that is consistent with its own environment, history, form, and character. In our case, we've focused on four things: expanding in an orderly way, maintaining urban form, enhancing our rural features, and creating special areas of unique design character. The result has been satisfying both to us and to our suburban customers.

CHAPTER 12

CHICAGO USES CIVIC LEADERS TO PLAN FOR THE FUTURE OF THEIR DOWNTOWN

Patricia K. Vaccaro

With four million square feet of office space under construction, a stream of one million business travelers per year, and a raft of new hotels, Chicago's Central Area is booming. Approximately 120,000 residents live in the area, up 45 percent since 1990, and the demand for housing is seemingly insatiable. A long-awaited revival is bringing State Street back to life, and North Michigan Avenue continues to be an international retail destination. Chicago's Central Area has managed to succeed — now it has to manage its success.

The Burnham Legacy

Daniel H. Burnham casts a long shadow in Chicago. The architect's 1909 plan for the city proposed straightening the Chicago River, bridging the river at Michigan Avenue, constructing bi-level streets, mandating alleys, setting aside land for parks, and creating tree-lined boulevards. Most of his proposals came to pass and continue to shape the city's development today.

"Chicago takes its heritage more seriously than any other city," says Philip J. Enquist, a partner with the Chicago-based architectural firm Skidmore, Owings & Merrill (SOM), which consults with the city on planning issues. "What other city, except maybe Washington, D.C., has a plan that's 90 years old and still referred to?"

Periodically, the plan has come in for retooling, notably with the 1956 zoning plan, which has been used as a model for several other cities, and the 1973 Chicago 21 Plan, which anticipated the highly successful residential developments at Central Station, Illinois Center, and Dearborn Park. The most recent update came in 1983, when the city was gearing up to host the World's Fair in 1992, as it had in 1893 and 1933. Chicago was awarded the 1992 fair, but the city administration then in office declined it, and the event was held in Seville, Spain, instead. Nearly two decades and a few surprises later, Chicago is back in planning mode.

To help chart the course of the Central Area in the 21st century, the city has assembled a steering committee of civic leaders and city department heads, supported by a

Originally published as "Planning to Succeed," *Urban Land*, Vol. 59, No. 9, September, 2000. Published by the Urban Land Institute, Washington, D.C. Reprinted with permission of the publisher.

working group of consultants and lead staff from public and private organizations. The steering committee and the Chicago department of planning have established seven task forces to examine the office, residential, and retail markets, tourism, transportation, urban design/open space, and educational/cultural issues.

Together, these groups will examine the challenges and opportunities facing the six-square-mile Central Area, which stretches beyond the traditional central business district (CBD), extending to Division Street on the north, the Stevenson Expressway on the south, Halsted Street on the west, and Lake Michigan on the east. These borders encompass districts as diverse as the tony Streeterville and Gold Coast neighborhoods, the downtown office district, the emerging Near South Side and Near West Side communities, Chinatown, and a swath of lakefront parkland.

The area's diversity makes the planners' task more complex, but it also gives them room to maneuver as they juggle competing demands for land with a projected development potential of 215 million square feet. "We have great potential to expand," says Patti Gallagher, the city's deputy commissioner for strategic planning. "The question is how to shape land uses for retail, residential, office, and so forth while preserving the city's special character." Completion of an action plan outlining priorities, financing, and management strategies is nearly a year away. But the major themes already are emerging.

Office versus Residential

Like most cities, Chicago experienced an office construction boom in the 1980s followed by a bust in the early 1990s as supply outstripped demand. While the commercial sector was limping back to a full recovery, something surprising happened — the residential market took off running. In 1980, just 8,000 people lived in the Central Area. A decade later, the number topped 80,000. Today, it has reached 120,000, with no slow-down in sight. Demand has spurred the development of projects ranging from condominium towers on the Gold Coast to commercial conversions in the Loop to whole new neighborhoods emerging south, west, and north of the Loop. There is only one catch. "If you build too much residential in the downtown commercial area, you'll risk running out of the land necessary for continued office, hotel, and other commercial uses," says Robert A. Wislow, chairman of Chicago-based U.S. Equities Realty LLC, who represents the Chicago Development Council on the Central Area Plan steering committee. "In Chicago, even though residences place a greater burden on city services than commercial buildings do, they are taxed at a lower rate, while commercial properties supply the lion's share of the city, county, and state tax base," he adds.

An imbalance of residential and commercial properties could hamper the city's economic growth and vitality. The problem is exacerbated by condominium ownership. While developing projects in South America, Wislow has seen firsthand the fallout from building condominiums in commercial zones. While a rental building could easily be acquired and the land converted back to commercial use, condominium ownership makes assembling property for redevelopment a Herculean feat.

"Chicago's greatest asset, and it's a rare one, is available land for continued commercial development," Wislow says. Unlike New York and San Francisco, both with limited land and restrictive zoning, Chicago has room to grow — room that helps keep commercial rents affordable, supporting business growth. "In San Francisco and New York, office rents have reached $75 to $85 a square foot, with some prime locations exceeding $100 a square foot," he continues.

"Chicago, with some of the world's greatest architecture and most technologically advanced buildings, has rents under $40 per square foot. Of the major world business centers, Chicago has the most attractive office rents going. International companies will look favorably on our lower rents, world-class architecture, and central location. They'll come here, stay, and expand — provided we protect our market advantage."

For Wislow, that means considering protecting the land between the West Loop train stations and the Kennedy Expressway for commercial use and possibly increasing densities in the areas within walking distance of mass transit stations. In the early part of the decade, with commercial development at a standstill, the issue received less attention, but now commercial development is taking off again. Projects under construction include One North Wacker and Dearborn Center at State and Adams streets. Plans are underway for an office tower at 191 N. Wacker Drive. Developers also are eyeing a site at Franklin and Randolph streets.

Even as the cranes are circling the core of the Loop, commercial development is edging out to fringe areas. The former Lakeside Press building on the Near South Side has begun a new life as the nation's largest telecom hotel, Lakeside Technology Center. Montgomery Ward's onetime headquarters and warehouse complex in River North is reemerging as another tech center, e-port @ 600 West Chicago.

But the highest concentration of fringe growth is in the area Wislow wants to consider protecting. A trio of mid-rise towers known locally as the three 550s — 550 West Washington, 550 West Jackson, and 550 West Van Buren — started the trend a couple of years ago, and the market has proven so robust that the developer of 550 West Van Buren is planning a second building, at 525 W. Van Buren Street. Quaker is moving its headquarters to a new building at Clinton and Monroe streets, west of the commuter train stations that now mark the edge of the downtown district. With trendy new condominiums to the north and the city's hottest new restaurants a few blocks west, residential uses could quickly engulf the area between the train stations and the expressway.

"It's important to have walk-to-work residential in the Central Area surrounding downtown," Wislow says. "But it's also important to have the ability to construct major office buildings within easy walking distance of the commuter trains, to provide space for business growth. Instead of looking only east of the train stations, we should provide for dense commercial development for the next 50 years west of the trains. At the same time, we should promote residential north of the river, west of the Kennedy Expressway, and south of Congress Parkway."

The Big Attractions

Office and residential are not the only contenders vying for space. The Central Area is booming with a variety of uses, all converging in what was once the unlikeliest of places — State Street. After losing customers to North Michigan Avenue and suburban malls in the 1970s and early 1980s, Chicago's historic downtown shopping street was converted into a pedestrian mall. Intended to make the street more shopper-friendly, the mall instead left the street deserted, not only by autos but also by pedestrians who found the isolation menacing. In a rousing turnaround, the city eliminated the mall, reinstating auto traffic and recruiting a wide diversity of projects.

Sears is returning to State Street after a 17-year hiatus, opening a five-level store in a recently renovated office building at Madison Street diagonally across from longtime Chicago retailer Carson Pirie Scott. Across from Chicago retail stalwart Marshall

Field's, owners of the long-vacant Block 37 site have presented a new plan for a five-story retail mall anchored by Lord & Taylor, a condominium tower, and a Marriott Suites Hotel. The site, cleared in the late 1980s for a development that fell victim to the real estate market collapse, has for several years housed a summer art program and winter skating rink.

In addition, Robert J. Mariano, the former head of Dominick's Supermarkets Inc., has launched plans for Mariano's Market Hall, designed by architect Lucien Lagrange and Associates to resemble an Italian village square or Les Halles in Paris. The four-story, 30,000-square-foot gourmet food market will offer fresh meats, seafood, cheese, produce, flowers, baked goods, and prepared foods. Already, Mariano is planning late-night hours to serve downtown office workers, residents, and two other groups that are enlivening State Street at nighttime — theatergoers and students.

Once a thriving mix of live venues and movie houses, Chicago's North Loop theater district has been hoofing its way to a comeback for nearly two decades. The first major success came with the redevelopment of the Chicago Theater in the mid–1980s. More recently, the district has spread along Randolph Street, where the Ford Oriental and Cadillac Palace theaters are adding to the live performance scene. This fall, one of the nation's leading regional theaters, the Goodman, is opening its new home in the district.

The Joffrey Ballet of Chicago also is planning to build new studios nearby. A long-awaited, 1,500-seat music and dance theater for performing arts groups is slated to break ground in the new Lakefront Millennium Park farther east on Randolph. And at the epicenter, State and Randolph streets, the School of the Art Institute is building the Gene Siskel Film Center, one of several education-related developments that are bringing a new group of young people downtown.

Today, the Central Area boasts more than 40,000 students south of the river alone — as many as the student population of Madison, Wisconsin, says Alicia Mazur Berg, the city's deputy commissioner for the Central Area. The number jumps to 75,000 counting the students north of the river at the University of Chicago, at Loyola and Northwestern universities, and just west of the Central Area at the University of Illinois at Chicago. Their presence is no accident. The city has made a conscious effort to draw educational institutions downtown and has encouraged them to expand their campuses.

Several years ago, DePaul University opened new facilities in the former Goldblatt's department store at State Street and Jackson Boulevard. A few blocks north, the School of the Art Institute is using the historic Chicago Building as a dorm. National-Louis University and Columbia College have expanded their downtown campuses. The John Marshall Law School and Roosevelt University also have maintained a long-term presence near State Street.

"State Street as a single project reflects the new life downtown," says SOM's Enquist. "It has cars again, people walking the street again. People have reawakened to the role a historic downtown plays in a region. I see it in downtowns across the country — for example, in Detroit and Houston, which abandoned their downtowns more than Chicago did. Now Chicago is leading the pack. We've created a safe, livable, inviting place."

New Neighborhoods

Two major shopping corridors with an international who's who of retailers, a bevy of restaurants, world-class cultural institutions, a newly enlivened theater district, acres of lakeside parkland, and a short commute to the office — if all the bells and whistles of Chicago's downtown scene do not account for the rush of city dwellers, architect John Lahey of Chicago-based Solomon Cordwell Buenz (SCB) has another theory. "Maybe it's partly because of e-business," he suggests. "Technology has tuned down interaction in the workplace. People want cultural and social interaction, and they're moving downtown to get it. They aren't afraid of the density. They're coming for the density."

Recently, SCB has designed high-rise residences such as the Bristol, the Fordham, and the Sterling in River North, and Park Place near the former Montgomery Ward headquarters. The area around the catalog retailer's onetime corporate campus is a hotbed of residential development, including Chicago-based Centrum Properties's 23-acre Kingsbury Park. Another architectural firm noted for its high-end urban residences, Lucien Lagrange and Associates, recently completed designs for Park Tower, 65 East Goethe, and 840 Lake Shore Drive.

Other developments, such as Kinzie Station, are cropping up west of the river in an area long devoted to railroads and industry and in the area once dominated by the Cabrini-Green public housing complex on the Near North Side. Longtime commercial player U.S. Equities is seizing the moment as well, planning a mixed-use residential and retail development called Grand Plaza on the former American Medical Association headquarters site just west of Michigan Avenue near the new North Bridge complex. In addition, the firm — in partnership with Victor Caccitore, Daniel Epstein, and Shelly Baskin — recently assembled the Central Area's largest parcel, bounded by Congress Parkway, 18th Street, Clark Street, and the Chicago River. The 61-acre site is earmarked for another residential and retail project.

"The fundamental issue is how to bring people to your downtown," says deputy commissioner Berg. "A lot of cities see the solution as a convention center or ballfield, but to make a downtown feel full of life, you have to have people living there." The new residential surge marks the latest twist in a trend SCB's Lahey has been watching since the creation of Sandburg Village on the Gold Coast in the 1960s. "Sandburg Village changed the way Chicago developed," he says. "The city had been in decline. Sandburg Village was a rallying point. The beatniks — not even the hippies yet, the *beatniks* — moved back from the suburbs and outlying neighborhoods to the heart of the city."

Through the era of loft conversions in the 1980s, downtown living remained the province of confirmed city dwellers. But, Lahey says, "Any movement becomes mainstreamed. After the lull of the early 1990s, the city became the place to be for young people out of college. It has become a widespread residential option, not just for the avant-garde elite. All sorts of people see living downtown as an option."

At this point, the vast majority of those who take the option are young professionals or empty nesters; only 3.9 percent of the Central Area's households include children. Accommodating the needs of all potential residents in the area, from children through seniors, will require more than urban energy. It will take small parks and playgrounds, schools, daycare centers, and grocery and convenience stores. It will take affordable housing — and parking.

As the profile of the city dweller has expanded beyond hard-core urbanites, the character of downtown residences has changed as well. While the old guard wanted a formal, urbane living environment, today's city residents want a less formal lifestyle, says Lahey. They want the conveniences of suburban living, and they want their cars. Once, the number of parking spaces equaled 55 percent of the residential units, Lahey explains. Now, developers are specifying a ratio of one to 1.5 spaces per residence. "People want to have a car even if they don't use it. And big garages are hard to integrate into the urban fabric." The influx of autos explains why so many of the new residences are located near expressways, he notes. It also points to a significant challenge facing Chicago planners.

Transit Issues

Chicago boasts one of the nation's largest transit systems. Last year, the Chicago Transit Authority recorded 500,000 daily trips by rail and one million more by bus. Metra, the area's commuter-rail system, logged 220,000 daily trips, up 35 percent since 1983, and expects a 52 percent increase by 2020. While the numbers look impressive, the system is feeling the strain.

"The transportation system is in dire need of repair. The Blue Line is falling apart, and the rest of the El (Chicago's elevated train system) structure is 100 years old," says Peter Skosey, vice president, external relations, for the Metropolitan Planning Council. Capacity issues also dog the system, spurring plans for a light-rail circulator system in the early 1990s; however, the circulator project died, and planners now are looking at creating dedicated bus lanes that would roughly mirror the planned circulator path. "We had great foresight," Skosey notes. "We could have said, 'We told you so.'

"How can we think of accommodating the future growth of downtown if we can't bring in more people?" Skosey asks. "And cars are not an option." Already, the roadways handle 815,000 auto trips to and from downtown every day. Traffic is projected to grow seven percent by 2020, and the existing roadway network cannot expand to absorb the increase, according to SOM's report to city planners.

As U.S. Equities's Wislow notes, concentrating future office development between the Kennedy Expressway and the train stations would reduce the burden by keeping auto traffic west of the historic downtown streets. Ensuring that cultural and entertainment attractions remain convenient to autos is another matter. From the standpoint of tourists and visitors, attractions are located "for beauty and convenience," Skosey says. "People can drive in now. We have to be careful we don't kill the goose that laid the golden egg" by choking it with congested roadways.

Managing Development

Efficient transportation. Affordable housing. Competing land use issues. The road ahead is paved with challenges, but Chicago's city planners are pleased with their progress and optimistic about the future. Much credit for Chicago's success goes to the long economic boom and an aggressive administration, planners say. "One of the surprises has been just how long this boom has kept going, and the depth of the residential market," says deputy commissioner Berg. "What's been nice about this boom is that it's spread out, beyond the high rises along Lake Shore Drive. More and more of the city is affected."

"Many of the things that had been talked about before Mayor Daley came into office got done on his watch — the Lake Shore Drive relocation, Theater Row, State Street," deputy commissioner Gallagher notes. "We're in very aggressive development mode." Adds SCB's Lahey, "Chicago realizes we don't need to entice development so much as to manage it."

CHAPTER 13

CLEVELAND USES PRIVATE PLANNING GROUP TO IMPROVE ITS DOWNTOWN AND LAKEFRONT AREAS

Ruth Eckdish Knack

"Pub is pub. Good, bad. Pub is cool." So said former Chicago Bears running back Raymont Harris two years ago in respect to some truly bad press. And if one believes that all publicity is good publicity, then Cleveland has it made.

In the '70s, television commentators — and comedians, too — had a field day with "the mistake on the lake," the city whose river caught on fire, that had a laughable mayor, and whose finances were in disarray. The bad news peaked in 1978 with a declaration of bankruptcy. Meanwhile, the city continued to lose population. Today it's down to 500,000, almost half of what it was in the 1950s.

Now the headlines are about the "comeback city." In the last 10 years, Cleveland transformed its skyline with a series of crowd-pleasing projects, particularly the $300 million Gateway Center sports complex and the lakefront Rock and Roll Hall of Fame. The Flats, the low-lying riverside industrial district, has become a hot spot for nightlife, and the 19th century Warehouse District has been reborn as a residential area.

Mayor Michael White, who was elected to a third term in November, has also become a media celebrity. Last August, *Time* included him in a feature on the "new pragmatist mayors," along with Chicago's Richard Daley and Milwaukee's John Norquist.

But publicity has its downside, including the suspicion that the rewards of prosperity are not being distributed equally.

Downtown First

Criticism came from all sides last May when the nonprofit group called Cleveland Tomorrow released *Civic Vision 2000 and Beyond*, its plan for downtown.

While many observers saw the plan as a much-needed diagram for future development, some, like Steven Litt, the architecture critic of the Cleveland *Plain Dealer*,

Originally published as "Cleveland: The Morning After," *Planning*, Vol. 65, No. 1, January, 1999. Published by the American Planning Association, 122 South Michigan Avenue, Suite 1600, Chicago, Illinois 60603-6107. Reprinted with permission of the publisher.

complained about inadequate public participation. Others, including David Beach, editor of the environmental newsletter, *EcoCity Cleveland*, worried about overdevelopment of the Lake Erie shore. Gadfly columnist Roldo Bartimole railed about the tax breaks and low-interest loans that benefit downtown developers — "socialism for the rich."

It's the charge that downtown is benefiting at the expense of the neighborhoods that produces the quickest response from Stephen Strnisha, Cleveland Tomorrow's deputy director and a former aide to Mayor White. "Downtown is the city's economic engine. It's important for everyone," he says.

Cleveland Tomorrow started out in the early '80s as an economic development group, the result of a survey by McKinsey & Company, the international management consulting firm commissioned by a group of local chief executive officers. The CEOs, says Strnisha, were concerned that northeast Ohio was not getting its share of manufacturing-related research — despite the presence of such institutions as the Cleveland Clinic and Case Western Reserve University.

McKinsey recommended that the CEOs set up an organization that would create a venture capital fund and stimulate development in other ways as well, for instance by identifying opportunities in the emerging biotechnology industry. It should be an exclusive group, the consultants said, made up of top company officers and tightly focused on a few strategic goals. One model was Pittsburgh's Allegheny Conference.

Today, the organization has some 50 members, and a four-member professional staff. Keeping the staff small allows flexibility, Strnisha says. "If an initiative requires ongoing effort, we spin it off into a new group." An example: Neighborhood Progress, Inc., which helps community development corporations with neighborhood projects.

Physical development was not part of the original agenda, but worthy projects kept coming up, Strnisha says. For instance, Cleveland Tomorrow helped raise funds to restore the four theaters in Playhouse Square, the city's 1920s theater complex. It also created a $50 million development fund to help finance several of the projects identified with downtown's turnaround, including the rock museum — which lately has been losing attendance. And it led a premium seating campaign for the Gateway Center stadiums.

In late 1996, the group took on a different type of project — a downtown plan, more specifically an update of the downtown portion of the city's 1990 general plan. Thus began an unusual private-sector foray into public planning. Substantial funding for the plan came from two well-known local philanthropies, the Cleveland and Gund foundations.

Filling in the Gaps

The new plan's title, *Civic Vision 2000 and Beyond*, reflects the idea of building on the last plan, which was called *Civic Vision 2000*. "We didn't want to reinvent the wheel," says Strnisha. "Our idea was to coordinate and fill in the gaps."

The recommendations released last spring focused on two areas: the city's traditional commercial spine, the Euclid Corridor, where empty office space is being converted into apartments, and the lakefront.

The lakefront is already the site of an eclectic collection of attractions, including the Great Lakes Science Center and the William S. Mather Museum, which occupies a 66-year-old oreboat. Just west of the science center, the $200 million Cleveland Browns stadium is rising, the result of a deal made by Mayor White with the National Football League to replace the old Cleveland Browns, whose owner moved them to Baltimore.

Consultant Jane Thompson of Boston, whose firm redesigned Chicago's Navy Pier, focused on North Coast Harbor just off East Ninth Street, a site that offers a splendid view of the city's skyline. To improve access, the plan calls for extending the lakefront transit line and possibly realigning the Shoreway, the adjacent highway, thus providing better access to Burke Lakefront Airport and to the new convention center that the plan calls for.

Although the recommendations are now in the city's hands — the planning commission adopted them in July — Cleveland Tomorrow is still involved. Strnisha says a committee is being organized to talk about implementation, including the best location for the convention center. "Candidly," he says, "I think it was good for city officials to stand back from this process. Now we can both be at the table to figure out how to get things done."

Strnisha also has a ready answer for those who fear that the recommendations will make Cleveland look too much like other cities. "There's a lot of Cleveland in what's being proposed," he says. "We know that this is still a manufacturing town. But people here like to do the same things as people in other cities."

The City's Role

City planning director Hunter Morrison stresses that, even though created by a private group, the Cleveland Tomorrow document is part of a public planning process. It fits into what Morrison jokingly describes as "sort of an apostolic succession of plans."

That history starts with the 1903 "Group Plan," whose legacy is the grouping of civic buildings surrounding a mall designed by Daniel Burnham. The first general plan was done in 1949 under planning director Jack Howard. It was updated in 1959

and again in 1988 and '89 under the *Civic Vision 2000* title. That plan, which won an APA national award in 1992, is now being updated and will incorporate the Cleveland Tomorrow recommendations in the downtown portion.

There's a new wrinkle in the current effort. The plan will be coordinated with a reorganization of the city's police districts (something that was last done in the 1930s, Morrison says, when "Untouchable" Eliot Ness was the city's public safety director). The entire plan will be computerized, using the planning department's geographic information system.

"It's a great deal for the neighborhoods, which will have much better access to up-to-date information," Morrison says.

Morrison describes what his department is doing as "development-oriented planning" — a phrase likely never to have crossed the lips of his predecessor, Norman Krumholz, AICP, who served as city planning director from 1969 to 1979, and who practiced what he called "equity planning."

A Cleveland native, Morrison received a planning degree in 1974 from Harvard's Graduate School of Design. He worked for the now-defunct Hough Area Development Corporation until 1980, when he became assistant planning director. He says he caught the eye of the newly elected mayor, George Voinovich (later governor of Ohio and now U.S. senator) because of his neighborhood work. A year later, he was named director of the city planning department.

"Initially," Morrison says, "the issue was to rebuild the department," which he says was demoralized following Krumholz's departure. At the same time, a task force appointed by the new mayor recommended that the planning commission and staff move away from the social planning that was its hallmark under Krumholz and toward more traditional, land-use planning.

A New Tack

The first step in that direction, says Morrison, was to update the general plan and the outmoded zoning code. The residential sections were tackled first, Morrison says, with provisions added for planned unit developments.

Under Mayor White, the revitalization of neighborhood commercial centers has become a focus. "Mayor White said we should look for the traditional heart of the community, the place where the movie theater used to be, and the drugstore. We've identified over 30 of those places," says Morrison. A case in point: a 150,000-square-foot supermarket in the blighted Church Square community on the east side. "It has been phenomenally successful," he says. "It makes the neighborhood a better place to live."

To get developments like this off the drawing boards, planners must be able to work with developers, Morrison says. It also helps to have a close relationship between the city's planning and development departments. "In most cities," he says, "the planners are in hiding somewhere in the attic."

Under Mayor White, related departments have been put in clusters, each under the oversight of one of the mayor's executive assistants. Planning, community development, and economic development are in one such cluster, coordinated by Ken Silliman, a planner and lawyer who has been in the mayor's office since 1995. "The result," says Silliman, "is a much higher level of coordination than in most cities."

Different Strokes

For Morrison, planning is a process "that reduces risk," thus creating a better investment climate, in the neighborhoods as well as downtown. For Krumholz, planning is a far broader activity. "City planning

should encompass the whole range of problems the city must deal with," he says, social problems as well as physical ones.

In Krumholz's view, Morrison and his staff have limited themselves — "unnecessarily, I think" — to the nuts and bolts of planning. "They haven't raised many questions about the broader issues" such as the wisdom of the tax abatements routinely given to developers. "If you believe that the planner's job is to find out what the private sector wants and to help them do it," then this department is doing the right thing, Krumholz says. "I disagree."

These observations come from a man the *Washington Post* recently dubbed Cleveland's "preeminent Grinch." Krumholz, president-elect of the American Institute of Certified Planners, now teaches urban studies at Cleveland State University — a good post for observing what's happening in the city.

And a lot of what's happening is good, he says, both downtown and in the neighborhoods. Mayor White deserves credit, he adds, for channeling community development funds to community development organizations.

"But for most people who live in the city, things are worse," Krumholz says. "The institutions they depend on — the public housing authority, the transit agency, and particularly the schools — are in worse shape." Even a federal empowerment zone designation — and the promise of $177 million in grants and loans — has had few apparent results so far, he says.

In the Hough neighborhood, the site of some of the nation's most violent urban riots, some 100 new houses have been built on city-supplied land and with generous tax abatements — ranging from $150,000 to $700,000. "But who are these houses for," Krumholz asks, "when the median household income in Hough is still not much above $10,000?"

A Keeper

Cleveland is the kind of place diehard city lovers root for, a still somewhat muscular manufacturing center, with a diverse, hard-working population and an impressive history — capital of the Western Reserve, birthplace of John D. Rockefeller and Standard Oil. Remnants of that history are visible everywhere, from the statue of surveyor Moses Cleaveland in Public Square, once a village green, to the freighters on the Cuyahoga River, signs of a great inland port.

And if a city's health is measured by the state of its downtown, Cleveland, with $3 billion in investment since 1990 and another $3 billion called for in the recent downtown plan, is doing well. Rick Cole, AICP, the former mayor of Pasadena, California, worked in Cleveland in the late 1970s. He says he's amazed whenever he returns to see the transformation of the city. "Downtown has had a genuine comeback," he says. "The question is whether a fixed downtown constitutes a fixed city."

The answer depends on a variety of things, including the global economy. "Cities like ours are always going to be affected by swings in the global marketplaces," says Cleveland Tomorrow's Steve Strnisha. "We still have two international banks based here, but that could change. That would have a big effect on us."

Regional competition is another threat, affecting the city as well as its suburbs. The nonprofit group, EcoCity Cleveland, working with APA researchers, has begun to formulate a statewide "smart growth" plan — an encouraging sign to many observers.

Closer to home a major problem is the city's public school system, which was placed under state control a few years ago. A state law passed last summer puts Cleveland Mayor White in charge.

Meanwhile, well-wishers hope that the center holds and that the trickle down effect will spread development from the downtown to the neighborhoods.

CHAPTER 14

DENVER USES TRANSIT SYSTEM TO ENHANCE DOWNTOWN ACCESS FOR BOTH RESIDENTS AND TOURISTS

Sam Newberg

It was a long time coming, but downtown Denver has realized a transformation in the past ten years that is matched by few other American cities. Restored warehouses with swanky restaurants and upscale urban lofts, light-rail transit with ridership above projections, an office vacancy rate of less than five percent, recreation paths along the waterfront, new stadiums for professional sports teams, one of the few successful pedestrian malls in the United States — and a new, international airport that makes getting there that much easier — all in the shadow of the Rocky Mountains.

Downtown Denver as it exists today is a combination of public and private cooperation, successes of the past, a plan enacted in 1986, and a prosperity in the 1990s that increased the population of Colorado by 30 percent. What is known today as the Downtown Denver Partnership, a nonprofit business organization that works to keep downtown healthy, was formed in the 1950s. One of the first steps taken was Dana Crawford's historic renovation of Larimer Square in the 1960s, and the 1982 dedication of the 16th Street pedestrian mall. The oil crash of the 1980s put Denver's back to the wall. The private sector had its hands tied, and the public sector stepped in. In 1984, Mayor Frederico Pena appointed a steering committee to oversee the creation of the downtown area plan. The plan, issued in 1986, set forth a visionary course for the city. Four overall goals were established for downtown Denver: to be economically healthy; to be the social and cultural center of the region; to be beautiful and full of people and activity; and to be a good neighbor to the city's other neighborhoods.

Thanks to a good economy, coupled with good transportation into downtown and a large number of residents, downtown Denver currently is economically healthy. With a performing arts complex, several sports complexes, the Denver Art Museum, a convention center, and many galleries and restaurants, downtown Denver is the cultural and social center of the region. Organized street sweeping of the 16th Street mall and other efforts have beautified downtown Denver and filled it with activity. The Downtown Denver Partnership works with surrounding neighborhoods to organize

---

Originally published as "Denver's Center," *Urban Land*, Vol. 60, No. 5, May, 2001. Published by the Urban Land Institute, Washington, D.C. Reprinted with permission of the publisher.

acceptable growth and development that are compatible with its surroundings and that are beneficial for the city overall.

Five critical needs were outlined in the plan: maintaining a vital retail center in downtown; developing people connections among downtown's activity centers; improving access into downtown; enhancing distinct districts in downtown; and providing housing downtown.

Due to the marketing efforts of the Downtown Denver Partnership and good property management in retail projects, the retail market in downtown Denver currently is both distinct and vibrant. The 16th Street mall, the spine of downtown, offers free shuttle-bus service that provides easy access to most of downtown. The planned expansion of both 16th Street and the light-rail system will improve connections among downtown's activity centers. The light-rail system, a streamlined bus service, and improved road access and parking have made the downtown area more accessible. Thousands of housing units are proposed or under construction in and around downtown.

The Birthplace of Denver

Lower Downtown (LoDo), the birthplace of Denver, is considered the most distinctive area in the city. The downtown area plan emphasized the importance of enhancing districts such as LoDo. Today, it is home to many restored warehouse buildings, which are used as office, retail, hotel, and residential space.

LoDo, which was rezoned from industrial to mixed use in 1981, was declared a local historic district in 1988. The Downtown Denver Partnership created a Lower Downtown Business Support Office that, with financial support from preservation groups and the state of Colorado, encouraged renovations. More than 20 buildings in

LoDo have been renovated since 1991, and there are nearly 1,400 housing units in the area.

Preservation has been a successful venture throughout downtown, not just in LoDo. A selective preservation overlay district for downtown Denver covers historic buildings. Only older buildings are required to be reviewed for preservation purposes. Buildings throughout downtown have been restored or converted into office and retail space that competes in rental rates with the newest skyscrapers.

There has been new development as well, such as Denver Pavilions, a 350,000-square-foot entertainment center anchored by Niketown, Hard Rock Café, a Virgin Records megastore, and a 15-screen United Artists theater, with 50 other local and national retailers. Denver Pavilions borders on the 16th Street mall shuttle bus route, making it readily accessible from anywhere in downtown. The project's completion in the late 1990s signaled the true revival of retail in downtown Denver.

With regard to the office market, Integra Realty Resources ranked downtown Denver the number one city for investment in 2001. Downtown Denver has more than 25 million square feet of rentable space, and Class A space has a vacancy rate of under five percent, down from 20 percent in 1990. A new mixed-use project located on the 16th Street mall called 16 Market Square provides a transition between LoDo and downtown proper, combining 183,000 square feet of office space with 23,000 square feet of first-floor retail space and 25 for-sale penthouse condominiums. In addition to 16 Market Square, which opens this year, a new 40-story office tower is due for completion next year. These two projects are the first new office construction downtown has seen since 1985.

Downtown Denver has 5,000-plus rooms in 16 hotels, six of which were built or renovated in the 1990s. Hotel occupancy rates for downtown are over 70 percent, which is higher than the national average.

Just beyond LoDo and Union Station lies the Central Platte Valley neighborhood, which consists mostly of vacant land and the new Commons Park along the South Platte River. The integration of this neighborhood with downtown was envisioned in the downtown area plan. Residential development is already occurring. Over time, the street grid of downtown and LoDo will be extended into the Central Platte Valley. Later this year, the 16th Street shuttle bus will be extended to serve this neighborhood.

Along the course of Commons Park are the Children's Museum, Colorado's Ocean Journey, Six Flags Elitch Gardens amusement park, the Pepsi Center, and the new Denver Broncos stadium. More than 2,000 housing units also are planned for this area. Commons Park is an amenity for the emerging neighborhood and for visitors.

Packing Them In

Stadium development is as popular in Denver as anywhere in the United States, and the past ten years has seen three new stadiums built. Beginning in 1995 with Coors Field in LoDo, home of the Colorado Rockies baseball team, each of these stadiums has been built in or immediately adjacent to downtown. The Pepsi Center, which opened in 1999, is home to the Denver Nuggets basketball and Colorado Avalanche hockey teams. The new Broncos football stadium, located next to the team's old Mile High Stadium, is due to open later this year.

Coors Field is considered the most impressive of the new stadiums. Awarded an expansion baseball team in 1991, Denver chose not to build a stadium along an interstate surrounded by parking lots, but instead to put it on the edge of LoDo, with a brick exterior that evokes the architecture of the surrounding old warehouses. Because

downtown's historic preservation legislation was in place, property owners were discouraged from tearing down historic buildings for stadium parking. Instead, the baseball stadium stimulated adaptive uses throughout the area and attracted people to downtown restaurants and galleries. Visitors regularly use the free shuttle bus on the 16th Street mall as part of a day spent downtown at a baseball game, art museum, or other attractions in between.

At the opposite end of the 16th Street mall from LoDo, the State Capitol building sits across Civic Center Park from Denver's city hall. The park is host to summertime concerts and other events, and is also flanked by the Denver Public Library and the Denver Art Museum.

Also located within two blocks of the 16th Street mall are the Denver Performing Arts Complex and the Colorado Convention Center. The arts complex includes seven theaters and one concert hall, and is the second-largest performing arts complex in the United States. In November 1999, voters approved a $289 million expansion to the convention center, including a 1,100-room convention hotel, scheduled to open in 2003.

At Home and on the Move

Approximately 25 percent of the office workers in downtown use some form of public transportation to get to work. Denver's public transportation system has been improved greatly in the past ten years with the opening of a light-rail transit line that bisects the 16th Street mall. All buses into downtown are routed to a station at the end of the 16th Street mall, from where riders can make easy connections to the free shuttle.

A light-rail spur is planned to connect the existing light-rail line with Union Station, and to serve along the way the Auraria

Higher Education Center campus (located on the southern edge of downtown), the Pepsi Center, the new Broncos football stadium, and Six Flags Elitch Gardens. The extended 16th Street mall will also reach Union Station. Additional train service from Union Station is planned, including possible service to Denver International Airport and Boulder.

A substantial goal of the downtown area plan was to add housing. The core population in LoDo and the central business district is approximately 3,700 residents, up from 2,700 in 1990. The Downtown Denver Partnership is surveying the 115,000 downtown employees to assess housing needs. Its goal is to construct more housing that serves the needs of downtown workers first, which not only helps reduce commuting traffic into the city, but also makes the area more vibrant.

The success of the downtown Denver renaissance is leading to redevelopment in surrounding neighborhoods, which are growing. Their population stands at 65,000, up from 58,000 in 1990. Thousands of new housing units are planned or are under construction.

Post Properties is constructing 949 rental units in a three-phase new urban project located in the Uptown neighborhood, which is just east of downtown. When completed, the development will have approximately 30,000 square feet of retail and live/work space.

Two blocks southeast of the State Capitol, in the Capitol Hill neighborhood, a 145-unit apartment building recently has been completed. Named Capitol Heights, the project incorporates ground-level retail with residential units above. The Capitol Hill and Uptown neighborhoods also contain some of Denver's oldest housing, much of it Victorian in style.

New housing projects in the Central Platte Valley include the Flour Mill Lofts (in a former flour mill) and Commons Park West, a 340 unit rental project.

With thousands of new housing units, three new stadiums, an enhanced public realm, a new light-rail system, and historic restored warehouses, Denver has an amenities advantage unmatched by most cities.

The collective imagination and a city-led, consensus-driven downtown area plan have helped Denver recover from its hard times in the 1980s and solidify downtown's position as the true center of the region.

CHAPTER 15

DENVER METRO AREA VOTERS RAISE REVENUES FOR SCIENTIFIC AND CULTURAL FACILITIES

Jane Hansberry

On November 8, 1988, during the worst regional recession in decades, citizens in metropolitan Denver, Colorado, voted three-to-one to increase their sales tax to support the region's scientific and cultural facilities. That day marked the beginning of a new division of local government in Colorado — the Scientific and Cultural Facilities District (SCFD).

The 1988 vote was an extraordinary event for three reasons. First, it was counter-intuitive that citizens would vote for a tax increase in such bad economic times. Second, it was a vote to provide public support for arts and cultural organizations at a time when many pundits doubted the public's willingness to support culture with tax dollars. Third, the vote established a regional basis for supporting cultural organizations, many of which were located in the core city. The region that was created comprised Denver and the five surrounding suburban counties.

Background

Several events led to the November 1988 vote to support the scientific and cultural facilities. First and foremost was the loss of state funds to the institutions. As a result, trustees developed a legislative strategy, and a bill outlining the cultural district was introduced into the state legislature. Then, cultural organizations launched a campaign to sell the cultural tax.

Loss of State Funds

In 1982, the City of Denver's major cultural institutions, namely the Denver Art Museum, the Denver Zoo, the Denver Botanic Gardens, and the Denver Museum of Nature and Science (referred to hereafter as the "Big Four"), lost the state funding they had enjoyed for half a century. The City and County of Denver (Denver is a combined city/county jurisdiction) already provided nearly half these institutions' annual budgets, and they were unable to make up

Originally published as "Denver's Scientific and Cultural Facilities District: A Case Study in Regionalism," *Government Finance Review*, Vol. 16, No. 6, December, 2000. Reprinted with permission of the Government Finance Officers Association, publisher of *Government Finance Review*, 180 N. Michigan Ave., Suite 800, Chicago, IL USA 60601 (312/977-9700; fax: 312/977-4806; e-mail: GFR@gfoa.org). Annual subscription: $30.

the shortfall. Denver was experiencing a loss of revenue and population to the suburbs that exacerbated a regional and state-wide recession and population emigration.

The institutions were forced to seek new sources of funding. They set up foundations and raised fees, but neither of these strategies, nor others that they employed, were able to mitigate the loss of state funds. In fact, the strategies of new and increased fees had driven attendance down, furthering financial losses and curtailing planned exhibits and programming.

A Strategy Takes Hold

In 1983, faced with rapidly deteriorating finances, the trustees of the four institutions began to discuss and explore their options. A chance encounter between a Denver Art Museum trustee and a trustee from the St. Louis Art Museum would prove fortuitous. From this meeting, the Denver trustee learned of the St. Louis Metropolitan Zoological Park and Museum District, which were created in 1971 through a referendum. The St. Louis District provided a regional base of support for the city's museums and zoos with property tax revenues. The Denver trustee took hold of the idea as a possible framework for how the Denver cultural organizations might proceed.[1] A regional funding base would provide a more equitable basis of financial support than reliance on the City and County of Denver alone. Surveys of attendance and membership rosters supported this plan by indicating that the majority of visitors to the four cultural institutions were residents of suburban counties outside of Denver.

From 1983 to 1986 when the first enabling legislation for the creation of a tax district was proposed, trustees from the Big Four institutions worked through political and legislative strategies. In the past, these institutions had viewed each other as competitors and had very little history of collaboration. They had learned, however, that the best legislative and political case could be made together, and not as separate entities.

The strategy was to find legislators willing to sponsor enabling legislation for a Denver metro-area sales tax district encompassing Denver and the surrounding suburban counties—Adams, Arapahoe, Boulder, Douglas, and Jefferson. These were the same boundaries as the Regional Transportation District and would prove to be a boost for the cultural district concept because a "regional footprint" already was established.

The proposed rate of .1 percent sales tax would raise $13 million. The plan was to direct 75 percent of the revenue to the Big Four, and give the remaining 25 percent of the revenue to the six counties' boards of county commissioners (and Denver City Council) for a locally controlled distribution to smaller cultural organizations in each county. A proposed selling point would be the lean administrative structure, which allocated less than one percent of revenues to administration of the tax. The tax would be created by the legislature and ratified by a vote of the citizens in the six-county region.

The Legislature

In January 1986, a bill outlining the cultural district was introduced. Initial debate centered on the questions of whether public funding for culture was an appropriate use of taxes and what percentage of the tax burden should be shouldered by Denver and by the suburbs. However, the discussion soon became argumentative even within the cultural community. With the introduction of the legislation, the entire cultural community became aware of the Big Four's plans. The major performing arts organizations, not included in the legislation as drafted, argued that they had been left out, while the smaller cultural organizations at the county level argued that, since they were written into the legislation, they wanted some input as to the shape of the proposed district.

These intra-cultural community arguments took place during the Colorado State Senate Local Government Committee hearings on the bill. The committee told the factions to go away and work through their issues and come back in two weeks. Despite the compromise solution hammered out at that time, the bill died when it was sent to the House side for review, mainly because of the infighting among the various cultural organizations.

Regrouping for Success. The group was convinced that it needed to hire professional political talent to develop and implement a legislative agenda. A political consultant was hired in 1986 for the task of "herding the cultural cats" and cultivating new legislation for 1987. The efforts proved successful. House Bill 1138 was introduced in the 1987 session. It encompassed the framework for the creation of a six-county district that would collect and distribute a tenth of a percent sales tax to three "tiers" of cultural organizations: 1) the Big Four, 2) the major performing arts organizations, and 3) the smaller cultural institutions. In April 1987, the legislation passed and was signed into law by the governor on May 22.

The Campaign

The campaign to promote the cultural tax that ensued is remembered for its creativity, focus on message, and penetration of the region. Polling indicated that the campaign would be best served by focusing on the most popular institutions, such as the zoo. The campaign highlighted the benefits of supporting cultural organizations, arguing that culture was not only good for the individual, but it was also good for the community's quality of life and economic well-

being.

The cultural organizations provided the bulk of the campaign funding (approximately $750,000) as well as its labor power. They also provided resources for the look and feel of the campaign's collateral pieces and ads. A particularly effective television ad was one in which a small boy is kept from entering a museum wing by a guard who says, "Sorry, son, this exhibit is closed." Another campaign asset was the late actor Raymond Burr, a great friend to Denver, who appeared in public service announcements on behalf of the cultural tax.

On November 8, 1988, when more than a half million voters voted yes (by a ratio of three-to-one) to create the new tax, they were also saying yes to a regional system of supporting culture.

Creating the New District

As prescribed by the enabling legislation, the Scientific and Cultural Facilities District (SCFD) had a board of directors in place at the time of the vote. Each county appoints a representative to the board to serve for no more than two consecutive three-year terms. In five of the counties, these appointments are made by the boards of county commissioners, and in Denver, the appointment is made by the Denver City Council. In addition, the governor appoints three members of the board, who are also term-limited to no more than two terms, for a total of nine board members.

The board's duties as outlined in the enabling legislation include: hiring staff, providing for the distribution of SCFD tax funds and the reporting and review of those funds, and calling for and administering an election for the renewal of the tax.

The initial SCFD tax had a sunset of June 30, 1996, unless otherwise renewed. On November 4, 1994, the voters renewed the SCFD through June 30, 2006.

The enabling legislation provided the SCFD distribution formula of 65 percent to the Big Four or "Tier I," 25 percent to the mid-sized performing and exhibiting organizations or "Tier II," and 10 percent to the smaller cultural groups operating at the county level (the "Tier III" organizations). These percentages were adjusted in the 1994 renewal to 59, 28, and 13 percent, respectively, to reflect changes in audience and changes in the number of Tier II and III organizations.

Although the SCFD statute provided a framework for the district, the policy and procedural work necessary to implement the statute was considerable. An example of this work was the process undertaken to develop the Tier II accounting and auditing procedures. Unlike the Tier I organizations which are named in the statute, Tier II organizations are only functionally described in the statute. In order to qualify for Tier II status, an organization must meet the statute's primary purpose test, be a nonprofit organization or agency of local government, have a minimum operating budget of $700,000 (in subsequent legislation this number was adjusted for inflation), and provide public benefit. Once an organization met these requirements, they provided an audit of their previous year's attendance and their previous year's operating budget. This information would be a part of their Tier II certification process and would determine how much of the Tier II funds each organization would receive, according to a formula that averaged the attendance and budget figures and then proportioned that average against the projected Tier II total funds.

The income side of the equation proved to be a relatively straightforward auditing process; the attendance side of the equation proved more challenging. The SCFD Board brought the auditors of the likely Tier II organizations together to work with them on devising workable auditing practices for auditing attendance. The questions that were addressed included how to handle classes that the organizations might sponsor, that is, how to weight a class series of two sessions as compared with a series of 10 sessions. Another question surrounded whether or not the number of tickets sold or the number of tickets actually used should be the base for auditing.

The class-session question was answered by counting each individual session of a class or workshop series. The ticket question was answered by auditing the number of tickets sold. It was also necessary to understand the differences in ticketing policies and operations of the exhibiting organizations as contrasted with the performing organizations. The work of the organizations' independent auditors was an integral part of the SCFD Tier II auditing and certification procedures, and established early on the district's style of working directly with the field, and not developing policy and/or procedure in isolation.

The Tier II formula provides that the larger organizations receive more funding, per the intent of the statute that the SCFD would reinforce the public's support as expressed through their patronage and attendance. And though it is a "the-rich-get-richer" formula, there have been new entrants to Tier II nearly every year, with the number growing from seven organizations in 1989 to 19 in 1999.

Tier III — The Wild Card

The Tier I organizations were named in the statute and the probable Tier II organizations were well known. In that first year of funds distribution, though, no one knew what to expect from Tier III. Just as with Tier II, Tier III was described in the statute, and eligibility criteria were outlined. An organization needed to have the statutory primary purpose, be a nonprofit organization or agency of local government, and provide public benefit. In short, provide all of the criteria of Tier II, with the exception of the $700,000 budget threshold.

By statute, each county appointed a cultural council whose job it was to oversee the distribution of Tier III funds. Those six councils worked with the district to develop application and grant making procedures and protocols. The district board understood that beyond statutory compliance, each county was free to develop rules of procedure and policies appropriate for their county's resources and needs. Like Tier II, Tier III has grown; from 1989 to 1999 the number of Tier III organizations grew from 159 to just greater than 300.

The impact of Tier III funds on local government has been substantial. Because local government agencies are statutorily eligible to receive SCFD funds, many municipalities have been able to expand their arts and cultural commissions' programming. A number of these municipal arts and cultural commissions also provide a re-granting function to small cultural organizations and a nexus of information and referral for those small cultural organizations. The City of Brighton, for example, developed an Arts and Culture Department in 1995 that has sponsored an annual "CultureFest," celebrating the many cultures of the local people; "Brass Blast" bringing the best of brass to perform in Brighton; and "Art Awakenings," designed to inspire all citizens to celebrate their creativity through the arts.

Since the Vote

Since the SCFD began, its revenues and distributions have grown from $14.9 million in 1989 to just more than $33 million in 1999. The number of institutions receiving funding has doubled to more than 300. The region's economy has recovered from the depths of the recession of the 1980s and is now thriving. Concerns about growth management and infrastructure capacity have replaced those of job loss, office vacancy rates, and population emigration.

The SCFD also has become a part of the regional landscape. Since the initial voter approval in 1988, SCFD was reauthorized by voters in 1994, thus fulfilling the "sunset" provision in the enabling legislation. Another reauthorization vote will be held sometime before 2006.

In November 1998, the Scientific and Cultural Facilities District celebrated its 10th anniversary by throwing a "Community Thank You Celebration." More than 45,000 people throughout metro Denver enjoyed free programming at 90 venues throughout the region.

The long hours spent creating the district and working the campaigns (for initial approval and renewal) have forged strong bonds within the cultural community. For instance, in 1990, after market research demonstrated that the major performing arts organizations collectively were only reaching 11 percent of metro households, those organizations came together and pooled a portion of their SCFD funds to create joint marketing and public relations programs. Donor and subscriber lists were shared and merged. Joint campaigns to "discover yourself in the arts" were launched. The guiding principle of the cooperation of these institutions is "to do together what we cannot do singly," reflecting, perhaps, the very spirit of regional cooperation that created the district itself. The results of these campaigns have been dramatic; there has been a marked increase in participation in arts and cultural events in the past decade.

The Public Benefits

In 1999, according to "The Economic and Social Impact of the Scientific and Cultural Facilities District" study produced by

Deloitte and Touche and the Colorado Business Committee for the Arts, total attendance at SCFD organizations was 9.3 million visits. (Those visits consisted of approximately 7.1 million paid, 1.8 million free, and 440,000 reduced rate admissions.) In contrast, the combined home-game attendance of the Denver Broncos professional football team, Denver Nuggets basketball team, Denver Avalanche hockey team, and Colorado Rockies baseball team was 5.8 million visitors.

There is a recognition on the part of the cultural organizations that receiving SCFD funds translates into a higher level of responsibility to the community. The entire cultural community has pitched in to supplement arts and science education in schools by providing school tours, school contracts, and after-school programs. In 1999, SCFD organizations provided 2,700 programs to underserved populations including children at or below the poverty level, people of diverse ethnic backgrounds, the elderly, and people with disabilities. In addition, more than 489,000 people enrolled in paid and free courses offered by SCFD organizations.[2]

The economic impact and benefits of the SCFD are as impressive as the social impacts. The same study reports an estimated $844 million in gross economic impact when the operating expenditures, capital expenditures, and audience ancillary spending by patrons of the organizations are totaled. Of that figure, the impact of cultural patrons who came from outside Colorado and stayed overnight was more than $130 million. Throughout 1999, SCFD organizations employed nearly 7,000 people and paid more than $15 million in payroll, seat, and sales taxes.[3]

Economic Development

Since the SCFD was created in 1988, Pittsburgh, Kansas City, and Salt Lake City have created cultural districts, each tailored to the resources and needs of their respective regions. Other urban areas and regions are studying the issue as public support of culture is increasingly seen as an investment in a region's present and future quality of life. There is a growing awareness of the role that the arts and culture play in developing an educated workforce and, on the other side of that coin, in attracting an educated workforce.

More and more evidence is indicating that the arts are a fundamental part of education. In one state study, reading comprehension was shown to improve when children took drama classes in addition to their regular classes. In a study that included multiple cities, at-risk children who participated in an arts program consistently scored higher in core subjects than children not placed in the program.[4]

It has been demonstrated that quality accessible cultural amenities are considered by businesses to be a prerequisite for attraction and retention of qualified employees. As technology increases the mobility of the workforce and allows for "virtual" industry structures, there will be concomitant changes in the nature of labor recruitment. The traditional model of attracting residents to a city or town based on employment opportunities may be shifting. In the future, the quality of life that states and communities provide will become an increasingly important element in attracting residents.[5]

The essential ingredient for the formation of cultural tax districts remains the development of public support for the concept and for raising taxes to fund it. This support may be more readily available than is commonly known. A 1996 Louis Harris survey on the arts showed that by a three-to-one margin U.S. citizens are strongly in favor of supporting arts and cultural organizations with taxes. The survey showed that 67 percent of Americans support local government arts agencies giving financial support to the arts, 63 percent believe that state governments should fund the arts, and 57 percent support federal support of the arts.[6] These numbers should be encouraging for regions contemplating an increase in the support of their arts and cultural institutions through a regional mechanism.

The Greater Denver Chamber of Commerce launched the "Year of Regional Cooperation" this year. The theme's goal is to continue reaching out to other public, private, and nonprofit-sector organizations to look for regional solutions for future regional issues and challenges.

Notes

1. McCarthy, Mike, "A Short History of the Scientific and Cultural Facilities District," produced on behalf of the Scientific and Cultural Facilities District, 1993, page 4.

2. "The Economic and Social Impact of the Scientific and Cultural Facilities District," study conducted by Deloitte and Touche and the Colorado Business Committee for the Arts, Denver, CO. October 2000.

3. Ibid. page 4.

4. "Eloquent Evidence: Arts at the Core of Learning," National Assembly of State Arts Agencies, 1998.

5. National Survey: Business Support to the Arts 1998, Business Committee for the Arts, Inc. 1999.

6. *The Washington Post*, Friday, June 21, 1996.

Chapter 16

DuPont Uses "New Urbanism" Concepts to Plan for Downtown Civic Center

Spencer A. Johnson

New urbanism — with its diverse neighborhoods, narrow, tree-lined streets, and residents who walk to stores, interact with their neighbors, and watch the world go by from their front porches — is a concept that most people find hard to fault.

Sometimes referred to as neotraditional planning, new urbanism emerged in the late 1980s in response to disillusionment with the low-density, single-use zoning of housing developments, office parks, and shopping complexes that characterized post–World War II suburban development. The orderly, peaceful suburbs that once offered escape from the crime and congestion of big cities have given rise to their own set of social, economic, and environmental problems, chief among them increased traffic congestion, pollution, and a disturbing sense of sameness and isolation that has people yearning for more engaging, community-minded environments.

While the premise of new urbanism fulfills that desire, because of problems it has in meeting market realities, its implementation is less successful. New urbanism does not always address the needs of the players — developers, commercial tenants, and homebuyers — as it must if it is to succeed. Before hailing new urbanism as the answer to quality of life issues, it is useful to look at the obstacles it presents for development and to explore ways to overcome them.

The Town Centers: Chicken or Egg? A defining principle of neotraditional town development is the notion of a town center — a commercial and social hub surrounded by housing no more than a quarter-mile stroll away. Although it is a great idea in theory, it presents the chicken-or-egg conundrum in practice. Does one first build the essential components of a new town and then attract homebuilders or build homes first and then attract commerce? Both are necessary for success, but experience indicates that a food store, for example, cannot wait for a community to build up around it. At the same time, homebuyers are reluctant to invest in and then wait for these services, meanwhile driving several miles to the nearest shopping district.

The key is to serve a new community's needs while providing commercial establishments with a viable market from the

Originally published as "Changing the Grid," *Urban Land*, Vol. 59, No. 7, July, 2000. Published by the Urban Land Institute, Washington, D.C. Reprinted with permission of the publisher.

start. A town center therefore may have to be close to a highway or an existing neighborhood or have high visibility. Sometimes a major anchor is enough to create a destination, but most new towns are built around a neighborhood shopping center, not entertainment or power centers that require extensive parking.

While new urbanism prescribes that commercial structures be physically centered within their future market area, evidence suggests that town centers are better positioned at the edge of new communities so that they are able to take advantage of existing adjacent developments.

Narrow Streets, Wide Problems. New urbanism advocates narrow, tree-lined, porch-fronted, double-sidewalk neighborhoods that encourage casual strolling. While this certainly curtails traffic, speeding, and noise, it often fails to meet local code requirements for street widths or fire access codes for street widths and turning radius. Until municipal codes are modified, planners and developers will continue to encounter problems in getting approval for narrow-width, dedicated streets.

Locking into the Grid. While well-suited for flat sites, the formal grid advocated by new urbanism often hinders ideal land use, especially in locations with uneven terrain. Most jurisdictions have minimum standards for lot widths and setbacks. Most project developers, however, want a mix of products, from starter to luxury homes. The builders who buy these parcels are looking for pads on which to build their products. Gridded street patterns on rolling or steep terrain using narrower lot widths complicate pad construction. Generally, small lots work best on flatter land and wide lots work best on steeper ground, where drainage and preservation of vegetation are more easily accommodated.

Clustering, rather than the tree-lined street layout, fulfills the requirement of creating open space while maintaining the needed density to make the overall development feasible. Yet clustering simply does not fit the models of development permitted in various jurisdictions. Coving — finding the best locations for lots to take advantage of views and existing vegetation and then routing streets to the lots — has produced good results. Residential parcels end up where they make sense in terms of view, buildability, size, and configuration, with fewer intersections, shorter streets, better efficiency, and more value per lot. Often, the topography is such that steep slopes need to be maintained and some coved streets will be unsuitable for lots on both sides. By maintaining existing vegetation between coved streets, the physical stability and character of the site can be kept while giving the lots breathing room.

The original new urbanist comprehensive land plan for the city of DuPont, in Washington State's south Puget Sound region between Olympia and Tacoma, required some interesting changes to make it more market sensitive. DuPont began as a company town, with more than 100 houses, a church, a general store, and a hotel in a village now listed on the National Register of Historic Places; the DuPont company operated an explosives plant adjacent to the historic village for nearly 70 years. In 1951, residents were allowed to purchase their homes, and the city was incorporated. DuPont closed the plant in 1976 and sold its 3,200 acres to the Weyerhaeuser Real Estate Company (WRECO), a subsidiary of Weyerhaeuser Company in Federal Way, Washington.

Today, DuPont is home to approximately 1,400 people and its population is projected to grow to about 10,000 by 2020. Since 1985, WRECO has worked closely with the city of DuPont to develop a comprehensive land plan that meets both its goals and the city's, as well as the directives of Washington's Growth Management Act. The act makes planning mandatory for the state's fastest-growing counties and the cities in them, and it requires five-year updates of all plans.

In the early 1990s, WRECO brought in planning consultant Peter Calthorpe of Calthorpe Associates, Berkeley, California. The resulting scheme for the area, called Northwest Landing, is an example of a new urbanist community — the plan included nearly 4,000 residential units set within more than 400 acres of green space, with 1,200 acres zoned for commercial and industrial use. City residents, fearful of losing the historic integrity of the village, demanded that a 300-foot green "buffer" surround the development and that access be limited to just one paved road.

About 400 acres of Northwest Landing have been developed to date, including a mix of 700 single and multifamily residential units and businesses employing nearly 3,000 people, including the State Farm Insurance Company regional headquarters and a major Intel research campus. However, by 1999, a number of issues arose that required substantial changes to the Calthorpe plan.

The most significant change concerns the consent decree area, a 666-acre parcel contaminated during the time that DuPont operated its explosives plant. Weyerhaeuser and DuPont already have agreed to remediate the area to the level established by the state's department of ecology. Under the city's 1995 comprehensive plan, the parcel was designed for a mix of retail, office, and approximately 1,100 housing units; however, the Weyerhaeuser and DuPont companies had since adopted a policy that precluded building homes in the area of the former DuPont explosives plant to eliminate any potential conflict between future residential uses and prior industrial uses. Consequently, a new site was needed for the displaced housing.

Retail also was a major concern. "Market analysis and experience indicated that the previous plan contained too much retail, too widely dispersed, to be supported by both residents and the greater market area," explains David Brentlinger, WRECO's general manager for Northwest Landing. "For Northwest Landing to become a vibrant community, we needed a more viable, accessible plan for retail."

Finally, the school board reduced the number of proposed new schools from five to three, and a site reserved for a high school under the 1995 plan was no longer available. In 1999, WRECO asked Callison, a Seattle-based planning and design firm, to help update the plan.

To the degree that commercial uses attract people to an area and encourage them to support community businesses and interact with neighbors, commerce is considered critical to achieving the social ideals of new urbanism. Yet too often commerce is not located where it needs to be to succeed.

Northwest Landing's 1995 comprehensive plan called for pockets of retail to be distributed among the residential neighborhoods, which ranged between two and ten housing units per acre, along with a town center to be located at the development's physical center. The idea was to provide stores and services in conjunction with civic space within walking distance of homes. However, market studies showed that the only sustainable retail outlets dictated by the 1995 plan were ATM machines. DuPont simply could not support that much retail, that widely dispersed. Retailers require residents before they will open stores. In addition, until basic commercial services are established — food stores and banks, for example — homebuyers tend to be reluctant to invest. To attract commercial users, Callison's plan clustered all the retail in an area already zoned for mixed use under the 1995 plan, west of the State Farm Insurance headquarters and along both sides of Center Drive north of the intersection with I-5.

No longer buried at the geographical center of the town, DuPont Center, as it is now called, is nonetheless the heart of the town, envisioned as a mix of residential and commercial activities that borrows some of the best attributes of historic town centers. With a variety of commercial uses, multifamily residential development, public spaces, a post office, and possibly other civic buildings, DuPont Center should become the city's social, civic, and commercial hub. Its location, which can be accessed from I-5, is considered essential to its retail success. The commercial element of DuPont Center draws beyond the population of the city: by accessing a larger market area, it should support a wider range of retail types and businesses and provide a greater variety of shopping, entertainment, and services for residents — good news for those who have been waiting patiently until they no longer have to drive ten miles on the freeway to get groceries. In fact, one of the area's first tenants, a Japanese restaurant, sold out of food during its first day of operation. Meanwhile, as the commercial center grows, new residents should be attracted to Northwest Landing, fostering the synergy necessary for a vital community.

The consent decree area now is zoned for a business and technology park and a golf course. To make up the 1,100 units formerly designated for that area, Callison used a strategy that not only achieved the desired number of units but offered more variety at less cost to the environment, thus lessening the hardship on homebuilders while creating more marketable housing choices. The net density increase was slightly less than one unit per acre.

The transfer of business and technology uses to the consent decree area freed up two parcels to the north and east of the historic village of DuPont. Although protected wetlands — Edmond Marsh — limited how these parcels could be laid out, they did allow for the development of distinct neighborhood clusters of a total of 800 units on 361 acres with unique natural features. Pub-

lic concerns about the comparative isolation of these parcels are mitigated by the network of trails that filter through Northwest Landing.

To regain the remaining two-thirds of housing units, a fundamental change was made in the planning for the Yehle Park and Hoffman Hill villages. Rather than forcing a grid over hilly terrain, the new plan reconfigures roads to follow the topography, requiring less grading and allowing home lots to fit the site better. Areas above 30 percent grade were uniformly declared off limits to construction. This more natural approach is less disturbing to the land and saves trees, vistas, and other natural features that homebuyers appreciate. It also is easier to develop. Meanwhile, the flatter areas still incorporate a more traditional grid with alley loading. In Yehle Park, taking the streets up to the lots resulted in an additional 40 residential units, including creation of Oak Savannah, which preserves a stand of oaks as open space surrounded by multifamily housing. In the larger Hoffman Hill neighborhood, approximately 460 units were gained, while increasing the density by less than one unit per acre.

Callison's revised plan for Northwest Landing preserves the ideals of the new urbanism plan set forth by Calthorpe by maintaining an environment that provides a variety of opportunities for living, working, and playing, while encouraging a small town development pattern that promotes a sense of community. But Callison's plan, which currently is being considered by the city of DuPont, balances these objectives with sound economic development by concentrating a mixed-use center near the freeway so that it works for both residents and nonresidents alike; by expanding business areas to strengthen the city's revenue base; and by creating site-specific residential neighborhoods that are more attractive to homebuilders and buyers.

The ideals of new urbanism should not

be compromised by the means used to achieve them. Changes to new urbanism's framework, along with a better understanding of how to attract commercial and housing developers, should ultimately result in creating more successful developments that can accommodate today's lifestyles in engaging and distinctive communities.

CHAPTER 17

GRAND FORKS REBUILDS ITS OLD DOWNTOWN CREATING OPEN SPACES AND WALKWAYS

Diane Suchman

Even for the hardy and resilient citizens of Grand Forks, North Dakota, 1997 was a tough year. Located at the eastern edge of North Dakota, Grand Forks is home to hard-working Midwesterners who pride themselves on their ability to thrive despite the city's long, harsh winters. The winter of 1996–1997 was extraordinary, however, even by Grand Forks's standards. It lashed the city with record storm after record storm, piling up a total of nearly 100 inches of snow. Spring brought more blizzards, followed by rapid warming and heavy rains. The rains and melting snow caused the rivers to swell and surge. When the Red River rose to 55 feet above sea level (more than double the 26-foot flood level), it broke through its earthen dike. Water flowed freely over the city, until more than two-thirds of Grand Forks was under water and nearly all the city's 50,000 citizens had to evacuate their homes. The city water system was contaminated, and the sewage treatment plant had to be shut down.

Downtown Grand Forks, which is adjacent to the river bank, was especially hard hit. Streets, basements, and the first floors of all buildings were awash with sewage-fouled floodwater, mud, and debris. Fires raged in 11 downtown buildings during the flood, wreaking further destruction. Torrents of water also flooded homes in adjacent neighborhoods and flowed over and beyond the city, across the plains of North Dakota.

When the floodwaters finally receded, the city, under the leadership of Mayor Patricia Owens, began the arduous job of cleaning up and rebuilding. U.S. Secretary of Housing and Urban Development (HUD) Andrew Cuomo moved immediately to help and pledged $171 million in aid to the city. As part of its assistance effort, HUD offered the city the services of a ULI advisory services panel, which visited Grand Forks last September.

Re-Imagining Downtown

The city of Grand Forks began to consider how to organize its recovery effort by taking a hard look at its downtown. Even

Originally published as "Rebuilding Downtown Grand Forks," *Urban Land*, Vol. 57, No. 2, February, 1998. Published by the Urban Land Institute, 1025 Thomas Jefferson Street, N.W., Suite 500 West, Washington, D.C. Reprinted with permission of the publisher.

before the devastating flood, downtown Grand Forks, like many U.S. cities, had begun to evolve from being the region's primary office and retail center to being its residential, governmental, and educational center. Over the past 20 years, changes in retail development and spending patterns had resulted in the movement of many stores and services to suburban locations, particularly after a regional mall was built in the southwestern part of the city. Many downtown businesses had been replaced by professional services and entertainment uses, while other storefronts remained vacant. In an attempt to compete with the shopping mall and other retail outlets, an indoor shopping center, City Center Mall, had been developed downtown by closing a street and connecting buildings on either side with a roofed enclosure.

Since the flood, many of the businesses that had remained downtown have relocated, have closed completely, or are in temporary space and have no definite plans for permanent relocation. Although government offices and schools are expected to rebuild in their existing downtown locations, the future of many of the retailers and professional service firms is uncertain.

The flood therefore has presented the city and its citizens with an opportunity to ask basic questions about the role and function of downtown. Some people believed the downtown core was obsolete and that perhaps the city should not devote resources to rebuilding it. Others felt that the downtown should be redeveloped, not simply as it was before, but in a way that reflects today's changed market realities.

With this in mind, the city's charge to the ULI panel was to determine, in the light of current market conditions and trends, what role downtown Grand Forks should play in the regional economy and to suggest rebuilding strategies that would enable it to fulfill that role. A great deal of useful planning work was done before the panel's arrival, including preparation of a report issued by Grand Forks' Re-Imagining Downtown Committee, a plan known as the River Forks plan, an interim business program, and more. In preparing its recommendations, the panel reviewed these reports, briefing materials prepared by the city, and information gleaned from interviews with more than 100 individuals.

Envisioning a New Heart for Grand Forks

The ULI panel advised that downtown Grand Forks be redeveloped in a way that asserts its historic role as the symbolic, physical, and functional "heart" of the region. To that end, the panel envisioned the city core as an exciting gathering place, with restaurants, specialty shops, entertainment, and festivals; public open space along the river; governmental, educational, and financial offices; and housing that offers easy access to downtown amenities, and, when possible, views of the river. The proposal also included a traditional town square that would serve as the main public space and focal point for the entire community.

The panel found that downtown Grand Forks has an essentially strong and stable economy founded on agriculture, retail trade, wholesale distribution, aerospace technology, and education. Key economic forces include the University of North Dakota, which has 13,000 students, faculty, and staff, and nearby Grand Forks Air Force Base, which employs 12,500 people. The city also functions as a metropolitan service center and provides retail stores and services to a 17-county area of 210,000 people in eastern North Dakota and western Minnesota.

The city's urban core seems to have many strengths on which to build. From a financial point of view, millions of public dollars have been invested in buildings, infrastructure, and community facilities downtown, which include a central high school, the city hall, the county courthouse and administrative offices, public safety offices, and a federal building. There also has been significant private sector investment. Despite the flood, underground utilities are in reasonably good condition. There is little crime, and the city is considered safe. The central business district is surrounded by generally stable and well preserved neighborhoods. In addition, downtown Grand Forks has remained a viable and affordable residential location. Before the flood, multifamily housing downtown served the needs of the elderly and university students. These generally affordable units were typically fully occupied, and waiting lists were common.

Downtown Grand Forks remains the geographic center of the metropolitan area and is one of the most accessible points in the entire region. The downtown area is small and well defined, with a grid street system that creates an urban scale and character that is unique in the Grand Forks metro area. The proximity of city and county government offices downtown provides an opportunity for the two systems to work together and employ a large, stable population of workers who represent a potential market for other business activity downtown. In addition, there is significant unmet demand for both replacement and new development in all segments of downtown real estate: residential, office, entertainment, public sector, and hotel uses.

The city also embodies the heritage of Grand Forks, with a collection of historic buildings that is admired throughout the West. Although it lacks a defined physical and social focal point, the downtown area — and particularly the riverbank — continues to serve as the gathering place for citywide community celebrations. Little riverfront infrastructure is in place, however, and little effort has been expended to capitalize on the river as one of the city's major assets and gathering spots.

Containing — and Celebrating — the River

The panel proposed a conceptual land use plan for downtown Grand Forks that includes a flood protection system; creation of exciting public spaces along the river, including a traditional town square; clustering of land uses by development type; and streetscape and infrastructure improvements.

The first order of business was to recommend ways to contain and celebrate the river. To make the area safe from future flooding, the panel, after consulting with the U.S. Army Corps of Engineers, advised creating a flood wall, part of which would be architecturally integrated into the historic buildings parallel to the river along the east side of Third Street, thereby preserving both sides of that street. All major streets would pass through the wall, allowing physical and visual access to the river. Movable flood gates would secure open passages during periods of flooding. The gates also would present opportunities for public art to mark and enhance the entrances to the river. At the same time, the panel suggested both making the river more efficient in its hydraulic flow and enhancing its value as an aesthetic and recreational amenity by creating a weir, an underwater dam, that would raise and widen the river's surface area. To accommodate the wider flow of water, reconstructing approaches to bridges would enable water to flow beneath them.

According to the panel, the river is the key to establishing a sense of place in downtown Grand Forks. To realize its value, the cities of Grand Forks and East Grand Forks were encouraged to work together to create a bistate Red River Park that would feature a landscaped esplanade anchored by the proposed town square, which is located at what is now City Center Mall. The town square would serve as a formal "living room" for civic and cultural events, provide a balcony overlook to the river basin, and be the point of transition from the flood wall into the park. The park would include regraded shorelines landscaped with natural flora, pedestrian promenades, hard-surface hiking and jogging paths, and, at the upper reaches of the floodway, baseball and football fields. Marinas, bicycle paths, and other amenities also could be included.

Repositioning Downtown

Next, clustering development downtown into three districts was recommended. Each cluster would emphasize a particular type of land use: a residential, retail, and entertainment district in the few blocks near and overlooking the river and the proposed town square; a financial district that would provide a first-class, high-profile home for financial institutions and professional service firms; and two government and educational centers that would build on existing clusters of public uses flanking the proposed financial center location. The activity centers would be connected by street-level retail activity, upper-floor apartments, and civic amenities such as street trees, lighting, paving, sculpture, fountains, and banners. Initial development would be concentrated within a five-block area to create a compact, walkable environment that would be attractive to downtown residents, workers, and visitors.

To reposition downtown Grand Forks so that its market potential would be maximized, the panel recommended that the city embrace the strategic elements of the nationally recognized Main Street Program of the National Trust for Historic Preservation, which consist of economic restructuring, through a business retention and recruitment program; organization, enabling downtown businesses to collaborate; design guidelines and assistance that emphasize historic preservation; and marketing strategies that present

downtown as a unit to both investors and consumers. To encourage historic preservation, the city was urged to support retention of cultural landmarks and to work with the Historic Preservation Commission to develop a reuse strategy for individual historic buildings.

The panel suggested that the existing River Forks Commission (RFC) assume responsibility for marketing and promoting downtown, river-related events, and the region, using its delegated legal powers. RFC also would be responsible for developing the bistate Red River Park and ensuring good communication between Grand Forks and East Grand Forks. Also advised was that an autonomous public/private subcommittee of RFC, to be known as the Downtown Development Committee (DDC), be established to create and implement the plans and budget for rebuilding downtown Grand Forks.

Progress in rebuilding downtown Grand Forks was thought to require public/private partnerships. The panel suggested that the DDC encourage a stronger private sector role by preparing and marketing "packaged" development opportunities for desired projects when appropriate.

Both short-term and longer-term strategies to revitalize the downtown area were recommended. Short-term projects include completing demolition of unusable structures; clearing, grading, and seeding lots as an interim measure to prepare them for development; creating a skating rink/farmers market; engaging a historic preservation consultant to prepare site-specific development proposals; and rehabilitating existing housing in key areas. As an important early but highly visible step in establishing confidence and investment momentum downtown, the panel suggested that the city take the first step toward creating the recommended financial center downtown by negotiating an equitable and mutually beneficial lease with First National Bank and interested attorneys and accountants as soon as possible. Longer-term projects include developing site-specific plans for infill and new housing, assembling sites for strategic development, addressing zoning and other regulatory issues, hiring a director of development, and preparing a detailed infrastructure improvement plan budget.

Since most market-rate downtown projects initially will not pencil out financially without some public funding, the panel recommended that the city allocate $50 to $70 million of its community development block grant (CDBG) allocation for the rebuilding of downtown and outlined various ways that the city could leverage its investment. The use of public funds would be essential for stimulating both initial revitalization projects and private investment, and it should be viewed as an investment that will pay future dividends to the entire community.

Taking a Regional View

The panel also looked across the river. East Grand Forks is about to complete its own ambitious comprehensive redevelopment plan, and the community's leadership is prepared to make a significant investment to implement it. In its final comments, the panel stressed that its suggestions for Grand Forks and the proposed plans for East Grand Forks are complementary, interdependent, and mutually reinforcing, and it urged the two cities to work closely together in implementing their downtown redevelopment plans.

Much of what the citizens of Grand Forks are proud of in their downtown was built by an earlier generation at the turn of the century. In about two years, there will be a new source of pride, based on what *this* generation gives to the future citizens of Grand Forks and East Grand Forks.

CHAPTER 18

HAMPTON APPROVES NEW TYPE OF BUSINESS IMPROVEMENT DISTRICT

Lawrence O. Houstoun

No longer content to leave economic development to government agencies, tens of thousands of business and property owners in more than 1,200 North American locations have taken the reins themselves by setting up business improvement districts. Their focus: improving property values, adding jobs, and increasing their own profits.

This movement toward self-help management has been going on for 20 years, mostly in the downtowns of major cities. But business improvement districts are now cropping up elsewhere as well — for example, in highway commercial strips, university and hospital clusters, and even industrial areas. The districts described here grew from a local government plan or policy or are designed to implement plans or policies. Each required public-private cooperation.

Edge City

By the early 1990s, the diverse owners of the 1,800-acre commercial center along Mercury Boulevard in Hampton, Virginia, knew they were losing market share to newer, larger retail areas elsewhere in the Tidewater region. Hampton's vast edge city includes Hampton's Coliseum, hotels and restaurants, and more than three million square feet of retail space.

To stay competitive, Mercury Boulevard property owners in 1995 took the advice of Richard Bradley, then president of the International Downtown Association, and decided to work with a consulting team to consider setting up a business improvement district. The city favored the idea because the tax revenue it was collecting from Mercury Boulevard businesses was topping out at $17.8 million and showed signs of slipping. When approved by the city in 1996, Coliseum Central became one of the first districts in the U.S. located in a large commercial area oriented to highway, rather than to central business district, markets.

With an organization and financing in place, the district's executive director, Peter Gozza, convinced his board that the area needed a plan to convert "1,800 acres of asphalt and aging commercial buildings" into a popular center for the entire Hampton Roads area. The 20-year blueprint for revitalization, written in 1996, has five major proposals,

Originally published as "Smart Money: New Directions for Business Improvement Districts," *Planning*, Vol. 64, No. 1, January, 1998. Published by the American Planning Association, 122 South Michigan Avenue, Suite 1600, Chicago, Illinois 60603-6107. Reprinted with permission of the publisher.

one of them being that Mercury Boulevard should be narrowed and landscaped. The other four: a pedestrian mall near a new movie complex, an entertainment-retail center near the Coliseum, an environmental center on 60 wooded acres, and a boat canal. Preliminary plans for the waterway show a canal leading from the lake at the Hampton Coliseum into the heart of the shopping district, after the fashion of San Antonio's Riverwalk.

Gozza is now using the plan to solicit state and federal funds for this $60 million project. One possibility is to link the development with an extension of Interstate 664, which will need stormwater retention ponds.

Like a downtown, Coliseum Central must draw customers attracted to a locale, not just an individual store. So Gozza is trying to create a sense of identity for the area — something that has been missing until now. One innovation is "Courtesy Kids," four teams of four teenagers each, who serve as a hospitality force, carry packages, open doors, sing, and clean up. These talented young people have given merchants a more positive view of teenagers and have made the area friendlier for shoppers.

Some may question why a tool of downtown revitalization should be used to bolster a suburban development. But Hampton's political and business leaders felt there was no competition between Coliseum Central — with its highly mobile regional market — and the city's small, waterfront-oriented downtown (which has its own business improvement district).

It's Institutional

University City District in West Philadelphia grew from a tragedy. Only after a University of Pennsylvania faculty member was killed there in 1996 did the concept of a district emerge.

University City lies immediately west of Philadelphia's popular Center City — a two-square-mile area where many university people live. Center City's business improvement district provides cleaning, security, and landscaping services that are among the best in the nation, enhancing attractions such as theater, nightclubs, restaurants, hotels, office towers, and department stores.

The contrast between the two locations could not be greater. While University City houses the beautifully restored Thirtieth Street Station and three attractive campuses — Penn, Drexel University, and the Philadelphia College of Pharmacy and Sciences — most of the remaining 100 blocks there are marginal. Once proud residential streets are poorly lighted and choked with weed trees, and beyond these streets and the campuses are acres of parking lots, roaring traffic, ugly vending trucks, and graffiti.

John Fry, executive vice-president of the University of Pennsylvania, launched the remediation effort in 1996 by hiring consultants and visiting the heads of major nonprofit groups and public agencies, securing their agreement to participate in what soon became cleanup, security, visual improvements, and marketing. So little commerce remained in University City at that point that business representatives were not included at first. But after four months a nonprofit corporation was formed and a five-year budget created.

The University City District's nearly $4 million annual expenses are being shared under a series of multiyear voluntary agreements by the two universities and the pharmacy college, the University of Pennsylvania Health System, the University City Science Center, Amtrak, the West Philadelphia Partnership (an alliance of neighborhood organizations), and several multifamily residential property owners. In addition, University City District will seek state and federal funding for infrastructure, visual improvements, and signage. Paul Steinke, formerly with Philadelphia's Center City District, was appointed executive director of the University City District in September, 1997.

University City District may now be one of a kind — an improvement district that is not dependent on municipal property tax assessments. But inquiries from comparable areas elsewhere in the country indicate interest where several institutions can support a district even when commercial properties are absent.

Industrial Site

The Bunker Hill Special Improvement District in Paterson, New Jersey, is one of the few business improvement districts based in an industrial area. Now three years old, the district's management corporation consists of a nine-member board whose industrial property owners (plus a city council member, as mandated by New Jersey law) administers a $175,000 annual budget. Every member of the group is a volunteer; there are no paid employees.

Both Fortune 500 companies and international firms are represented among the 200 property owners in the district. John Ressie of the Bascom Corporation is chairman of the district's board.

Sixty percent of the group's revenues are spent on security, about 30 percent on sanitation and beautification, and the balance on public relations and special projects. A private security service provides 24-hour mobile service within the square mile service area. When the district's burglar alarm is activated, security guards typically arrive before the police do. Other tasks the district has undertaken include graffiti cleaning, fence repair, and fighting dumping by roofers and others.

When the district was being organized, opposition came from some of the industrial property owners, residents (who were to be charged a $5 annual fee), and one city council member, who objected to business improvement district assessments on principle. Once the district was approved, however, residents were dropped from the project and the idea became so popular that the city formed a second district, this one downtown.

New Jersey law is the most flexible in the nation with regard to assessment formulas, specifying only that there needs to be a relationship between charges and benefits. Some districts use square footage, share of property taxes, or type of use as the basis for assessment. Districts do not have independent bonding authority, although long-term capital improvements can be financed through business improvement district assessments with municipal bonding authority. Ressie says that the board of the Bunker Hill district will seek grants, not bonds, to finance infrastructure improvements there.

Ongoing operating expenses are financed through payments based on assessed valuation, with a minimum annual payment of $125 per property. Each assessment represents the property's share of the district's total assessed valuation. Owners of large properties may pay between $10,000 and $12,000 a year.

Entertainment Venue

Lark Street in Albany, New York — separated from downtown by the massive state office complex — is a pleasant mix of restaurants, specialty shops, residential buildings, and a supermarket. By 1995 this 10-block-long area had become somewhat shabby but still had plenty of energy.

Early support for a business improvement district came from George Leveille, the city's director of economic development. Sharon Ward, a former city alderman, and Lark Street businessman Tom Rowland co-chaired the planning phase. A consulting team hired by the city found that local people were especially interested in nighttime security, parking improvements, holiday lights, and joint advertising directed at state and private office workers.

When opposition surfaced from the adjacent Townsend Park neighborhood, this area was excluded from the service area. The Lark Street business improvement district, the city's first, was approved by the city council in 1995.

By the fall of 1997 the Lark Street Neighborhood District Management Association had survived the turnover of both the chairman and the director and now has a lot of successes under its belt. Executive director Vicky Stoneman and board chairman Bill Allen have made the district a major force in revitalizing the area, despite a shrinking budget. Property reassessments have reduced the district's annual revenues from $90,000 in 1995 to $70,000 in 1997.

The district contracts with Homeless and Travelers Aid for sidewalk cleaning four hours daily. A local security firm provides uniformed officers, who patrol on foot during the evenings from May to September. The extra security people have been helpful in moving panhandlers, breaking up fights, dispersing teenagers, and responding to merchants' complaints.

Reflecting a common theme among business improvement districts in commercial areas, entertainment and cultural offerings are important here. "Art on Lark" attracts artists and craftspeople for a weeklong event in the spring. In September, "Larkfest" offers three stages of live entertainment with special presentations for children. And holiday events are offered in October and December.

What's Coming Up

Because the downtowns of most large cities already have business improvement districts, the next decade's growth will necessarily include nontraditional settings — very small places, nonprofit clusters, industrial areas, and highway strips. New York City and Philadelphia each already have half a dozen small business improvement districts with yearly budgets of under $100,000.

Look, too, for more partnerships with residents, more concern for public open space, and more programs that serve residential properties where property values are high. These efforts might better be called "civic improvement districts."

Expect more hybrid financing, with greater attention being given to combinations of commercial property assessments and multiyear voluntary agreements, like University City's, where the institutions share common problems and can agree on a unified program to enhance their environment.

Where the conventional wisdom once held that universities, residents, business interests, and industrial firms must be kept apart, planners can now be more ambitious in proposing business improvement districts to solve common problems. The notion that one size fits all is obsolete — if, indeed, it was ever valid. A new generation of business improvement districts is coming.

CHAPTER 19

HARTFORD REVIVES RIVERFRONT TO STIMULATE INNER-CITY TOURISM

Steve Starger

You could talk about a long history of tobacco farming; the major transportation hub of Bradley International Airport in Windsor Locks; the jet engine manufacturing giant Pratt & Whitney in East Hartford; the towering financial, insurance and investment home offices in Hartford; the capital city's rich store of nationally recognized arts and cultural institutions; the suburban communities that have transformed Hartford County's diverse towns into class-driven enclaves; the few working farms that still exist here and there throughout the county.

And, perhaps the most significant feature of all, the Connecticut River, whose 400-plus miles meander through Hartford County on the way to Long Island Sound to the south. The river, a major navigable waterway that nourished the county's history and growth, gives Hartford its most visible symbol of vitality.

Assets ... and Challenges

In recent history, there have been seismic shifts in Hartford County: Steady mi-

grations from the cities to the suburbs have created new, autonomous societies but have left depleted urban areas in their wake, in effect creating two separate and not so equal societies; the wrenching evolution from a manufacturing to a service-oriented economy has cost jobs and businesses but also has held the promise of new opportunities for those equipped to take advantage of them.

Hartford's plate currently is running over with an embarrassment of new development proposals and visions for revitalizing the city. The recent fever to remake and restore the city to a new version of its former glory has put Hartford into the public consciousness in much the same way that revitalized urban centers like Providence, Indianapolis and Baltimore have. Those cities may in fact be models for Hartford visionaries to consider, but Hartford has its own particular range of assets and challenges.

All of this development excitement has come out of an extended period of struggle by Hartford to salvage what many have seen as a dying city. Hartford has absorbed a

Originally published as "Reinventing Downtown Hartford," *CT Business*, Vol. 1, No. 4, November/December, 1998. Published by Nolan Media, LLC, Cromwell, Connecticut. Reprinted with permission of the publisher.

number of shocks in the wake of the region's socio-economic sea changes. The city has been plagued by financial downturns, a school system seen as racially segregated and bereft of resources, reigns of terror by warring gangs, and a steady drain of its population to the perceived safety of the suburbs.

Major Projects Proposed

For all of its problems, Hartford also has such advantages as a rich, multiethnic core population, a thriving arts and entertainment scene, long-established neighborhoods that feed into the downtown sector, and, of course, the invaluable resource of the Connecticut River.

Tallying the pluses and minuses, Hartford in 1998 — although more than three-and-a-half centuries old — remains a work in progress, which can bode well in terms of creating a high quality of life for its citizenry but can also offer a jolting rollercoaster ride.

Hartford is rebounding from its latest thrill ride, the crashing of the heady financial boom times of the 1980s. The last decade in Hartford, like Connecticut and the country at large, was marked by an almost insatiable lust for acquisition and expansion. Corporate mergers and dizzying deal-making created mega-banks and real estate empires that looked great on the surface but which all too soon collapsed like the proverbial house of cards.

From the stock market crash of 1987 on, the party atmosphere quickly turned noxious in the halls of power. Corporations that had expanded as if pumped with helium began to deflate, expelling assets and personnel. "Downsizing" became the favorite euphemism for job loss. The economic landscape resembled a village ravaged by vandals.

But out of that bleak scenario has sprung a series of development projects that, even if a small percentage reach completion, will have enormous impact on the entire city and will have the potential to restore Hartford to a vibrant center of life, culture and commerce.

Among the major proposals on the boards for Hartford are:

- Adriaen's Landing, a billion-dollar, multifaceted development complex that would encompass a good portion of downtown near to and linking with the river.
- Redevelopment of the old G. Fox and Co. site at 960 Main Street as a multiuse facility anchored by the Shaboo Nite Club, a resurrected version of a former eastern Connecticut night club and concert hall that, in its heyday, was one of the East coast's major entertainment venues.
- Purchase and redevelopment of the Hartford Civic Center, a high-profile but problematic downtown mall and arena that has seen more downs than ups in recent times.
- A plan to develop the neighborhood around Trinity College as a cooperative effort between the college and neighborhood organizations, and initiatives to locate Capital Community-Technical College and a University of Connecticut training center in downtown areas.
- A $15 million city bond to renovate and expand the Hartford Public Library.
- A $30 million proposal to build a 950-seat theater addition to the Bushnell, one of Hartford's oldest performing arts centers.
- Six Pillars of Progress, a $300 million plan developed by Gov. John G. Rowland to help fund and generate funding for numerous economic, education, and cultural projects over the next decade.
- Various proposals to build new hotels, offices, and residences throughout downtown to bring a core population back to the city.

Adriaen's Landing: Massive Plans

Proposed by Robert W. Fiondella, president, chairman and chief executive officer of Phoenix Home Life Mutual Insurance Co., Adriaen's Landing is, simply in terms of dollars, the most ambitious plan of the lot.

The plan, unveiled at a meeting of the Hartford City Council last May, includes a convention center and stadium; a 700-room convention hotel; a 14-screen movie complex; a Riverfront Discovery Center with aquarium, space station and history museum; affordable housing; and a network of shops, nightclubs and other recreational amenities.

Also planned is a riverfront pedestrian arcade that would provide walking access to the river, a multiuse sports complex and an intermodal transportation system featuring water, rail, pedestrian, vehicular and air traffic. An underground parking lot with more than 4,000 spaces is also proposed.

Promoters of Adriaen's Landing estimate that the project will generate 7,000 jobs and breathe considerable life to Hartford's economic doldrums. The big consideration, of course, is the price tag.

The current phase of the project involves seeking the needed $500 million in private funding and pursuing some $150 million in federal funding to cover environmental cleanup of the proposed site, housing and transportation costs. A feasibility study also must be done and the city must agree to donate the land, which encompasses the old Hartford Times building, owned by the city's pension committee.

At this point, work is continuing on developing architect's plans, raising the public portion of the funding, and generally drumming up support for the project among business people, community groups and developers, says Jon Sandberg, a spokesman for the project. Sandberg says he expects those efforts to continue into early next year.

The city has applied for environmental cleanup funds on behalf of Adriaen's Landing, and the project's leaders will also be talking about funding with the Capital City Economic Development Authority, the group that also controls the $15 million earmarked for the Civic Center makeover, Sandberg says.

Neighborhood organizations throughout the city "have been genuinely supportive" of Adriaen's Landing, Sandberg says, but added that they also have raised such concerns as traffic congestion and the possibilities for jobs and job training connected with the proposal.

For all of its glittering promise, Adriaen's Landing remains at this point a kind of shining vision on a hill, with some major questions and financial challenges yet to be addressed.

But, Sandberg says, "we're as anxious to get working as people are anxious to have us get working. There's a lot of work to do on a project this complex."

Linking the Resources

The short list that includes Adriaen's Landing and the other major development projects begins to boggle the mind. Add to them ongoing projects by Riverfront Recapture Inc. to link the city to its riverfront and to the riverfront of East Hartford, the continued redesigning of the I-84/91 interchange through Hartford to restore links to the city and some neighborhoods, and initiatives by local and regional arts and downtown councils, planning groups, think tanks and the Rowland administration, and Hartford appears to be a kind of giant Lego set looking for the right builders. That's preferable to being compared to a piece of Swiss cheese, as Hartford has in the recent past.

Why this sudden spurt of activity now?

"It was time," says Rie Poirer, a spokesperson for the Greater Hartford Growth

Council, an economic development agency that serves the Greater Hartford region. The council created the MetroHartford Millennium Project, a coalition of area business leaders led by Pratt & Whitney President Karl Krapek.

"Over the past few years, there's been a cry for some kind of cohesive strategy" from business leaders in Hartford and surrounding towns, Poirer says. "We finally had the plan when we put together Millennium. It's really a broad mix of people, and it's the people who can get things done."

The group is charged with overseeing the "action agenda for the region," Poirer says. That means bringing the various downtown development plans into a cooperative situation to reach the resources they need to realize their proposals.

"The myriad activity is a happy problem," Poirer says. "Millennium's role is to provide synergy."

As an example, Poirer pointed to the group's receiving requests from developers who want to build housing downtown that would connect the downtown to the city's neighborhoods. "If the neighborhoods aren't connected, then we've failed," Poirer says.

One proposal to link the neighborhoods to downtown is the so-called "Circuit Line" route that would follow historic and architecturally significant sections of the city and ultimately tie together not only peripheral neighborhoods — such as Asylum Hill, North Meadows, Armory, and South Green — but many of the development proposals for downtown as well.

The Study

That idea was generated by a survey of downtown development activity by Ken Greenberg, a consultant with Urban Strategies Inc. of Toronto, Canada, who was hired by the Hartford Downtown Council under its Action Strategy Plan, developed with the Millennium Project.

Greenberg began his study last March and was expected to complete the task by the end of September, according to Anthony M. Caruso, executive director of the Hartford Downtown Council. Greenberg interviewed more than 400 organizations, businesses and individuals to "get a feel for what the situation is in Hartford," Caruso said. Greenberg also looked at the Hartford Civic Center and the concept of a new downtown convention center in the context of Adriaen's Landing.

In terms of the Civic Center, Greenberg had worked with LaSalle Partners, a real estate development company that had been given exclusive rights by Hartford city government and Aetna Inc. to propose development plans for the Civic Center mall. Aetna owns the mall. Fifteen million dollars in state funds were earmarked for the mall's renovation.

But uncertainty about how the money would be used resulted in the city and Aetna reopening the search for a developer. The city is rebidding the project, but LaSalle Partners could still be in the picture, Caruso said.

Despite the stalling of that project and the snail's pace on others, Caruso is optimistic about the downtown activity.

"I think we're on the brink of some significant development," he said. "Obviously, these kinds of projects don't happen immediately, but this is the first time in a long time that we're on track to bring a good portion of these projects to fruition over the long term."

The Importance of the River

Perhaps the most visible reclamation project in Hartford — short of the impossible-to-miss construction on the I-84/91 interchange — has been in the works for nearly 20 years: Riverfront Recapture's massive effort to reunite the river with the city.

Driving through Hartford on the interstates, one can see real evidence of progress in the form of a walkway down to the riverfront on the Hartford side and continuing construction of a promenade to span the river and connect Hartford to the East Hartford side of the river.

Also planned with the walkway is a landscaped plaza over I-91, which will allow pedestrians to access the walkway to East Hartford. The walkway will be 18 feet wide and will be open to pedestrians, bikers and joggers, says Joseph Marfuggi, president and chief executive officer of Riverfront Recapture.

Other plans call for grassy terraces descending to the river from the plaza on the Hartford side, areas that could seat up to 2,000 people for performances and other special events. A bulkhead is also planned to be built along the river's edge to allow excursion boats and water taxis to operate from downtown, Marfuggi says. That construction is scheduled to be completed next summer, he adds.

Since the group was formed in 1981, Riverfront Recapture has raised about $42 million for design and construction, Marfuggi says. The organization was formed out of a public forum held at Hartford's Old State House in 1980 that focused on how the city could take advantage of its waterfront as other cities had done.

The river had been cut off first by flood-control dikes in the downtown area after the floods of 1936 and 1938. A flood-control system was installed in the 1940s that protected the river but also became a barrier between the city and the river, Marfuggi says. The construction of the I-91/84 interchange "finished off the job and made the river inaccessible."

Since the early '80s, Riverfront Recapture has built a network of public parks and riverwalks in Hartford and East Hartford, "literally taking people by the hand and showing them how to use the river,"

Marfuggi says. The river has been the site of numerous activities, such as the annual July 4 celebration, which attracts thousands to the riverfront, and such nationally profiled events as a big-money bass tournament held this past summer.

Marfuggi says, "The river is becoming a destination for visitors from outside the region. We're showing that we can use the river as a magnet to attract people. That's a new kind of economic development."

Making Use of Existing Resources

All of these visionary proposals for turning Hartford's economic vitality around are certainly exciting in the abstract, but they're also a bit dizzying. It seems basic that to have any kind of successful urban center, you need to start with an existing population that supports itself and its neighborhood with its own resources.

Hartford evinces vitality through numerous merchants' associations scattered across the disparate sections of the city. Whether in the north, south, west, east or downtown areas, these organizations of local business people share a mission of addressing challenges by adopting a general mission to the specific needs of their communities.

To connect the merchants' organizations and help them take care of business, Hartford's Office of Economic Development contracts with about a dozen different merchants' associations throughout the city, groups that already exist as independent entities usually affiliated with nonprofit organizations in their neighborhoods.

The city makes available $30,000 to each association from Community Development Block Grant funds, according to Hector Torres, Hartford's acting director of economic development. Typically, the money is used to hire a full- or part-time merchant coordinator who works directly with the associations on a near-daily basis.

How do such associations meld with the big development proposals saturating the city?

"The media are interested in the mega downtown projects," Torres says. "In reality, I've found that the majority of economic development in Hartford — and in most urban areas — with internal, existing businesses and the entrepreneurial activity that comes out of that."

But Torres also feels that the redevelopment picture is a good one for local businesses.

"These projects will certainly provide more life and more economic activity, not only for downtown, but for the neighborhoods," he says. "When you look at the entire picture, if we're able to generate economic activity downtown, that would certainly spill over into the businesses in the neighborhoods."

And, Torres notes, along with those developments come jobs. "If people in the neighborhoods can get jobs, they'll be spending some of their dollars at local businesses."

When all of the dust settles on the development frenzy in Hartford, the city will certainly be transformed. Exactly what the landscape will look like is still unclear. One thing is certain — to be successful, a transformed, economically vital Hartford must be conscious of all of its citizens and users, whether they live in Enfield, Avon, Manchester or within the city limits.

As the comedian Mort Sahl liked to observe: The future lies ahead. In Hartford and Hartford County, the glow seems to be brightening.

CHAPTER 20

HAYWARD USES TRANSIT VILLAGES TO STIMULATE DOWNTOWN REDEVELOPMENT

Ruth Eckdish Knack

In its first two decades, the San Francisco Bay Area Rapid Transit District concentrated on building up its heavy rail system — now 72 miles — and providing riders with parking. As a result, most of the 34 stations are surrounded by acres of surface parking lots.

Now, says Michael Bernick, one of BART's nine elected directors, BART should be moving in a different direction, creating high-density mixed-use "transit villages" around its stations. The idea got a boost last fall when the California legislature passed a bill that allows local governments to designate station-area redevelopment districts. Although the law, which Bernick helped write, doesn't include all the redevelopment powers he had hoped for, it does introduce the concept of transit districts, and that's a major step forward, he says.

In its early years, BART, which began operations in 1972, made several stabs at "joint development," seeking to attract office developers to build on agency-owned property. Little was accomplished, however. Then, about four years ago, the agency's property development department initiated a series of market studies and community assessments, which suggested that, at least for some stations, mixed-use development had a good chance of success.

Thinking Big

Of several plans now under way, the one for Oakland's Fruitvale station is the most ambitious. The station is important because it's a transfer point for the city of Alameda and its naval air base. But the surrounding, predominantly Hispanic commercial area is raggedy, and a huge parking lot separates the station from the shops on East 14th Street. A transit village plan spearheaded by the Spanish Speaking Unity Council, a local community development corporation, calls for new housing, a community medical center, and a revitalized retail strip.

The plan is a response to an earlier BART proposal for a new parking structure. "We opposed it," says Arabella Martinez,

Originally published as "BART's Village Vision," *Planning*, Vol. 61, No. 1, January, 1995. Published by the American Planning Association, 122 South Michigan Avenue, Suite 1600, Chicago, Illinois 60603-6107. Reprinted with permission of the publisher.

the council's executive director, "because it would have further separated the BART station from the neighborhood." Instead, the council pushed for a comprehensive neighborhood plan, lobbying to get about $300,000 in planning grants from the city.

U.S. Transportation Secretary Federico Peña gave the plan a boost when he visited Fruitvale in 1992. "He asked us what our vision was," says Martinez. "We explained that instead of having a vast sea of parking, we wanted housing and a pedestrian plaza linking the station to 14th Street." Over the next year, Martinez's group, working with BART and the city, received $475,000 in federal ISTEA funds to produce planning studies of the area. A financial feasibility and market assessment report, by Keyser Marston Associates of San Francisco, is due out this month.

In July 1993, BART learned that it would receive $750,000 in ISTEA enhancement funds to build the pedestrian plaza, and the council won $5.4 million in HUD's Section 202 funds for new senior housing. The city also agreed to locate a senior center on the site, and Martinez has applied to the U.S. Department of Health and Human Services for funding for a Head Start center.

The council is also talking with private housing developers and with a supermarket chain interested in opening a store on 14th Street. The city is now studying the area's zoning, with higher residential density a likely result, Martinez says. Meanwhile, the council is about to issue an RFP for a final site plan.

"There's not many times in life you're doing something you truly believe in," says John Rennels, Jr., senior real estate officer in BART's property development division. "For me, this is one of those times. Fruitvale is a classic example of a project that maximizes the value of the public infrastructure. By providing a mixed-use development that has a sense of community, you bring life and activity back to the station — and you put tax dollars back into the community."

Edge City Remake

The high-rise offices and hotel around the Pleasant Hill BART station make it a classic edge city. Forty percent of this unincorporated area just off the Interstate 680 ramp in Contra Costa County is built out. According to Robert Cervero, codirector of the University of California transit center, about 40 percent of the residents and 10 percent of the employees commute by BART.

In the late 1970s, says Bernick, the San Francisco planning firm of Sedway Cooke prepared a specific plan for Pleasant Hill calling for a wider range of development. Then came the market slowdown. Now BART is picking up pieces of that plan, focusing on the potential of shared parking. According to Bernick, a major movie theater chain is interested in the site for just that reason. "Their needs dovetail with ours," he says. "They need parking nights and weekends; we need it during the day."

An outlying station with even more potential — if the jurisdictional problems that surround it ever get resolved — is the East Dublin-Pleasanton station. It's part of the 7.5-mile BART extension being built in the median strip of Interstate 580. Some 20 acres of largely vacant land are adjacent to the station, which is in an unincorporated part of Alameda County adjacent to the Hacienda Business Park, and Camp Park, an Army reserve training facility.

Parking First

Parking is a major issue in every BART project. In Castro Valley, the nonprofit Bridge Housing Corporation of San Francisco cut its proposed development by a third to ensure adequate parking for BART commuters. The location is also in an unincorporated part of Alameda County.

"In the beginning, we hoped to do a project with 300 units," says Bridge senior project manager James Buckley. "But BART was concerned about parking, so we are now focused on a project of about 100 rental units, including some for seniors." The design, by Treffinger, Walz, MacLeod of San Rafael, calls for townhouses and apartments on a podium above the parking structure. It includes a police substation — a feature of several BART projects.

"At the moment, units in the $10.3 million development are contemplated to be below market rate," Buckley says. "We are working on getting low-income tax credits, and we will also ask the county for housing development funds." Bridge, the nation's largest nonprofit housing developer, built a similar complex in Richmond, near another BART station but on privately owned land.

At El Cerrito Plaza, the Koll Company of San Diego is using funds from a transit-related bond measure to build a parking structure. BART's John Rennels says the agency is now seeking financing as well for the project's housing component, to be built by the nonprofit San Jose Housing Corporation.

El Cerrito, a Contra Costa County bedroom community with many senior residents, already has one BART-related development, the two-year-old, 135-unit Del Norte Place. Now plans are under way for a similar project on a vacant site a block south. But El Cerrito's redevelopment program manager, Gerald Raycraft, says finding a mixed-use developer has not been easy. The current proposal, by Charles Oewel of Mill Valley, calls for 216 apartments in a three-story building atop a parking structure, 20,000 square feet of retail space — and a 20-screen movie theater.

The attraction for the movie theater, says Oewel, is BART's willingness to enter a shared parking arrangement with its 2,000 parking spaces.

Raycraft says the El Cerrito city council has gone on record as wanting to intensify development around the stations. A ballot measure narrowly passed by local voters in November amends the city's redevelopment plan to allow the redevelopment agency to incur new indebtedness — a substantial boost for additional transit-related projects, Raycraft says.

Retrofits

At several stations, BART's plans fall into the retrofitting category. Fruitvale is an example, as is Hayward, farther out in Alameda County.

John Rennels describes Hayward as a station "development has passed by." Located in a compact downtown characterized by its Art Deco facades, the station is viewed as a potential catalyst for renewal, particularly if a proposed pedestrian promenade connects it to the small shops of the four-block-long B Street Plaza.

As at the other stations, BART hopes to include housing, and Rennels says the city has recently acquired an appropriate site. Financing remains the sticking point for potential mixed-use developers, but Rennels says the California Housing Finance Agency is a possibility for the housing component.

Not in My Backyard

Not everybody thinks BART's transit villages are a good idea. Castro Valley's recently adopted specific plan calls for joint development around the BART station. But some local residents are skeptical of any proposals that include "affordable" apartments. "They're afraid of what mass transit could bring to their community," says one planner.

In Oakland a few years ago, the opposition of neighborhood residents helped kill a plan to rezone the area around the Rockridge station for higher density apartment development. Some neighbors also opposed the Rockridge Market Hall, the upscale shops that occupy the corner across the street from the station. But the market hall, which has offices above, was approved and has turned out to be a marketing — and design — success.

According to Rennels, the agency has learned from the Rockridge experience. "BART came in with a development plan without doing its constituency building," he says. "Now our philosophy is that we won't go into a community to promote development if it is not the wish of the community."

Last year, the agency hired the San Francisco planning and design firm of Kaplan, Diaz, McLaughlin to work with a citizen group in the neighborhood around the MacArthur Station in North Oakland. The busy station at the crossing of two BART lines has long seemed a likely spot for transit village development.

Kaplan, Diaz planner Morton Jensen says the firm is "seeking to develop consensus on what some alternatives might be not only for BART-owned property but for property surrounding the station." The process has taken time, he adds, "because it is a community with lots of opinions."

Three transit village alternatives will be described in the final report, Jensen says. All call for housing. The difference is the number and type of commercial uses.

The most ambitious of the three alternatives includes a large supermarket, which Jensen says has drawn some objections because it is likely to attract more automobile and truck traffic to the neighborhood.

Driving Force

Michael Bernick, the new chairman of BART's board of directors, has been on a mission ever since his election to the board in 1988. "I intend to continue to push along the transit village plans," says Bernick, an attorney with a San Francisco firm.

Bernick has a history of public interest work. For eight years, until 1986, he directed San Francisco Renaissance, a job training organization. Several years ago, he helped establish the National Transit Access Center, a research center that is part of the Institute of Urban and Regional Development at the University of California in Berkeley. He now codirects the center with planning professor and transit expert Robert Cervero.

Last year, Bernick and Cervero drafted the state's Transit Village Development Act, which was signed into law by Gov. Pete Wilson September 30. The act allows cities to designate quarter-mile-radius transit redevelopment districts around stations, and to grant density bonuses and tax breaks to developers in those areas. "We originally drafted it to give the districts redevelopment powers," including land assembly and tax increment financing, Bernick says. Political opposition killed those provisions, considerably weakening the incentives available to entice developers for transit-related projects.

But Bernick remains optimistic, even after the November elections, which had left funding for many public projects questionable. "I don't think transit investment is going to change much," he says. "I think rail transit is one of the few areas where you really have bipartisan support."

CHAPTER 21

HOUSTON MAKES PUBLIC IMPROVEMENTS TO ENTICE PRIVATE DEVELOPMENT

Charles Lockwood

For most of its existence, Houston's downtown was the city's economic, social, retail, and entertainment center. Yet in the last three decades, many downtown retailers, hotels, and businesses have closed their doors or deserted downtown for suburban locations, as in most U.S. cities.

Now, in a remarkable turnaround, businesses, grass-roots organizations, developers, and municipal officials are working together to transform Houston's once-moribund downtown into a vital urban center. Several billion dollars' worth of new projects have recently been completed, are currently underway, or are being planned. These projects — both new construction and adaptive use of existing buildings — cover a wide range of uses: residential, office, and retail space; hotels, entertainment venues, and restaurants; and civic infrastructure, including streetscape improvements and open-space projects.

"About ten years ago, people realized that downtown Houston could offer more than just office buildings that emptied out at 5:00 p.m.," says Robert Eury, president of Central Houston, Inc., a civic improvement organization whose members are large property owners and corporations. Eury also is executive director of the Houston Downtown Management District, which functions much like a business improvement district (BID). "Within the last few years, almost every single development market became active and strong simultaneously. Only hotels and retail have been a little slow, but they are catching up now," he adds.

Houston's downtown revitalization demonstrates the importance both of using freestanding public projects — like a new baseball stadium — and unifying infrastructure and urban fabric projects — like streetscape improvements — to jump-start private sector redevelopment. If Houston had decided only to construct private projects downtown, or only urban fabric projects, many observers believe the city would not now be enjoying the surprising revival of the urban area.

Catalysts for Reinvention

Several broad-based trends have sup-

Originally published as "Houston's Turn," *Urban Land*, Vol. 59, No. 2, February, 2000. Published by the Urban Land Institute, Washington, D.C. Reprinted with permission of the publisher.

FIGURE 1
Challenges to Reinventing Downtown Houston

Every city faces challenges when it tries to reinvent its downtown, but, as the following list suggests, Houston may have more than most:

- Streets are being robbed of vitality and street-level shops and restaurants of customers by an air-conditioned pedestrian tunnel and skywalk system that connects many downtown buildings, keeping people off the sidewalks.
- A lingering misconception exists among some Houstonians and visitors that downtown Houston is half-dead, ugly, and dangerous.
- The Houston region has approximately 20 other activity centers, or edge cities, which are relatively near downtown.
- The stock of old two- and three-story buildings that are suitable for redevelopment is limited.
- Downtown, which suffers from the absence of a people-pleasing urban fabric, is not a coherent whole. For example, the George R. Brown Convention Center has failed to attract adjacent development, even a hotel. Many downtown uses are separated from each other by overly wide streets and blighted sites that prevent the creation of the critical mass necessary to establish a pedestrian-friendly environment.
- More than 130,000 people work downtown, but the area has only 84,000 parking spaces. Houston needs to create downtown parking to serve new uses without further eroding the city fabric.
- Now that revitalization and redevelopment are underway, downtown property owners are upping their prices, making further development less feasible.

---

ported the downtown's revitalization, including Houston's economic rebound from the recession of the late 1980s to early 1990s, the diversification of the local economy from its overdependence on energy, the relocation of several companies such as Continental Airlines and NGC (now Dynegy Power Corp.) to the downtown, and decreasing urban crime rates. But several downtown-specific catalysts appear to have done the most to spark today's redevelopment activity.

"The first is the pervasive grass-roots redevelopment activity initiated by private business and organizations like Central Houston, Inc., and the Houston Downtown Management District," says Nancy Fleming, a principal of the Houston office of the SWA Group, an international land planning and landscape architecture firm. Both orga-

nizations are supporting or spearheading several downtown projects. Guy Hagstette, Houston Downtown Management District's director of capital projects and planning, reports that the organization is providing extra money for several publicly funded streetscape improvement programs to plant additional trees, provide better street lighting, and generate more on-street parking, strengthening projects that will benefit its members and the entire downtown.

The second major catalyst for downtown revitalization has been the strong municipal support that has led to major city-driven redevelopment projects. When Bob Lanier, a single-family suburban home developer, was elected mayor in 1991, he immediately became an inner-city development advocate. Then, in 1997, Houstonians elected Lee Brown, a prodowntown mayor who has supported several key projects, including the convention center hotel, the Main Street Project, the Cotswold 2000 Project, and a proposed light-rail system, among others. The city has provided financing and outright grants to projects that otherwise would be financially unviable. For example, the city created a tax-increment zone so it could subsidize approximately $4 million of the private sector redevelopment costs for the historic but long-closed Rice Hotel.

The third catalyst has been a growing public and private sector understanding that this city, which not only has avoided traditional zoning but also has scorned basic planning principles and actions, needs high-quality urban design initiatives. "You must create a template," says Kevin Shanley, a principal at the SWA Group, "a people-pleasing palette of streetscape, open space, transit, and buildings to encourage private sector development." Taken together, these three forces are helping to create a revitalized downtown Houston.

Streetscape Improvement Projects

Rather than undertaking individual improvement projects scattered around the 300-square-block downtown area, downtown Houston is reinventing itself through a series of programs that are helping to create a pedestrian-friendly environment, unify isolated pockets of activity, and reconnect different downtown districts into a cohesive whole. The catalyst for much of downtown Houston's redevelopment activity is the $177 million Downtown/Midtown Transit Streets Project, a large-scale streetscape redesign project funded by the Federal Transportation Authority and METRO, the Metropolitan Transit Authority of Harris County. The five-year project, which broke ground in June 1998, covers 26 downtown streets and seven streets in the nearby mid-town district. This project involves narrowing a number of overly wide downtown streets, widening some of the city's sidewalks, and installing new bus shelters, lightpoles, trees, benches, and information kiosks.

Last June, Ehrenkrantz Eckstut & Kuhn Architects of New York won a competition to develop the Main Street Project, a revitalization master plan for what the *Houston Chronicle* calls "the spine of downtown"—the once-bustling, now-shabby downtown main street corridor. The firm, which has completed some of the initial planning, reports that the project, if adopted, could taken ten to 15 years to complete.

The third major downtown streetscape project focuses on 100-foot-wide Texas Avenue, the widest street in downtown Houston and downtown's major east/west link, with the Theater District at the west end, a new ballpark at the east end, and the George Brown Convention Center nearby. The street also connects the historic district on the north with the more contemporary central business district to the south. However, because Texas Avenue is not used by buses, it could not be included in the Downtown/Midtown Transit Streets Project. Instead, the SWA Group, in collaboration with private groups such as the Houston Downtown Management District and Scenic Houston, prepared a streetscape improvement plan for Texas Avenue. The plan for the $950,000 project calls for constructing a 14-block-long promenade by widening sidewalks, creating on-street parking, and adding street trees and plantings, benches, and custom-designed light fixtures.

The first phase of construction, which targeted the blocks between Bagby Street and Main Street, began in June 1998 and was completed four months later. The second phase, which extends the project to the new baseball stadium, will be completed in time for the stadium's opening this April. It has been consolidated with the Cotswold 2000 Project, the last of downtown's major streetscape projects, which began in 1996 as a grass-roots undertaking. A group of private investors, in collaboration with then-mayor Lanier, wanted to make pedestrian-friendly street and sidewalk improvements — including narrower streets, broader sidewalks, fountains, angled on-street parking, and trees — on 93 blocks in the northern and most historic portion of downtown Houston.

In September 1998, the city took over the project and contracted with the Houston Downtown Management District to oversee management of Cotswold 2000's design and construction. The city retained oversight of parking, security, infrastructure, and other aspects of the project, and it is adding new drainage, water, and sewer lines. The $54 million first phase, which includes a 25-block area from the new ballpark to Sesquicentennial Park, broke ground last March and is scheduled for completion this fall.

Residential Projects

In 1995, there were approximately 900 apartment and condominium units in downtown Houston; at the end of this past year, there were nearly 2,000 units, with hundreds more under development or in the planning stage. However, they are not enough to feed the growing market demand. A study by CDS Market Research undertaken last May in conjunction with the Downtown Management District shows that 137,000 Houston metropolitan area households are interested in living in or near downtown. Much of the new downtown residential construction boom is credited to Houston-based developer Randall Davis, whose successful residential renovation of the historic Rice Hotel began to change things for Houston.

From its opening in 1913 until its closure in 1977, the 18-story Rice Hotel had been the heart of the city's social life. It sat empty for 20 years until Davis, in partnership with Post Properties of Atlanta, spent $32 million to renovate what was considered the grand old lady of downtown buildings into a 312-unit luxury loft apartment complex known simply as "The Rice." Just as the hotel's closure two decades earlier had symbolized downtown's decline, its rebirth in April 1998 symbolized downtown's resurrection. The apartments, which range in size from 500 to 2,800 square feet, rent from $650 to $4,000 a month; the building currently is fully leased.

With the Rice's success, other developers began buying up all the historic buildings they could find. Over a dozen rental and condominium projects have been completed recently or are under construction. For example, Spire Realty Group, another key player downtown, has turned the ten-story Southern Pacific Building on Franklin into the Bayou Lofts, 94 loft condominiums priced at $110,000 and up, with ground-floor restaurant and retail space.

Developers generally credit the surge in downtown housing development for the wave of new shops, restaurants, bars, and clubs. "These (residential) units are bringing back nightlife in what had been an after-hours ghost town," claimed the *Houston Chronicle* (May 23, 1999). By the end of this past year, more than 45 new restaurants, bars, and nightclubs had opened in downtown Houston.

Houston's suburban residents and visitors to the metropolitan area also appear to have discovered the new downtown. In the past two years, nearly 100,000 people more than in the early 1990s take part in downtown's nightlife each month, according to Gerard J. Tollett, director of the city of Houston's convention and entertainment facilities department. Downtown Houston also is home to a new nightclub scene that is drawing 20-something and older crowds to in-spots like the Spy Club, which has two levels of dance floors with DJ-hosted disco music, and the 804 Underground Lounge and Disco.

Reinforcing the Performing Arts

The performing arts have always been an important part of life in Houston. The city has its own symphony, opera, ballet, and theaters, all located in downtown's theater district. Today, new theaters, cinemas, galleries, and performance spaces are being added to the mix. For example, the $23 million first phase of Bayou Place, the Baltimore-based Cordish Company's redevelopment of the obsolete Albert Thomas Convention center — which had stood vacant in the theater district after the George R. Brown Convention Center opened in the 1980s — includes several restaurants; the Angelika Film Center and Café, with an eight-screen movie complex; a hall for music performances; and a pool parlor. Completed in December 1997, the first phase was followed by the 150,000-square-foot second phase, which broke ground last year and was 100 percent leased by last October. Another project is the $85 million Hobby Center for the Performing Arts, scheduled for completion in 2002, which is under construction on a seven-acre site adjacent to city hall. The new center will have two theaters — a 2,650-seat hall and a smaller 500-seat proscenium theater — as well as a restaurant and rehearsal space.

Office Buildings: Expanding the Base

Thanks to the office tower building boom of the 1970s and 1980s, downtown Houston has a skyline of high rises that, for almost a decade, suffered from a dearth of tenants. In 1993, the downtown office vacancy rate was more than 27 percent. By last February, however, the vacancy rate had dropped to 12 percent, and in some downtown areas it had dropped to between three percent and four percent. It now is almost impossible for companies to find large amounts of available Class A space downtown. Last summer, Houston-based Enron, the largest supplier of electricity and natural gas in North America and one of the biggest employers in Houston, broke ground on its new $200 million, 40-story, 1.2 million-square-foot office building at 1500 Louisiana, previously a parking lot. Developed by the Hines Company of Houston and designed by Cesar Pelli & Associate of New Haven, Connecticut, the silvery glass-façade building — the first downtown tower to be erected since 1986 — will be completed in 2001.

Most current downtown office projects are renovations of existing buildings, like McCord Development/AEW Capital Management's $35 million transformation of the old First City Main building into One City Centre, a 600,000-square-foot office building with a new parking garage. Levcor Realty is spending $30 million to renovate the 22-story Texas American Bank into 1001 McKinney, a 370,000-square-foot office development with retail space on the ground floor and a new parking garage.

Even speculative office development is returning to downtown Houston. Later this year, Century Development is scheduled to break ground on a $150 million, 35-story building at 1000 Main Street, across the street from Foley's Department Store. The Hines Company also has announced plans to build a 32-story, 600,000-square-foot office building on Texas Avenue.

Hotels

Throughout the 1990s, downtown

Houston had only 1,800 hotel rooms, divided among four hotels — much-smaller Austin, in comparison, had 3,625 — and it lacked even a convention center hotel. Without such a hotel, the new convention center could not operate at full capacity or generate a high-enough level of economic activity to benefit the entire downtown. After years of private sector delays, the city of Houston recently announced that it will finance and build a $180 million hotel with more than 1,000 rooms; it is scheduled for completion by 2003.

In the meantime, several downtown hotel renovation projects are underway. The $65 million conversion of the 15-story HRI/Humble Oil Building by New Orleans-based Historic Restorations includes three separate uses: a 191-room Courtyard by Marriott hotel, a 171-room Residence Inn extended-stay hotel, and 82 private condominiums and apartments.

Following a $25 million renovation by MHI Hotels of Maryland, the Whitehall Hotel will reopen this fall as the 255-room Crowne Plaza Cullen Center Hotel. Meanwhile, Rusk Development Limited Partnership of Baton Rouge, Louisiana, has paid approximately $5 million for the long-vacant 1915 limestone Texaco Building — "The most princely of Houston's early 20th-century skyscrapers," according to the *Houston Architectural Guide*— for conversion into a 325-room Ritz-Carlton hotel.

New Ballpark

A new $265 million, 42,000-seat Houston Astros baseball stadium with a retractable roof is scheduled for completion in March, in time for the opening of the new baseball season in April. The new ballpark, named Enron Field, is an example of the critical role played by public/private partnerships in reinventing downtown Houston. "When a new Houston Astros ballpark was being planned near the Astrodome," notes Houston Downtown Management District's Hagstette, "Central Houston, Inc., thought it should be downtown. So, the organization raised $100,000 to hire the HOK Sports architectural firm to study a downtown site. Central Houston then helped to convince the local political leadership to support a downtown location, and it led the citizens referendum to endorse that location." Next, Central Houston assembled and purchased the land for the downtown stadium, then turned it over to the Houston/Harris County Sports Authority, which had been authorized by the state legislature to build the facility.

"Sporting venues really get people to stay downtown, or come downtown, after 5:00 p.m.— that's what downtown Houston is really lacking," says Billy Burge, chairman of the Houston/Harris County Sports Authority. "So, 80 nights a year during the season, thousands of people not only will go to the game, they'll go to a restaurant or a bar, maybe do some shopping. And that will happen ten to 15 other nights a year for non-baseball events at the stadium," he predicts. Enron Field, expected to bring at least three million people downtown annually, already is spurring development activity nearby. Last September, for example, Trammell Crow Company announced that it wants to build a mixed-use project named Ballpark Place across from the stadium. In anticipation of additional future development, land prices near Enron Field already have doubled and tripled.

Looking Ahead

Much has been built — or is being built — in downtown Houston, yet many believe that even more needs to be done to sustain current redevelopment activity. Suggestions include:

Filling in the Holes. Several areas of

downtown Houston remain a patchwork quilt of vacant lots and boarded-up buildings next to high-rise office towers. The city should encourage low- and mid-rise, pedestrian-friendly construction in a variety of uses to create greater critical mass in the downtown, as cities like San Diego have done. Houston also should set up a site assembly program to create large lots to attract developers. "During the last big real estate boom in the late 1970s and early 1980s, there was a tremendous amount of land assembly, because many people assumed more high rises would come," says Central Houston, Inc.'s Eury. "Many of those assemblages are still intact — whole blocks, half blocks, three-quarter blocks — and they are all over downtown, including some of today's hot areas."

Expanded Residential Development. Unlike most other big city downtowns, Houston lacks a stock of charming and historic buildings that lend themselves to redevelopment. "Fortunately, developers are already scouting around for downtown sites that will support new construction of low-rise, loft-style apartment and condominium projects," notes Eury. "A recent survey of downtown Houston housing demand shows an increasing preference for high-rise living,"

he adds, "and some new high-rise projects already are on the boards for downtown."

Street Redesign. Downtown Houston's overly wide streets, originally designed to be wide enough to allow a mule team to turn around, reportedly intimidate many pedestrians and inhibit foot traffic. In addition, the downtown's one-way traffic patterns encourage high-speed traffic and hinder creation of a pedestrian-friendly environment.

Image. Despite what has been and is being built, the general consensus is that Houston's downtown still suffers from an image problem, which is not being helped by some of the city's new civic and institutional projects. New jails and courthouses, as well as single-room-occupancy buildings (SROs) for the homeless and others, can promote a negative, unsafe image of downtown Houston.

In recent decades, a number of half-dead U.S. downtowns have come back to life, creating a community hub, helping existing property owners and businesses, and improving the metropolitan area's image — all vital components in attracting new business, conventions, and residents. Baltimore did it in the 1980s; Cleveland did it in the 1990s; and now, many believe, it is Houston's turn.

CHAPTER 22

KANSAS CITY RENOVATES OLD TRAIN STATION TO JUMP-START DOWNTOWN RENEWAL

Zach Patton

Planners in Kansas City, Missouri, are beginning to think that the money they invested in fixing up their 87-year-old train station was money well spent. They're a little nervous, though, and they ought to be. Renovating the long-vacant Beaux-Arts landmark, reopened in 1999 as the centerpiece of downtown revival, cost a quarter of a billion dollars. Much of that money came out of taxpayers' wallets, earmarked by means of a regional sales tax increase.

The indicators are looking good. More than 1.3 million people showed up the first year to visit the building's interactive science museum, planetarium and laser-light show, see a concert or try out the theme restaurants and stores. Two local businesses lease space in the building, and the place is rented for conventions, civic celebrations and weddings.

But the promoters of the revival aren't declaring victory yet. They know too much about the fragility and riskiness of the whole station renovation idea. "These kinds of things are not for the faint-hearted," says Kansas City Union Station CEO Turner White, "but they can have tremendous

benefits for the cultural quality of life of a city."

Many planners cite the triumphs of New York's Grand Central and Washington, D.C.'s Union Station as an impetus for similar rail renaissance projects across the country. But the era of station renewal has also produced some failures. The rebuilt structures are nearly always jewels of historic preservation, but they can also be white elephants: Once the buildings are entered in the National Register of Historic Places, cities essentially are obligated to maintain them, regardless of cost or commercial viability. The effort can bring a city priceless benefits, but it is also difficult and extremely expensive, and — as more than one official has noted — it never really ends.

Indianapolis demonstrates the problem. That city's rail terminal, opened in 1888, was America's first true "union station" — multiple rail lines converging at a central hub. After peaking in the 1920s, rail traffic declined until the station finally closed in 1979, and the city began shopping for a developer. Seven years and over $50 million in renovations later, Indianapolis'

Originally published as "Choo-Choo Choices," *Governing*, Vol. 14, No. 7, April, 2001. Published by Congressional Quarterly Inc., Washington, D.C. Reprinted with permission of the publisher.

Union Station reopened as a festival marketplace with an adjoining hotel.

Financed through federal grants, city loans and private funds, the Union Station entertainment complex was regarded as the harbinger of redevelopment on Indianapolis' neglected south side. In the first year, 14 million visitors flocked to the nightclubs, shops and theme restaurants at the urban mall. Less than a decade later, however, Union Station had again closed its doors: The crowds had dwindled, and the tenants had all moved out. "It was a money pit," says Evert Hauser, the city's project manager for the station.

After the second closing in 1997, maintenance of the structure cost Indianapolis $100,000 per month. More than $9 million in repairs were required to replace what Hauser calls the cosmetic "Band-Aid fix-ups" of the first revitalization effort. Problems such as an inadequate gutter system and leaky skylights had to be dealt with before any further redevelopment could even be considered.

The experience in Indianapolis mirrored the failure of a similar festival mall project at Cincinnati's Union Terminal, which lasted less than eight years before closing in 1988. The price tags of these projects — Cincinnati spent over $20 million in public and private funds — have led some city planners around the country to question whether restoration of the structures is worth the cost, the headaches and the energy. A station, says Hauser, "is a pretty inflexible space. Even if you fixed it up as much as you could, it would still be C-grade space. It's never going to be grade-A space."

Notwithstanding all that, station fix-up projects continue to be popular with many local governments, and it's not hard to see why. "Train stations have a lot of resonance in terms of collective memory," says Hank Dittmar, president of the Great American Station Foundation. "As a symbol of revitalization, there's really no better.

Train stations are typically at the heart of the city, and renovating them is a public way to show a city's commitment to its downtown. And that demonstration of public faith catalyzes urban growth."

Dittmar's five-year-old foundation, based in Las Vegas, New Mexico, works with communities to make station reuse projects successful. Funded by private and corporate donations and through membership dues, the foundation is dedicated to restoring and preserving rail terminals through grants, information networking and the Most Endangered Stations Program, which highlights the terminals across the country in greatest need of preservation. Although the foundation focuses on those stations that maintain some transportation element in the renewal, its efforts have a broader impact than that. Dittmar's group produces a guidebook on station revitalization and a "how-to" manual for adaptive reuse of stations, and it also hosts yearly rail revitalization seminars.

Adaptive-reuse advocates emphasize that there are right ways and wrong ways to do the station fix-up process. Geography matters — a building that's located even a few blocks from the heart of town may have trouble drawing crowds. And the attractions inside can't just be curiosities. They have to be strong enough to bring locals back once the novelty wears off. Terry Sweeney, the real estate development director for the city of Indianapolis, concedes that while planners may have considered Union Station a centerpiece of that city, geographically and economically "it was an island. There was no reason to go back to the festival marketplace after a while. You need the right type of use that's going to bring people back."

Finding the right use is a tricky proposition for big cities and small ones alike. Joliet, Illinois, is a town of barely 80,000 people, but it has an impressive terminal building, designed by Jarvis Hunt, the architect of the station in Kansas City. The city bought the building in 1986, when it was crumbling, and began what would be a $6.5 million restoration effort — relatively ambitious for a town of Joliet's size. When the project was complete in 1991, the city waited for retail tenants to come, but they never did. Ten years later, they still haven't.

On the other hand, Joliet has been creative enough to keep the project from becoming a total disaster. "At first, while we were focusing on retail and specialty stores, we kept turning down requests to rent the place out," says Jim Haller, Joliet's director of community and economic development. Ultimately, Haller says, they decided single-event bookings were a lot better than nothing. Joliet Union Station is now rented for banquets, conferences, trade shows, weddings, car expos and high school proms. The building is also home to several county government offices. It's a far cry from the city's initial plan, but as Haller explains, "we're very flexible — we just want to be able to cover our expenses."

Indeed, flexibility may be the most important element of all. And cities gradually seem to be realizing it. In the past decade or so, railroad stations have been converted into municipal offices in Louisville, Kentucky, and Collierville, Tennessee; hotels in Chattanooga and Nashville; a bank in Albany, New York; and loft apartments in Memphis. After its failure as a mall, Cincinnati's Union Terminal was reborn as a museum of natural history, and the station in Omaha is a museum as well. The terminal in Tacoma, Washington, is now a federal courthouse, while Anchorage, Alaska, and Fargo, North Dakota, saw their stations become microbreweries.

Sometimes a festival marketplace turns out to be a failure, as it did in Cincinnati and Indianapolis, but sometimes the idea works. The festival mall at the old St. Louis station, a $150 million project opened in 1985, has done well, reminding visitors of similar spaces at Faneuil Hall in Boston and Harborplace in Baltimore. Steven Miller, a managing partner of St. Louis Station Associates, calls the project "the stone in the pond" of the city's urban renewal. It sees more annual visitors than the Arch, the zoo or the Cardinals.

It was an appreciation of the need for flexibility that ultimately led Indianapolis to the current incarnation of that city's terminal. After the festival marketplace closed in 1997, the city committed itself to repairing the damaged structure and to striking a diverse mixture of tenants. Today, Union Station houses a banquet and catering facility, but also includes an alternative school for at-risk students and a European-style go-kart center geared to corporate retreats.

This combination of tenants is certainly nontraditional, and it's clearly not a blend that a city could ever plan for. But, in the view of an increasing number of economic development specialists, it's the type of thinking that is most likely to breed success in the long run.

In short, cities are realizing that if they simply perform the fix-up work and then become complacent, they are asking for trouble, no matter how lavish the restoration job may be. "You have to reinvest and reinvent yourself periodically," says Terry Sweeney in Indianapolis. "Five or 10 years from now, tastes change, and you have to adapt."

Hauser, reflecting on nearly 15 years of difficult experience, agrees. "We aren't done," he says. "We never will be." Then he adds a tongue-in-cheek reminder of the ultimate instability of these ambitious projects: "Hopefully," he says, "we'll be breaking even in about three years."

CHAPTER 23

LAKE WORTH RESTORES SHORELINE PROPERTY TO REVIVE BEACHFRONT COMMERCIAL AREA

Paul M. Twitty

The term civic architecture often conjures up visions of important community buildings such as libraries, courthouses, or town halls. But in the city of Lake Worth, Florida, some of the most important civic structures are on the beach. A 19-acre site, Lake Worth Beach is 1,240 feet long and 560 feet deep. Unlike many Florida beaches, this site encompasses parking, a pool, restaurants, retail shops, and a fishing pier between State Road A1A and the ocean.

Although the beach has been a center of Lake Worth community life since before the city was founded in 1913, the existing beach facilities were not constructed until 1949.

A Mediterranean/revival-style casino and bath built on the site in 1922 were largely destroyed by a hurricane in 1947. Remnants of the original gambling casino survive within the shell of the 1949 casino-style replacement building, but the current structure has no historical significance. Also in 1949, the entire beach was scraped clean of native vegetation and converted to a vast surface parking lot to accommodate large numbers of tourists; today, 80 percent of the beach is paved. A freshwater pool was added in 1971 to replace an original saltwater pool that was filled in behind the casino building the same year.

The effects of more than a half century of use are evident in the shabby condition of most of the beach facilities. Over the years, there have been several efforts to rally public support to improve its appearance. In 1981, the Lake Worth City Commission solicited a comprehensive redevelopment plan, which was debated, changed, and ultimately abandoned four years later. Conditions continued to deteriorate until the mid-1990s, when the beach again became a matter of public discussion. Subsequent inaction has stemmed from a lack of agreement within the community about what the beach should become. At long last, through the efforts of both a determined mayor and the city commission, a shared vision for the beach has finally emerged—a core master plan produced by the Treasure Coast Regional Planning Council (TCRPC) and refined by a specially appointed beach steering committee, as well as Lake Worth residents.

Originally published as "Beach Structures," *Urban Land*, Vol. 60, No. 10, October, 2001. Published by the Urban Land Institute, Washington, D.C. Reprinted with permission of the publisher.

"The redevelopment of our beach is truly a grass-roots project; it's what our citizens want," notes Mayor Rodney Romano. "When I was mayor from 1993 to 1997, I was courted by a developer who wanted to redo the beach, but the resulting shopping mall concept was rejected. After I left office, the city went through the process again, as several hotel/resorts vied for the opportunity to develop the site. At a public meeting at Lake Worth High School in December 1998, our citizens rejected the various plans and clearly informed elected officials that the beach should be considered a public space and not be turned into a mall or hotel resort," he adds.

A charrette organized by the TCRPC was held with designers, planners, and various public interest groups in March 2000, and a preliminary plan was drawn up three months later. The city embraced that plan, and in September 2000 appointed a beach steering committee to improve it. Local planner Frank Palen led the 16-member committee, with the nine-member city planning and zoning board at its core, augmented by a mix of professionals and interested citizens.

"The beach appeals to a lot of people," points out Palen. "Yet initially, it was not clear how the beach was perceived by people. We conducted a survey and discovered there are many different perceptions. Some people want to sunbathe; others like to fish or just stroll on the pier. Then there's the group that sees the beach as a place to meditate and watch the sun rise. We have surfers, kids who clearly love to 'cruise' the beach, and tourists and residents who like to come to the beach to eat. We have one of the area's top restaurants: John G's is an institution. All these groups don't mix together, but each has an interest in what is going to happen at the beach."

Between September 2000 and this past May, the beach steering committee met 17 times to consider the TCRPC plan and the issues identified by the city commission, before presenting its report on May 23. "It is not a physical plan, it's a policy plan," emphasizes Palen. "We brought in experts on parking, finance, fiscal impact analysis, and we asked them all to assist us in making rational judgments and help validate the design.

"We had to come up with a shared vision and look at the beach as an economic asset, not just a physical asset. It is also a social asset, a gathering place in an urban setting. People get very passionate about the beach," Palen adds with a smile. "While there is a tendency to get caught up in side issues, the steering committee was committed to keeping the process moving. We needed to get people with very different views together and focus them on the main issue—what to do about the beach. My main concern was getting people to commit to the planning and design process. The plan is more likely to be accepted if people feel they have a real opportunity to participate and get their questions answered. That was not always true in the past, and I am pleased with the nearly unanimous consensus the steering committee achieved."

Romano was reelected mayor of Lake Worth in March after a campaign in which he focused on the beach plan and neighborhood revitalization, and he says he is intent upon moving beach redevelopment forward. In July, the city commission voted unanimously to accept the conceptual designs produced by West Palm Beach-based Schwab, Twitty & Hanser Architectural Group (STH), which is responsible for the final design for the beach redevelopment. Rather than wait for construction drawings, STH suggested to the mayor that he and the design team expedite the process and go immediately to the state of Florida to begin a dialogue with various state permitting agencies, especially the Bureau of Beaches and Coastal Systems zoning agency, and get them on board from the beginning. The city task force now is eager to market the project to the general public.

The design team recognized the beach — with its small-town attributes and charm — as the jewel of Lake Worth. The new plan calls for strengthening these attributes and improving and preserving the character of the beach as a historic focal point for the city and as an important amenity for its residents, which comprise a diverse community of first-, second-, and third-generation Americans, including African Americans, as well as Guatemalans, Jamaicans, Haitians, Finns, and a sprinkling of others of varied ethnic backgrounds. The new public entrance and proposed facilities are designed to announce an arrival to a unique public place.

Included in the project will be the casino building, a two-story structure comprising retail; John G's restaurant; conference and banquet space; and a common area. An upscale restaurant is planned for the second level. Another mixed-use group of buildings will feature retail, public locker rooms, a lifeguard station, and a common area. Also included in the plan are a parking garage, a picnic pavilion, restrooms, a fishing pier, and a pool equipment building. The total building space is about 145,000 square feet, but retail and restaurant space has been limited to 22,000 square feet.

"There will be a lot of open space, a simple circulation plan, and the area will be barrier free," explains design architect Ron Wiendl. "It was a conscious decision to create interaction among spaces. The retailers will have high exposure to visitors coming from the garage, but retail is limited to avoid competition with downtown Lake Worth."

The design of the new structures is Mediterranean/revival, reminiscent of, but not a replica of, the architecture of the original casino building. STH has recalled some of the architectural features of the original casino building — e.g., domes, gables, etc.— and there are a lot of similarities to the old

facility because the city and the citizens want the new buildings to reflect the character of the past. But there is no gambling; the casino name remains for historical purposes.

The existing Olympic-sized pool will remain in its present position, with the casino building at one end, and the new mixed-use building, locker rooms, and lifeguard station, which flank the children's pool, at the other end. "This allows for more visibility and pedestrian circulation, and provides a direct connection between the pool and the beach," notes Wiendl. "Bathers will enjoy the use of the freshwater pool rather than the ocean on a windy day."

Currently, the road along the beach has multiple traffic lanes. But the new beach promenade will no longer be an automobile circulation area conducive to cruising; it will be a tree-lined, old-fashioned single-lane avenue where pedestrians can feel more secure and welcome. The 500-foot-long promenade also can be closed off for festivals and other cultural events.

The parking garage in the STH plan will hold 200 cars, which will eliminate a lot of surface parking and enable the creation of open space — something the public demanded. Some beachfront parking will remain for seniors and emergency vehicles; a total of 650 spaces will be available, with 120 off-site spaces at the entrance to the beach complex. According to Romano, plans call for Lake Worth citizens to be able to purchase yearly parking passes, while tourists and other visitors would pay a daily fee to use the beach.

The garage, located midway between the casino building and the other mixed-use buildings, will have the character of a retail structure, with tower pods for vertical circulation at the corners. A trellised area will be visible from State Road A1A and from the Lake Worth Bridge. An effort also has been made to make the parking garage visually appealing since it is so highly visible. Visitors approaching over the Lake Worth Bridge will have views of the entire complex and the beach.

Public buses and the Lake Worth Trolley can drop visitors off at the main entrance, and the Lake Worth Bridge provides walking access from downtown Lake Worth. A traffic roundabout proposed for the main entrance to the beach on State Road A1A requires further coordination with the state department of transportation.

John G's restaurant will have an outdoor dining patio connected to a large park on the south. Another elevated terrace with a view of the pool will be located on the north side of the building. From this area, visitors can be seen coming from the garage to the beach and retail patrons can visit the beach and pool. The second-floor conference facility is intended for use by city residents as well as to support the city's hotel and motel industry, which currently lacks comparable meeting space. One of the city's directives is that John G's restaurant stay open during construction. Phasing the redevelopment calls for keeping the existing structure open until the new building is complete, then the old casino building will be demolished.

The fishing pier — one of only two such piers in Palm Beach County — with its restaurant is an important component of the beach complex. While the pier will remain untouched, several options were considered for the pier entrance/restaurant complex, including demolishing and rebuilding it, or renovating it. Plans currently call for creating direct pier access, a new restaurant, and an entry kiosk, providing a gateway to a more inviting and attractive public space.

The beach site's landscape plan, created by West Palm Beach–based Glatting, Jackson, Kercher, Anglin, Lopez & Rinehart, aims to integrate the new buildings and swimming pool into a lush Mediterranean garden alongside the ocean. According to landscape architect David Barth, mature trees and other foliage will be used to enhance the promenade and the pool and to shade walkways. Decorative concrete block paving will be used to link the buildings to the ocean and pier. The main entrance will be planted with avenues of palms and ornamental shrubs to help create a grand entryway.

"The obvious citizen concern will be how we pay for all this," points out Romano. "We wanted to do the beach redevelopment ourselves," he notes. "I feel financing is best served by a bond issue. A workshop has been scheduled to discuss financing options, and if we all agree the best way to finance is with general obligation bonds, a referendum will go before the voters next March. Everyone agrees we have to do the project and we have to raise the funds. We plan to ask our citizens for $19 million. If we can go to Washington and get a $1 million endowment or obtain money from a private source, that will be wonderful, but we must be committed to raising $19 million."

The preliminary budget of $19 million is the actual cost of doing the project. This estimate includes the $14.5 million construction cost escalated over two years at the rate of inflation, a contingency fund to protect the citizens from unforeseen environmental conditions, plus fees, permits, and the actual cost of producing the bond referendum. "We need to consider how much more use will occur with the improved facility. We anticipate generating $1.5 million in revenue against the needed $1 million for maintenance and staffing. This would give us a half million dollars to put back into this general fund," adds Romano. "The fact that the city is retiring an old bond before this new one starts is helpful. A family with a $125,000 house with homestead exemption will pay only $70 more a year in taxes.

"The process has been long and tedious, but at last consensus reigns, and the redevelopment of Lake Worth Beach is nearing realization," says Romano. "Downtown revitalization began five years ago, and the citizens were very involved. They took it upon themselves to be involved in the beach revitalization planning, too."

Romano says he is optimistic about the beach plan, but not complacent, noting that he plans a very active community sales campaign. "Historically, our citizens have said they don't want to spend money. But, as we have gone through this process, their support has been overwhelming. Their approval will be reflected in the passage of the bond issue next March," he adds. "I think of Lake Worth as an 80-year-old debutante. Our city has a lot of charm and history. It's time to strut our stuff."

CHAPTER 24

LITTLE ROCK MAKES IMPROVEMENTS TO REDEVELOP ITS DOWNTOWN RIVERFRONT AREA

Robert J. Gorman and Nancy Egan

Little Rock, Arkansas, is enjoying a makeover. The national press has focused its attention on the arrival of the Clinton Presidential Center, the nation's next presidential library. But the real story begins with the vision of local government and its residents. Strong, creative leadership and civic involvement have reshaped this quiet southern river town in the last decade. When Bill Clinton became president in 1992, Little Rock drew national attention for the first time since the desegregation of Central High School in 1957. This is the story of how citizens of Little Rock leveraged their existing assets with the political momentum of the Clinton election to create a more attractive and dynamic city.

Ten years ago, Little Rock's central business district — like that of many other cities that suffered from the ground-zero approach to redevelopment prevalent in the 1960s — was the requisite collection of office and parking towers and "soon-to-be-developed" vacant lots. Although there did exist a handful of historic structures and several buildings of architectural significance, the downtown lacked the focus and vibrancy

that results from a thoughtful urban plan. With Clinton in Washington, Little Rock was on camera. Local leaders recognized the economic prize that the presidential library represented and committed to creating an environment for this once-in-a-lifetime, urban development opportunity.

As this was not the city's first attempt at revitalization — earlier efforts had failed — Little Rock officials realized that a long-range vision and specific, short-term development objectives were needed. George Wittenberg, director of the Donaghey Project for Urban Studies, the urban planning arm of the University of Arkansas at Little Rock, recalls, "The city was ready to get serious. We looked around the country at other cities to see what had been done, and we took a very hard look at what we had failed to do before. There was a new confidence in Little Rock following Clinton's election, and we were able to translate that into a sense of urgency." Business and civic leaders represented by the Downtown Partnership worked with the Donaghey Institute and MRA International, a Philadelphia-based development strategy firm, to

Originally published as "Revitalizing Little Rock," *Urban Land*, Vol. 60, No. 9, September, 2001. Published by the Urban Land Institute, Washington, D.C. Reprinted with permission of the publisher.

define and accomplish their goal: to develop a business strategy to enhance Little Rock's competitive position as a business center and regional leisure destination.

Facing Facts

The consulting team's 1994 study revealed both the challenges and the potential gains of an accelerated economic development program. First the tough realities — Little Rock is the center of a region with a relatively small population, and competitor cities within a 150-mile radius boast entertainment and recreational offerings that the city cannot match.

However the city's natural riverfront location offered an attractive physical asset on which to build a strategy. Little Rock possessed substantial vacant land and, while there was little public financial support available to initiate development there, a few privately funded projects were beginning to create a critical mass. A revitalized River District would provide an identifiable destination within the city and would reconnect the downtown to the historic riverfront and its geological formation, the little rock, from which the city derives its name.

A number of existing assets in the River District needed upgrading: the Central Library and the Museum of Science and History were due for new facilities; and the Convention Center, the Camelot Hotel, and River Park needed attention. Finally, a number of "missing assets" were identified that would give the River District a distinctive draw and enhance the existing properties.

Inventing the River District Area

Barry Travis, the executive director of the Little Rock Convention Center and Visitors' Bureau, describes the redevelopment process: "Like pieces of a jigsaw puzzle, Lit-

tle Rock is re-creating itself as new projects are finished and other projects are announced. This is a very exciting time." Today, the majority of the facilities outlined in the 1994 plan are in operation. Development has recaptured the waterfront to create a bustling hot spot in the heart of the city.

The River Market. The lively farmers' market has become the rallying symbol for the transformation of the entire district. Its food stalls, eateries, and year-round events — from the seasonal farmers' market to holiday ice-skating — have changed the way both locals and visitors view the River District. The initial $5 million investment in the market served as a catalyst for further development in the River District.

Operated by the Little Rock Parks and Recreation Department, the market comprises 18 businesses in the Market Hall and two 7,500-square-foot pavilions on its river side. The pavilions, including the plaza area, house more than 100 vendors and host many other events throughout the year. They attract approximately 75,000 visitors to the farmers' market each year. Started in 1974, the market, which has been in other locations, continues today to be very successful during its six-month run each year from May through October.

The Alltel Arena. This state-of-the-art facility originally was slated for the River District. The decision to locate it in North Little Rock directly across the Arkansas River from the River Market in Little Rock was made, in part, to reinforce the concept of the two-sided riverfront destination. Today, the arena draws hundreds of thousands of people to the central Arkansas area, increasing the vitality of the entertainment/recreation sectors on both sides of the river.

Costing approximately $7 million to build, the arena provides seating for more than 18,000. It opened in October 1999 and during its first year hosted 30 concerts, eight

Arena Football League games, 35 Arkansas Razorblade hockey games, 22 basketball games, and 100 meetings and reception events, attracting more than 711,000 people. The local economic impact already is estimated to be more than $2 million.

Statehouse Convention Center. The $23 million expansion of the Little Rock Convention Center and Visitors' Bureau doubled the size of the convention center, increasing it to 192,000 square feet and making it a strong, regional contender. The existing center already was drawing 450,000 to 500,000 visitors per year. Now, the expanded center has the size and flexibility to compete on a new level.

Little Rock Central Library. The new, $15 million facility provided a needed boost to the River District revitalization efforts. The Little Rock Central Library was a pioneer, having made an early commitment to renovate and occupy an existing warehouse. Since its opening in the fall of 1997, the number of visitors has doubled.

Museum of Discovery. This museum has been a Little Rock institution for more than 70 years. Relocated in another refurbished warehouse, the museum contains 50,000 square feet — three times the original size. The $10.6 million expanded museum attracts 200,000 visitors per year.

The River Amphitheater. This tented structure has been home to warm-weather events for a number of years. Recently, permanent seating, restrooms, and performer facilities have helped enhance the amphitheater.

The Doubletree Hotel. Doubletree Hotels, along with a local development group, completely renovated the former Camelot Hotel, investing $8 million to bring the facility up to the standard of its competing hotels, the Capitol and the Excelsior. The remodeled hotel provides an entryway to the main spine of the River District.

Seeding the Future

The fast-track redevelopment program began to pay off in 1997, when the city selected the Little Rock River District over other sites, including the University of Arkansas at Fayetteville, as the home for the Clinton Presidential Center. Little Rock's City Board of Directors approved the use of $1.2 million from its 1998 economic development budget to pay for the first year's estimated debt service on $15 million of a total $22 million revenue bond issue. This move did not increase taxes. The bonds are earmarked for the acquisition of land for the center, the removal of railroad tracks, and the transformation of the Arkansas River's Rock Island Bridge into a pedestrian bridge.

James L. (Skip) Rutherford, who has been responsible for organizing the planning of the center, comments, "This commitment to urban development creates a catalyst that will influence additional community development on both sides of the Arkansas River. We see the Clinton Presidential Center as part of a larger vision of the future of Little Rock."

With a solid commitment to action, a coalition of the Downtown Partnership and city leadership, including the mayor's office, the Convention Center and Visitors' Bureau, the Greater Little Rock Chamber of Commerce, Fifty for the Future (an organization of senior business executives), and private investors, has changed the image of the city. Each project, whether it is a public or private initiative, is an impressive contributor on its own.

As local businessman and civic leader Jimmy Moses says, "Our first decisions are still reverberating as additional projects expand our original vision. We are filling the gaps and redeveloping older properties to take advantage of the real estate value that has been created. And I wouldn't rule out another major new project based on increased interest in the city."

The timing of the River District's redevelopment could not have been better. Little Rock's economy mirrored the nation's, giving locals and out-of-town visitors more disposable income to spend. Major national trends toward downtown living gave a boost to several older properties in the district as they were converted to residential lofts. A variety of new businesses have flocked to the area — now a flourishing collection of restaurants, florists, retail outlets, and even a satellite studio for a local television station — which hosted more than 250,000 visitors in 2000.

With their success in revitalizing the historic River District and securing the Clinton Library as the centerpiece for an expansion of the area, Little Rock's leaders — all dedicated citizens — are celebrating a renaissance in their community. They are committed to the quality of life, as they are to the economic vitality, of their city. They understand that urban renewal requires the improvement of both and have included them successfully in the revitalization of Little Rock.

Observers are stunned by the turnaround. The community leadership defined a vision, created a plan, and followed a clear strategy for implementation with remarkable speed. Little Rock's story provides a compelling scenario for other cities hoping to renew their urban core.

A Checklist for Success

Towns and cities across America share a dream of revitalizing their downtowns, their forgotten waterfronts, or faded retail districts. All too often, pursuit of a single magic project that is expected to turn everything around — be it an aquarium, a planetarium, or a museum — sidetracks civic leaders. Little Rock could have waited for the arrival of the Clinton Library. However, cities that have been successful in attracting a blockbuster project usually begin with a series of smaller, related projects that build

confidence without breaking the budget, thereby creating a platform of support for a large-scale attraction. Although each opportunity is different, the lessons of Little Rock's success can be readily extrapolated to suit other locales. Essential criteria include:

- Long-term political and community leaders with the patience and perseverance to nurture a plan over time.
- A clear sense of the possibilities scaled to the place, and a marked sense of "optimistic realism." These will keep doubters at bay in the critical early stages.
- A vision articulated in a way that captures the imagination of the community. Professional planners and other advisers often can sell the concept more successfully than the local support team.
- A strategic plan for implementing the vision. It is important to have a tactical game plan as well as a compelling goal — dreams fade when no visible action exists.
- A management entity that can "act" and take responsibility for implementing the plan. Most cities have term limits for elected officials, making it imperative to have an organization that will ensure continuity.
- Early successes that can enhance the community's ability to maintain a sense of momentum. Realistic first targets and an integrated marketing program help to set a sustainable pace.
- Borrowed successes. Linking the plan through shared amenities to initiatives already underway (i.e., streetscapes, transport systems, or marketing programs) accelerates the sense of achievement.
- Critical mass. If the program encompasses too much territory it ceases to be a precise destination in the eyes — and feet — of the visitors.
- Funding through a variety of sources. The dream should be realizable to a certain degree when taken in smaller steps that can be financed quickly.

CHAPTER 25

MADISON INTEGRATES LAND-USE AND TRANSPORTATION PLANNING TO CURB SPRAWL

Ruth Eckdish Knack

On May 22, the Dane County Regional Planning Commission in Madison, Wisconsin, is expected to vote on a controversial new land-use and transportation plan. Three months ago, the commissioners told state officials that they needed more time to review the "Vision 2020" plan, which had drawn criticism from both rural township supervisors, who complained that it was too much centered on Madison, and Madison residents who contended it was too automobile-oriented.

Both sides agree on one thing: that Madison is a special place. Last summer *Money* magazine put it at the top of its list of "best places to live," and a recent *American Health* story said its low crime rate and good schools help make it the "healthiest" city for women. It doesn't hurt that Madison occupies a splendid site. "No other city of the world, so far as I know, has naturally such a unique situation on a series of lakes," planner John Nolen wrote in 1908.

Madison is at the center of one of the "urban constellations" identified by retired University of Wisconsin landscape architect

professor Philip Lewis. Within this four-state, upper Midwest "Circle City" constellation, Lewis has written, live 17 million people. They threaten to fill in the relatively undeveloped "driftless" area at the middle, part of the landscape that was spared by the glaciers thousands of year ago.

The city's twin anchors are the 40,000-student University of Wisconsin campus and the elegant state capitol. Both are major population draws, helping the population of Dane County grow from 292,000 in 1970 to 390,000 in 1994. By 2020, according to the new plan, another 100,000 newcomers will bring the total to about 490,000.

During the same period, the plan estimates that 57,000 new jobs will be added — in state government, the university, and the high-tech businesses that are increasingly moving into the area. To house the newcomers, the plan estimates that 40,000 new dwelling units will be needed.

To planners in New York or California, those figures, based on projections by the Wisconsin administration department, may not seem like a big deal. But to rural

Originally published as "Go Badgers, Fight That Sprawl," *Planning*, Vol. 63, No. 5, May, 1997. Published by the American Planning Association, 122 South Michigan Avenue, Suite 1600, Chicago, Illinois 60603-6107. Reprinted with permission of the publisher.

Wisconsin residents, they evoke Chicago-like images of high-density development, traffic congestion, and social problems.

Madison has already seen some rather large demographic changes, including a growing homeless population. University of Wisconsin planning professor Jerry Kaufman, AICP, describes Madison as a "threshold" city because of the changes that have taken place in the last 15 years. Minority peoples — Hispanics, African Americans, and Asians (including a large Hmong population) — represented 10.5 percent of Madison's population in 1990, "probably more today." That's enough, says Kaufman, to have significantly altered the perceptions of long-time residents.

Hot Issues

"We are suggesting some things in the Vision 2020 plan that are very controversial for some people, both from a land-use and transportation standpoint," says Robert McDonald, AICP, director of transportation planning and a 22-year veteran of the Dane County Regional Planning Commission staff.

Among the red flag issues are the plan's recommendations for higher residential densities throughout the county (five dwelling units per acre rather than the current average of three to four), that the countywide balance of single- and multi-family housing approach 50-50, and that outlying communities provide a broader range of housing types (e.g., affordable housing).

"Some people interpreted that to mean rent subsidies, although that's not what we're saying," McDonald says.

The plan's transportation section includes a recommendation for a new transit corridor running from Middleton west of Madison through the central Isthmus area to the eastern suburbs. But the plan also lays out $373 million in road capacity improve-

ments — including new west and north beltways — that are likely to be needed by 2020, based on the plan's projected congestion levels.

The result, according to a recent opinion piece in *Isthmus*, the area's weekly newspaper, will be to make Dane County look like the "concrete tangle around O'Hare Airport" in Chicago.

"There's a strong contingent that doesn't want to see any road improvements," McDonald says. But even with new rail and bus lines, he adds, "many of the trips will be suburb to suburb, and 97 percent of them will be made by auto. So we need to add capacity."

Tricky Part

According to consultant Charles Causier, AICP, it wasn't hard to get area residents to agree on goals for the new plan. Causier, who is director of planning services for HNTB in Milwaukee, initially shared consulting tasks with Lane Kendig, AICP, of Mundelein, Illinois, in effect becoming project manager when Kendig's role ended rather abruptly.

"There was a consensus," Causier says, "that you want to protect farmland, and have balanced communities with different types of land use so people can work and live in the same place. There was also an overwhelming sense that this is a wonderful area and that we want to keep it that way."

The tricky part, says Causier, was when the planners started saying where growth should go. There was tension from the beginning between the county's 26 incorporated cities and villages, including the city of Madison, and the unincorporated townships.

The RPC staff and consultants began by presenting 10 alternative growth scenarios, ranging from continuing current growth trends — in other words, sprawl —

to encouraging traditional neighborhood development like Middleton Hills, the 150-acre Duany-designed project west of Madison.

Two computer models were used to narrow the alternatives: One was the SAVES model (strategic analysis vision evaluation system), designed by Kendig to evaluate land-use development patterns. Those results were then fed into the transportation model, TRANPLAN. "We used it to figure out what sort of transportation system would be needed to serve each of the alternatives — as well as potential ridership and costs of light rail and busways," McDonald says.

The land-use and transportation connection was key to this process, McDonald says. "ISTEA (the federal Intermodal Surface Transportation Efficiency Act) requires all metropolitan planning organizations to update their transportation plans — and to consider land use. We did more than just consider it. Our new plan will actually merge our existing land-use and transportation documents. We wanted people to know the consequences of moving one way or another."

Don't Tread on Me

Not everyone wants to hear about the consequences. Vision 2020 strongly recommends that new housing and new jobs be directed to existing communities that are served by public water and sewer services.

To Robert Bowman, a retired University of Wisconsin professor on the board of supervisors in Cross Plains, an unincorporated town of 1,340 west of Madison, that's an example of the county's bias toward its largest city.

In 1964, Bowman bought a 30-acre tract in Cross Plains. Then in 1981 Wisconsin passed a farmland preservation act and Bowman's land became part of an agricul-ture preservation zone that allowed only one house per 35 acres. "A few years ago," he says, "our daughter wanted to build a house on our land, and we applied for a permit to split off five acres. But even though our land is rocky and hilly, unsuited for farming, the county would not grant a variance."

Bowman sued and eventually got his zoning. But the affair soured him on the county's regulatory process and led to his decision to run for supervisor, he says.

In Bowman's view, "the Vision 2020 process was designed to come out with a certain result. Under all 10 of the scenarios, Madison was free to grow," he says. "I took exception to the idea that there should be virtually no development in the countryside."

In a book called *Cities without Suburbs*, David Rusk, former mayor of Albuquerque, takes a different view of Madison's efforts to annex. Rusk's thesis is that cities that annex aggressively — as Madison did between 1950 and 1990 when its land area grew by 275 percent — do far better economically than cities that don't. He notes that Harrisburg, Pennsylvania, another state capital, grew by only 29 percent during the same period and is in a poorer position because of it.

"Annexation is not a dirty word," says former Madison mayor Paul Soglin, who did not run for reelection last month. The outspoken Soglin, who served as mayor from 1973 to 1979 and again since 1989, is used to attacks on this issue. Soglin says he sees Dane County being remade into something like the collar counties around Chicago, defined by a desire to convert farmland into subdivisions and shopping centers.

"When Madison annexes," he says, "it develops at eight times the density the towns do. And we provide housing, not just strip commercial. Meanwhile, the towns get to be part of the Madison community without having to pay for services."

Madison's Take

To ensure that the city's interests — particularly those of the central area, the Isthmus — were taken into account, Soglin appointed the Isthmus 2020 citizens task force, which is chaired by Richard Wagner, former chairman of the county board of supervisors.

"We frankly were not happy with all the consultants' projections," which allocated some of the new growth to outlying areas, says Wagner. "The land-use model seemed to emphasize trends that showed suburban growth. Our data showed that the Isthmus could accommodate a lot of that growth."

With the help of Todd Violante of the city's planning staff, the committee sponsored several events designed to show Madison residents what that growth could look like. In one exercise, flash cards were used to demonstrate concepts like "medium high density"; in another, participants were asked to move transparent rings on an aerial photo to find the best locations for new rail stops in a proposed transit corridor.

At the conclusion of this process, the committee decided that the Isthmus could handle another 4,500 housing units and, with adequate transit, another 14,000 jobs. Those figures were accepted by the regional planning agency for incorporation into the plan, Wagner says.

Like other Isthmus 2020 members, Anne Monks, longtime assistant to Mayor Soglin and a former city council member, believes that the larger Vision 2020 process failed in terms of public participation. "There was never an adequate plan for involving the public, and they never came up with anything that all those Dane County villages and towns could identify with as a statement of where they wanted the county to be going," Monks says.

Consultant Lane Kendig says the problem was an inadequate budget that included only four public hearings over three years. "You have to do more if you're really interested in citizen participation," Kendig says.

Money is also a factor in carrying out the Isthmus 2020 plan. Monks notes that many of the recommendations for more compact residential development and a "Main Street" approach to commercial areas would require new zoning.

"A lot of changes that the committee is asking for will lead to more work on the part of the city planning staff," she says.

What's Next

It won't be Paul Soglin who worries about finding the money for the staff needed to carry out those changes, however. The April 1 election gave Madison a new mayor and Dane County a new executive. Susan Bauman won the mayor's race over a fellow city council member, Wayne Bigelow.

In the county executive race, Karen Falk, who has a strong reputation as an environmentalist, won over the more conservative Michael Blaska, who had been chairman of the county board, where he was seen as a representative of the Dane County Towns Association.

Meanwhile, the regional planning commission staff is preparing for that May 22 vote on the new plan. "We're looking more closely at some of those roadway improvements in response to some of the criticism," says Bob McDonald. After a decision on the draft plan was postponed, a subcommittee was formed to attempt to balance some of the concerns voiced by area residents, he says.

According to McDonald, the commission's staff of about 12 planners did not grow for this project. "The ISTEA money did not filter down this far," he says.

After the commission acts, the plan goes to the state Department of Transportation, the Madison city council, and the

Dane County board. If they approve, and if the plan is also approved by the other local governments within the county, it will replace the present regional development guide and transportation plan as the county's governing documents.

How likely is implementation?

Bob McDonald is hopeful because the Vision 2020 plan does something that has never been done before in integrating land-use and transportation decisions.

But Lane Kendig says he's skeptical. "People talk about the Madison area becoming the Portland of the Midwest, filled with nice new neotraditional developments. But unless they're willing to change the basic zoning structure, they won't be able to do it. They're zoned for auto-oriented development."

"I think most people in this region want the things the plan calls for," says Jerry Kaufman. "They'd like to see more compact development and more transit. The question is whether we have the mechanisms to accomplish these things." Kaufman is talking about more than new zoning. "We lack metrowide institutions that could equalize the disparities between rich and poor communities," he says. "As a result, Madison tends to suffer from growth rather than benefit from it."

But the biggest deterrent to change seems to be the state. In 1909, Wisconsin became the first state to authorize cities to form planning commissions. But since that time, its planning record, with some exceptions such as the agricultural preservation act, has been negligible.

"We don't have a state legislative framework," says George Austin, Madison's planning director since 1983. In 1994, Gov. Tommy Thompson appointed a strategic growth task force to "develop a land-use vision for Wisconsin." The task force was charged with dealing with such issues as annexation and consistency of town and county plans and zoning codes. Its recommendations will eventually go to the legislature, but Austin says he's not hopeful that new laws will emerge any time soon.

Paul Soglin views Vision 2020 as "a modest beginning," but says he's not very hopeful about the future in a state with such timid politicians. "We lost the opportunity 20 years ago when we could have emulated the state of Oregon," he says.

There are bright spots, though, including the recent formation of 1000 Friends of Wisconsin, modeled after 1000 Friends of Oregon. And both the city of Madison and Dane County have been buying land to create some of the corridors and greenways called for by Philip Lewis.

At a 1995 symposium to commemorate John Nolen's landmark 1908 plan for Madison, neotraditional guru Andres Duany said of the Madison area: "This is one of the few places that is growing now that can still do it right." The Vision 2020 plan and the local efforts in support of it are a start.

CHAPTER 26

MINNEAPOLIS REVISES ZONING CODE TO ALLOW MORE FLEXIBLE DEVELOPMENT

Alan Ehrenhalt

On the corner of 19th Street and Nicollet Avenue, a mile south of downtown Minneapolis, there's a massive brick building that stood for decades as the headquarters of the Frenz garage and car dealership. After the business moved elsewhere, the building housed a storage company, and then, as the neighborhood around it declined, it fell vacant for a long time.

Then Steve Frenz, scouting around for a new close-in location for the still-thriving family automotive business, hit on the idea of opening back up at the original site, renovating the empty building, which he owned, and maybe putting some retail on the ground floor.

He found the city zoning ordinance standing in his way. Yes, the building had been a garage for 50 years, but once the garage closed, the property reverted to commercial use. His automotive business is by definition an industrial use. The land wasn't zoned for much except a store — notwithstanding the fact that it wasn't very attractive to stores, or it wouldn't have been empty all those years.

After months of tedious and expensive

effort, Frenz managed to get an "exception," and today the renovated building at 1 East 19th has not only a Frenz automotive business but also a flower shop on the Nicollet Avenue side. But he's the first one to admit that he got permission mostly because his family has some clout in Minneapolis and he knows his way around City Hall. "If I had been an immigrant applying for this exception," he says, "it never would have been granted."

There's something wrong with the Minneapolis zoning law. Nobody realizes that better than the city government. Written with the best intentions in 1964, and amended nearly 500 times, to the point of cumulative incoherence, the law now serves more to frustrate creativity and renewal than to encourage them. It arbitrarily places land and buildings in categories that bear no relation to the urban reality of the 1990s. In the words of Bob Miller, head of the city's Neighborhood Revitalization Office, "we've set it up so that zoning codes act against our best interest."

And so Minneapolis has embarked on the daunting job of rewriting the entire 350-

Originally published as "The Trouble with Zoning," *Governing*, Vol. 11, No. 5, February, 1998. Published by Congressional Quarterly, Inc., Washington, D.C. Reprinted with permission of the publisher.

page code. It has been working on the project, on and off, since 1989, and it isn't finished yet. But with any luck, a year or so from now it will have a whole new law — one that relaxes the rules and encourages new ideas instead of stifling them irrationally.

There's nothing egregious or particularly unusual about Minneapolis. Cities all over the country have discovered that their comprehensive zoning codes, many of them created in the 1920s and updated in the 1950s and '60s, long ago became more of a problem than a solution. Several big cities — New Orleans, Nashville, Cleveland, Toledo, San Diego — are at various stages of what the chairman of the Minneapolis council zoning committee admits is "the agony" of doing it all over from scratch. San Diego's new law won council approval just this fall. New Orleans is hoping to reach that stage this year.

Meanwhile, a whole group of other cities, realizing the need for change but reluctant to return to square one, are writing a new law on top of the old one, in what they call an "overlay" process. The mistakes of the 1950s and '60s aren't being erased, but the ideas of the 1990s are being placed alongside them. Neighborhoods or commercial districts that want to apply the new rules instead of the old ones will have the legal authority to do that.

In all of these efforts there is a bottom line, and the bottom line can be stated simply enough: Zoning has been rigid where it needs to be flexible. In attempting to prescribe the way communities should look, it has mostly made them look worse. It has sought to separate the residential, commercial and industrial lives of American cities, when it ought to have been looking for ways to mix them together.

"So much of what we have on the books today is 1950s zoning based on 1930s and 1940s ideas," says urban historian Laurence Gerckens. "It's about time things were changed. Zoning is one of the most im-

mutable things in the world once it's on the books, but the largest cities are in life-or-death circumstances. They have to look at zoning."

"You have to take a few chances," agrees Minneapolis' planning director, Paul Farmer, who presided over a similar rewrite a few years ago in Pittsburgh. "There are opportunities out there we don't know about. We want to try to allow good things to happen. Zoning can't make things happen. It can allow them to take place."

In seeking to replace the rigidities of the 1960s with an almost diametrically different approach to urban planning, cities are borrowing heavily from Andres Duany, Peter Calthorpe and the other prominent New Urbanists, the dissident architects and planners who preach a gospel of mixed uses, transit-oriented development, pedestrian-friendly streets and sustainable use of resources. In virtually every case, the planners seem at least conversant with the New Urbanist language, and sympathetic to complaints, such as Duany's, that in an effort to save cities, the previous generation of planners mainly served to hasten the process of urban decay.

If you listen hard enough, you can even hear an occasional good word nowadays for Houston, the city that repudiated zoning altogether and served as the 1960s model of what you get when there are no rules: an unappealing urban goulash of expensive homes next to gas stations next to tool-and-die plants. The new zoning writers are not interested in emulating Houston, but they now readily admit that in trying to avoid it, the last set of laws created something that was quite unappealing in an entirely different way. "I don't think anyone here would say we ought to be like Houston," argues Judy Martin of the Minneapolis Planning Commission, "but there's a perception that the hard and fast rules we put in in 1963 just are not the answer."

The history of zoning in America is a

series of waves. The first wave broke in the late 19th century, when it became clear that unregulated urban development was creating situations not only unattractive but literally nauseating — tar boiling, fat rendering and carcass cremation right in the middle of a residential block. Keeping these activities out of people's backyards was little more than common sense.

It wasn't until 1916 that New York City codified this common sense into a legal pyramid, with residential uses at the top, commercial in the middle and industrial at the bottom, and most land in the city reservable for one kind of use at the expense of others. This approach is still sometimes called "Euclidean zoning," not for geometrical reasons but because the U.S. Supreme Court approved it in the case of *Village of Euclid vs. Ambler* in 1926.

By the end of the 1920s, most large cities in America had a zoning code modeled after New York's. Some went further: Los Angeles invented the distinction between "single-family" and "multi-family" residential zoning, and between "light" and "heavy" industrial uses. But most of these first-wave zoning laws read pretty much alike. In general, they didn't try to dictate what a city ought to look like — they concentrated on giving some stability and order to what was already there and resolving the most serious problems in the least intrusive way possible.

It was after World War II that zoning got more ambitious, and started getting into trouble. In the mid-1950s, most big-city zoning laws were three decades old and clearly in need of updating. That need coincided with the emergence of a generation of planners and local officials who saw themselves making far-reaching decisions about the physical appearance of the city. They assumed that massive urban renewal would be changing the face of older neighborhoods anyway, and thought they could use zoning to determine what these neighborhoods would look like after the bulldozers went

away. "Zoning ordinances in the Sixties," says Paul Farmer, "were built on a presumption of massive clearance and renewal." Sometimes they were created expressly to foster renewal: In some cases, the federal government made grant money contingent on a comprehensive zoning rewrite.

The postwar zoning codes discouraged the old pedestrian-scale Main Street corridors that had flourished before World War II, and encouraged their replacement with strip-mall-like businesses that provided large amounts of parking. They took the idea of segregated uses and pressed it much further than the original versions had dared go. The more distance they could create between residential, commercial and industrial uses, planners reasoned, the easier it would be to dissuade residents from escaping to greener pastures. "When cities did zoning codes in the Sixties," says Minneapolis zoning activist Joni Herren, "they assumed what people wanted was something like a suburban experience. They thought if they gave them that, people wouldn't flee to the suburbs. But it wasn't true."

Segregated-use zoning was generally popular with banks and developers, which saw it as protecting their capital from unwanted neighborhood change. It enabled them to establish separate departments for lending to each of the three categories. But it forced planners into making predictions about the future of land that even the brightest of them couldn't make very intelligently. And it saddled communities with the results of those predictions for decades to come. When a parcel of land was zoned for one sort of use, and demographic changes made it more appropriate for a different use, one frequent result was that it ceased to be used at all.

In many cities, the only way to prevent these zoning codes from stifling renewal altogether has been to amend them on what amounts to a patchwork basis, creating what Stuart Meck of the American

Planning Association likes to call "Post-it" zoning. "It becomes like a zoning code with a bunch of Post-it notes attached to it," Meck says. "When there get to be too many Post-it notes, they decide to redo it."

That is a reasonable description of what has happened in Minneapolis. "It's not a code at all in a coherent sense," admits Blake Graham, the planning supervisor who is conducting the current rewrite. "It was established in a rigid, hierarchical era. You add 500 amendments to that rigid hierarchy, and it becomes very difficult to understand and use."

Sometimes it is so difficult to use that it simply isn't used, and the whole renewal process suffers. "Rezoning a parcel of land is not an easy task," complains Bob Miller of the Neighborhood Revitalization Office. "Zoning can take you out of having viable projects. It can be a real problem in terms of getting anything done at all."

Some of the complexities of the Minneapolis zoning law sound like they were written by Abbott and Costello. Let's say you own an apartment building, and you want to know whether you can build an addition to it. You discover that it is zoned R5A — general residential. You go to the codebook and it defines R5A as being the same as R5, but allowing a little more density. So you look up R5, and the basic meaning of that is a little denser than R4. In the end, you are back to R1, and you still can't make any sense of it. About all you can do is consult the planning department. "The only person who understands this is the zoning inspector," concedes Planning Commissioner Dick Little. "You have to rely on his interpretation."

But as confusing as the residential sections of the Minneapolis law may be, the problems are minor compared with those created by the sections on commercial and industrial property. The code sets up more than 20 categories of commercial use, and imposes tight restrictions on most of them.

If a piece of land is zoned B-2, for example, that means the 1963 planners meant for it to house small-scale "neighborhood" retail units, such as groceries or bakeries, but not wider-ranging "community" retail, such as pet stores, music stores or photography studios.

To read all the restrictions and qualifications, you might think that Minneapolis was a city with a precious supply of choice locations and a corps of tenants desperate to get one and willing to abide by almost any rules. In the 1950s, this may have been true, but in the 1990s, the exact opposite is close to the truth. Most of the city's old Main Street corridors are struggling to keep a semblance of commerce alive at all. The mom-and-pop bakeries departed years ago; these days, a carpet store is often a far more realistic possibility, but the code frequently discourages that, if it does not prohibit it altogether. Everyone involved with the zoning rewrite agrees this is a problem. "In many of these inner-city neighborhoods," say Blake Graham, "any kind of investment would be welcome."

One of the best examples is the community of Eliot Park, on the outskirts of downtown near the Metrodome sports stadium. Eliot Park was a flourishing commercial neighborhood a generation ago, but the combination of stadium congestion and general inner-city blight all but destroyed it in the 1970s. More than 20 percent of its original buildings have been torn down to make parking lots. Fewer than a dozen active retail businesses are currently operating.

Eliot Park could yet be revived by its proximity to downtown, but ideas for renovation of the buildings run up against the obstacle course of the zoning law. There are five abandoned gas stations zoned in a category that prohibits most other uses. Some of the neighborhood civic activists think there might be an opportunity to combine retail units with second-floor apartments, but the perception is that the code makes this difficult. A larger business willing to take a chance on locating in Eliot Park often encounters parking requirements that it cannot easily meet at reasonable cost.

"Minneapolis is like a lot of cities," says Planning Commissioner Judy Martin, "with a lot that's zoned commercial that can't support it. Why not remove the designation and let something happen?"

A few miles farther out from downtown is the wide, flat expanse of Lake Street, which was once home to the city's gaudiest auto showrooms, but fell into decay as the dealers moved to the more distant suburbs. It's a challenge to find uses for many of these buildings, but there are some. Many of the old auto facilities are convertible to light manufacturing, and there is currently a demand for light industrial property in Minneapolis — a much greater demand than there is for storefronts. Just in the past couple of years, Lake Street has attracted computer assembly, packaging, and metal-plating plants. So far, those new businesses have had to come in as exceptions to the general categories of the 1963 law. One of the goals of the current rewrite is to build in such flexibility by law, not by exception.

As in the case of the Frenz garage, the city may be hampering recovery rather than fostering it. "Minneapolis," says Steve Frenz, "has become very unfriendly to industry."

It doesn't take a degree in planning to see what Minneapolis needs: a new zoning code that pays less attention to the formal uses of land and more attention to the effect those uses have on the community. And that is the sort of law that the city is trying to come up with. "We're moving toward a much wider range of uses," says Planning Commissioner Dick Little, "but based on impact."

Under the proposed new code, virtually all small- and medium-scale commercial property would be in the same category, and the vast majority of business establishments would fit in it — a grocery story and a photo studio would no longer be considered different kinds of uses. Residential apartments above the storefronts would not only be permitted, but would carry incentives for the landlord. Light industrial tenants could be combined with commercial or even residential tenants, provided they produce "little or no noise, odor, dust or vibration." The restrictive industrial category would be reserved for the really heavy-duty uses, such as scrap yards, metal mills, and textile and plastics factories. In the view of Pat Scott, the longtime council zoning chairman, "the potential for combinations of things is going to increase."

In many ways, of course, reaching agreement on the larger issues is the easy part. No one in Minneapolis disagrees that segregated-use zoning deserves to end. The really tricky part of the exercise will be rezoning the city, block-by-block and parcel-by-parcel, in accordance with the new mixed-use principles. That could still take years — which is why so few cities, at this late date in their development, are willing to undertake it.

Nevertheless, early signs in Minneapolis are that the creation of a new zoning law, even in intricate detail, does not inevitably mean organized combat among local interest groups. In the 35 years since the last code was written, the politics of Minneapolis land use law has changed enormously. The banks and development companies that dominated the 1963 effort are no longer intense participants: Minneapolis is an aging, built-out city now, and they don't see many lucrative investment opportunities within its borders. "We don't get lobbied by developers," says Planning Commissioner Judy Martin.

The Minneapolis Community Development Association, the city's primary business recruitment office, obviously does care about development. But it also knows that the mega-projects it is interested in are likely to attract sufficient support from the mayor and city council no matter what the zoning code says. How Minneapolis is zoned on a block-by-block level is not the sort of question the MCDA recruiters spend their time worrying about.

In 1998, unlike in 1963, the real players in the zoning rewrite process are the neighborhoods, the places like Eliot Park that perceive their survival to be on the line. It is the neighborhood activists who have tried to put the entire process in their direction. "Neighborhoods get it," says Planning Director Paul Farmer. "They understand it. I don't think they understood it in the Fifties."

The influence of the neighborhoods is evident in Minneapolis in virtually every aspect of the new zoning law. But the clearest evidence of neighborhood power is the creation of overlay districts — residential areas that will be free to write their own standards for the way streets and buildings ought to look, even if the standards differ from what prevails elsewhere in the city. In a sense, the overlay districts represent a step away from the freedom of combination and experiment and back to rules and requirements — except that instead of the auto-influenced rules of the 1960s, they will reflect the New Urbanist values of the 1990s. The overlay districts will encourage mixed uses, but the mixture of those uses will be very much subject to the dictates of community opinion.

A district has already been established, in Linden Hills, an affluent enclave in the southwest corner of the city. According to the new code, the Linden Hills civic association will be free to restrict car traffic, limit curb cuts and off-street parking, require storefronts to come up to the street, and impose numerous other regulations in the interest of creating a desired aesthetic quality to future neighborhood life.

The overlay concept is proving highly attractive these days, not only to cities such as Minneapolis that are rewriting their en-

tire codes but also to others that are trying to avoid the tedious multi-year ordeal. Overlay districts can simply be grafted on to an existing law, and this is what a number of cities are beginning to do. Austin, Texas, amended its zoning code last year to create what it calls "traditional neighborhood districts," requiring a street grid, increased residential density and substantial open space. Fort Collins, Colorado, chose to keep its basic code but create individually designated neighborhood design standards, drafted with the help of the New Urbanist architect Peter Calthorpe. Fort Collins has banned any future gated communities and decreed that all new subdivisions have at least three separate entry points. Orlando, Florida, which went through a full rewrite of its zoning law in the 1980s, changed it substantially this year to make room for an overlay-style concept.

Overlay zoning is an attractive answer for the Austins and Orlandos of the country, fast-growing cities that have been nimble enough to keep pace with changing demand over the past decade. What is doubtful is whether overlays represent much of a solution for the older Frost Belt cities that have been laboring under the burden of entire codes that are 30 to 40 years out of date. Those cities probably need to do something more like what Minneapolis is doing — start over again from scratch, as tedious and time-consuming as that is. And then they need to keep adjusting their laws rather than essentially letting them go for 20 years, as most of them normally do.

"You're never done with this," says zoning historian Laurence Gerckens. "By the time you finish it, the conditions that led you to rewrite the law are eight or nine years old. The city is constantly evolving. Zoning has to be constantly changing. We ought to be quietly making changes every year instead of stockpiling them for a generation."

CHAPTER 27

NASHVILLE INVESTS IN RIVERFRONT TO STIMULATE DOWNTOWN REDEVELOPMENT

Jim Constantine and *Hunter Gee*

Downtown Nashville today is a world apart from that of just ten years ago, when the city center labored through the urban schizophrenia of many downtowns. By day, it was a bustling central business district for banking, commerce, law, and government services. By night, it was a place that people fled for their havens in suburbia. Most windows in the city's office towers fell dark after nightfall. The evening cityscape was punctuated by the blinking of a few neon signs along Lower Broadway, a once-proud boulevard tracing west from the Cumberland River that became weighted with pornography shops, souvenir vendors, and honky-tonks.

Now a series of public/private initiatives has produced a virtual renaissance within the city's former fallow core. Downtown streets are active both night and day as people are being drawn to new offerings of entertainment, major league sports, art, music, and education. While Nashville residents may view the change as having happened overnight, it actually has been a long time in the making.

In the late 1980s, the problems of the declining downtown were being attacked on a number of fronts by a variety of public and private groups, all of which recognized the importance of a strong core to a healthy city. One such effort was an economic revitalization program created to preserve the buildings and provide an economic stimulus for the historic areas of Broadway, Second Avenue, and Printers Alley, which became known collectively as the District.

The idea for the District originated with the Broadway Committee, an ad hoc group consisting of the mayor's office, the Metropolitan Development and Housing Agency (MDHA), the Metro Historical Commission, the Metro Arts Commission, and Historic Nashville, Inc. Using a four-point revitalization plan, based on the Main Street Program of the National Trust for Historic Preservation, the District program sought to:

- Organize property owners into committees that would increase the downtown community's involvement;
- Establish specific design guidelines that would retain the area's character;

Originally published as "Reactivating Downtown," *Urban Land*, Vol. 60, No. 10, October, 2001. Published by the Urban Land Institute, Washington, D.C. Reprinted with permission of the publisher.

- Market vacant properties to business owners and private investors; and
- Restructure the area economically.

Created with an MDHA grant, the program continues today as an active conduit for downtown revitalization.

Initially, confidence was generated by a few pioneer success stories, most notably the preservation of several blocks on historic Second Avenue and the restoration of the Merchant's Hotel, which reopened in 1988 as a restaurant and continues as a popular spot for lunch and dinner. Separately, the Ryman Auditorium, historic home of the Grand Ole Opry, was restored in 1994 and operates today as a world-class music venue and tourist center in the shadow of the 33-story BellSouth Tower, completed the same year.

In many ways, Nashville's renaissance is tied to the city's reorientation to its riverfront. The 68,000-seat, $292 million Adelphia Coliseum, home of the NFL's Tennessee Titans, opened in 1999 on the Cumberland's east bank. Across the river, a battery of public venues has transformed the once-blighted Lower Broadway into a busy center of sports and entertainment for all ages. The new 20,000-seat, $144 million Gaylord Entertainment Center has been the site of performances by the likes of Luciano Pavarotti and Elton John, and also is the home of the Nashville Predators, which in 1998-1999 set the record for highest attendance for a new NHL franchise. Several arts, cultural, and civic projects have opened this year, including the $50 million Frist Center for the Visual Arts, the $37 million Country Music Hall of Fame, and the city's $50 million main library.

"Twenty years ago, Lower Broadway was considered among the seediest spots in the city," notes Gerald Nicely, MDHA director. "The riverfront was a blemish on downtown and, frankly, it was not friendly for pedestrians. By the early '90s, major re-

tail had marched to the suburbs. There were no wholesome entertainment venues or decent restaurants to attract families, professionals, or tourists. The buildings there were historic, but many were in decline.

"We realized that to improve the situation in the District, we needed to do more than save buildings," he adds. "We needed to renew the historical significance and sense of place within the entire area. We wanted people to have a feeling of arrival when they were in the District."

Through MDHA grants, federal tax incentives, and intense marketing and recruiting, investment on Lower Broadway and Second Avenue got a shot in the arm. Restaurants and music venues returned. For example, crowds now swarm Riverfront Park for Dancin' in the District, a weekly free concert series held during summer months.

"It's been amazing to witness the transformation of the area, particularly Lower Broadway, from an unsavory section into a place enjoyed by crowds," says Nicely. "It has positive energy that is evident now on any given night. This is an indication that we can continue to improve the image and outreach of our downtown and make it *the* destination in Nashville. It also enables us to achieve future quality growth that is balanced and complementary to what the community has created."

There is a reason for such optimism. Mayor Bill Purcell was elected last November by a broad coalition in response to his emphasis on the improvement of neighborhoods throughout Davidson County. Purcell subsequently spearheaded the creation of Nashville's first Civic Design Center, which brings together Vanderbilt University, the University of Tennessee, private sector partners, and leaders in historic preservation. The mayor has assigned his new planning director, Rick Bernhardt, a proponent of new urbanism, to work with the local think tank.

Nashville Urban Venture, LLC, a private sector partnership of developers and investors who understand urban revitalization and historic preservation, currently is focused on a way to complement the downtown progress. One ingredient is missing, they say, if Nashville is to experience a true urban renaissance: a strong residential component in an urban mixed-use neighborhood.

About two years ago, Nashville Urban Venture assembled a planning team including Looney Ricks Kiss (LRK), an architecture, planning, research, and interiors firm in Princeton, New Jersey; Manuel Zeitlin, a Nashville-based specialist in restoration architecture; and RPM, Inc., a Nashville-based traffic engineering firm, to focus on a blighted downtown industrial area just south of Nashville's historic Union Station. The area is bounded by Interstate 65 and a large-scale active railroad complex that serves the suburban CSX rail cargo hub in Radnor Yard located miles to the south. Historically known as the Gulch, it is located within a stone's throw of the burgeoning revitalization of the District and the legendary Music Row area.

Topographically, the Gulch is a depression running along the western edge of the old downtown core that has provided a natural lane for rail lines since the 1800s. Over the decades, it housed an asylum and served as a neighborhood for railroad workers and merchants near Union Station. Since the 1950s, the Gulch has become an out-of-sight, out-of-mind place for warehouses, light-industrial manufacturing, and service companies, with a patchwork of low-tax properties and a number of older buildings, some dating to the 1920s.

Working within the concept of an urban plan, the Nashville Urban Venture team designed a $400 million, 30-acre mixed-use area to establish the Gulch as a central component in the fabric of the city's downtown renaissance. The development team visited cities with districts similar to

the Gulch, conducted a regional market analysis based on demographic data to determine profiles for potential residential and commercial users, and conducted qualitative focus-group research and a design charrette to obtain information on designing and renting condominium products. This assessment proved that there was a strong market in Nashville for a neighborhood that was very urban in character and unlike anything that currently existed. As a result, the team devised highly tailored rental apartment, condominium, and retail concepts; entertainment themes; and workplace opportunities in various locations within the Gulch. The plan has evolved through an ongoing process of detailing and refinement with feedback from various prospective users and marketing consultants. In addition, an extensive financial analysis was conducted to demonstrate the viability of the completed project and its positive impact on the economy of the region as well as on city tax revenues.

The resulting master plan for the Gulch emphasizes neighborhood and a sense of community, and features moderate-density residential uses, including affordable housing. It calls for the restoration of old buildings and the development of new structures to provide an array of lofts, flats, rowhouses, and condominiums. High-tech offices with an industrial edge will be located adjacent to and intermixed with the homes, which will have views of the downtown skyline. Parking will be situated along tree-lined streets featuring retail necessities, cafés, and boutiques, all punctuated by green spaces.

Following an initial planning period, Nashville Urban Venture invested private capital in acquiring properties in the area. In the meantime, the group launched the development of specific office properties and apartments, all presently operating or under construction.

Just over a year ago, the team began discussing its plans with MDHA, and after extensive review, they obtained the endorsement of Mayor Purcell. MDHA's board named Nashville Urban Venture as redeveloper of the area this past May, which enabled the group to use tax-increment financing, and the government has indicated its willingness to provide about $7 million in needed infrastructure improvements. To date, Nashville Urban Venture has purchased the 22 acres called for in the plan it submitted to the MDHA and is working with individual property owners to incorporate additional parcels.

"The Gulch will be a centerpiece for individuals, families, and companies moving into Nashville," explains Joe Barker, managing partner of Nashville Urban Venture. "It will appeal to those who have found the urban lifestyle attractive in other cities. The Gulch also will draw residents throughout our region who seek a progressive and distinctive shopping district in a downtown setting, hopefully making a significant dent in reducing suburban sprawl in our region."

According to the plan for the Gulch, there needs to be a balance between glamour and grit, uniting establishments that range from hip to historic. No single architectural style will dominate, and creative design from multiple architects and developers for individual buildings is considered paramount. Established urban design principles will guide the Gulch development, melding Nashville institutions like the Station Inn with new restaurant concepts and entertainment venues. "For many locals and visitors, the Station Inn presently highlights the area and helps define who we are as Nashvillians," comments Bill Barkley, a partner with Armistead Barkley, developers of the Gulch project and partner in Nashville Urban Venture. "It will add a diverse layer of interest to the unique personality of the Gulch."

The skyline of the Gulch is sculpted with three- to five-story buildings, with taller structures placed in carefully planned locations to take advantage of topography and to capture dramatic views of the downtown. Urban residential stoops and more than 120 storefronts are expected to stimulate visual interest along wide sidewalks. Contemporary forms and materials will be juxtaposed with traditional brick warehouses. On-street parking will be provided where possible throughout the district, with parking structures located behind or beside buildings, screened with landscaping, fencing, and/or other structures. Signs will be designed to complement the buildings and not obscure architectural elements or detailing.

At least 20 percent of the residences in the Gulch will be defined as affordable housing, as determined by federal Department of Housing and Urban Development standards. "Diversity is the key to making this project work," stresses Steve Turner, senior partner of Nashville Urban Venture. "We want the Gulch to embody many aspects of a larger city's urban neighborhood, which means different cultural influences in everything from dining to shopping to living. The Gulch is designed to have people interact with one another professionally and socially, forming a vibrant, sustainable community." A network of public green spaces at six locations and plazas will serve as focal points of activity within the Gulch to enhance neighborhood interaction among those who live and work there.

Its location at the center of an active rail complex will allow the Gulch to serve as the hub for commuters to and from the downtown area. Adjacent to the Clement Landport, which serves as a multimodal motor transportation hub, the Gulch is planned to link commuter rail passengers with light-rail transit, buses, and shuttles. A commuter rail line has been proposed along the existing tracks, which could link outlying communities with the Clement Landport.

When completed, the Gulch will offer

350,000 to 400,000 square feet of retail space, 750,000 to one million square feet of office space, 100,000 square feet of hospitality space, and two million square feet of resident space — making it a district accessible by foot or mass transit where people can live, work, shop, and spend leisure time.

"As the Gulch project progresses, I think people may wonder why an urban neighborhood downtown has not existed before now," Barker adds. "In one sense, we are responding to and expanding upon an existing downtown community. In another sense, we are building something completely new that we think will excite present Nashvillians and newcomers."

CHAPTER 28

NEW BEDFORD USES OLD STREET PATTERNS TO REVITALIZE AGING WATERFRONT DISTRICT

David Spillane

The commercial redevelopment of decaying industrial waterfronts is a worldwide trend, with countless examples in cities throughout North America, Europe, and Asia. But for communities that still rely heavily on industrial economies but seek economic diversification through waterfront tourism and recreational uses, the displacement of waterfront industry is neither economically supportable nor political feasible. For these communities, the challenge often is to integrate new commercial and tourism uses with continuing port operations. While merging old and new waterfront functions can present complex planning, development, and political challenges, melding these diverse uses can create authentic and compelling urban environments that represent unique economic and community assets.

Over the last three years, the citizens, elected leaders, and business community in New Bedford, Massachusetts, and the neighboring town of Fairhaven have prepared a blueprint for the future of their waterfront. The plan calls for expanded tourism as well as heavy investment in port industries. Once the capital of the world's whaling industry and later a textiles center, New Bedford, with a population of 100,000, is Massachusetts's fourth-largest city. The downtown's National Register of Historic Districts attest to the 19th century wealth that flowed into the downtown from the seaport. New Bedford is known as one of the nation's major commercial fishing ports, ranking first or second nationally for more than two decades. But by the mid-1990s, vacancy levels within the downtown were growing and there was limited evidence of public or private investment in the downtown or adjacent waterfront. Meanwhile, questions were being raised about the future viability of the fishing and seafood industry.

Though in many ways unique, New Bedford's experience illuminates the challenges and opportunities that face other communities seeking economic diversification from their waterfronts as they strive to hold onto key industrial assets. Several factors are significant:

• the critical role of a master plan;
• the opportunity for distinctive place mak-

Originally published as "Creative Connections," *Urban Land*, Vol. 59, Nos. 11/12, November/December, 2000. Published by the Urban Land Institute, Washington, D.C. Reprinted with permission of the publisher.

ing, where history, industry, and tourism meet;

- the significant economic potential of low-cost waterfront initiatives, such as the encouragement of tourism-oriented excursion boating services and the use of waterfront open areas for special events and festivals;
- the need for public investment and public sector leadership; and
- the importance of creative thinking in addressing environmental liabilities in a way that promotes environmental restoration and economic development.

After three years of sustained public effort to shape a master plan, New Bedford is ready to transform its waterfront with a wave of new initiatives. Combined public and private sector investments in excess of $250 million are anticipated over the next five years. Projects that were only dreams a few years ago are now being funded and built. Public optimism is at an all-time high — and the private sector, long shy of New Bedford's struggling downtown and waterfront, is giving the city a second look. The recently completed 150,000-square-foot Compass Bank headquarters in the downtown is the largest private investment in a decade.

The signature project of this first wave of waterfront development is the transformation of Route 18, an urban renewal-era highway that in the 1970s severed the connection between downtown and the waterfront. Using combined federal and state funding of $15 million secured in 1998, the project will reestablish the network of streets that once connected downtown and the waterfront, removing the barrier that for three decades has left downtown stranded like a beached whale — at significant cost to the local economy. The New Bedford Whaling National Historical Park, one of the nation's newest parks, is up and running, introducing New Bedford's diverse history and wa-

terfront to a national audience. Cruiseship service was initiated to New Bedford in 1999, establishing it as a port of call on trips to more established tourist destinations such as Martha's Vineyard and Nantucket. The proposed New Bedford Aquarium, no more than a fantasy in 1996, has successfully passed some key fundraising thresholds and secured site control, allowing transformation of a hulking waterfront power station into a destination attraction. The number of annual visitors is projected to be about one million. Hotel development also is being advanced, with the construction of a 150-room hotel on a publicly owned downtown site. Recently established water taxi and launch service between New Bedford and Fairhaven connects a community with more than 900 recreational boating slips to New Bedford's National Park area, its Whaling Museum, restaurants, and other attractions.

The fishing industry is benefiting from recently completed pier improvements that are reducing wear and tear on the 265-vessel fleet. New Bedford's strength as a national and international seafood industry center has been reinforced by major seafood processing firms that are planning to expand substantially and by the influx of new firms attracted to the city's newly established waterfront industrial park. A new $4 million roll-on, roll-off freight ferry terminal, first proposed in 1997, has opened for business to Martha's Vineyard, with future service planned to Nantucket and other ports.

A full-scale, $120 million harbor cleanup project is beginning a decade-long implementation phase under the jurisdiction of the U.S. Environmental Protection Agency (EPA) and the Army Corps of Engineers (ACOE), setting the stage for a subsequent restoration of the harbor's natural environment. The state is extending Boston's commuter rail network to New Bedford with a terminal to be developed in the harbor area. Emboldened by the success of these efforts, the city is evaluating the relocation of the major cross-harbor bridge in conjunction with substantial harbor dredging. It is a project that has the potential to reconfigure the entire harbor area and significantly expand the port's capacity.

Master plans are especially important for communities seeking to combine tourism with industry in waterfront settings. The visions, values, and perspectives of downtown business owners, historic preservationists, developers, and those in the fishing industry are inevitably different; mutual trust is never a given, and suspicions often are rife. "An essential aspect of the master plan is to negotiate formal agreement among these groups," says Matthew Thomas, city development attorney and redevelopment authority member who served as the city's point person on its harbor master plan effort.

An overarching "vision" that can be supported by all constituencies is crucial. In New Bedford, Tony Souza, executive director of the Waterfront Historic Area League (WHALE) and chair of the broadly representative 12-member Harbor Master Plan Committee, articulated a theme that was central to securing consensus: the fishing industry would be "the star of the show." This was a strong unifying concept that illustrated the industry's importance both to tourism — as reflected in the themes of the national park and the proposed aquarium — and to seafood processing and other port industries.

While New Bedford and Fairhaven formally began the master plan process in late 1997 with the selection of a consulting team, years of community discussions had in many cases begun to define the projects that ultimately would be integrated into the formal plan. Through the early and mid-1990s, WHALE and the city's cultural institutions and nonprofit groups had successfully made the case to establish the national park and had led a series of effective community visioning efforts focused on the waterfront.

With the 1997 election of New Bedford mayor Frederick Kalisz, Jr., the city administration made major waterfront renewal a top priority, and it has provided political leadership in the master plan process.

New Bedford's attraction to visitors is based on the appeal of its working waterfront, which is occupied for the most part by the fishing fleet. Relocating it to make way for tourism-oriented uses was never seriously considered. As Souza recently told an *Architecture-Boston* roundtable discussion: "We're not trying to create something we're not. We are a seaport. And if tourism plays a role in that, it will be because people are attracted to what we are." The master plan mixes tourism and port industry along the downtown waterfront, leaving the fishing fleet untouched, but along the edges of the piers it creates a series of flexible open areas that can be used for port industry or for public waterfront festivals. A central terminal for commercial charter and excursion boats and the historic schooner *Ernestina* will be created to allow visitors not only to look at the harbor but also to experience it firsthand by traveling out into Buzzards Bay. Two new waterfront restaurants will open in this area. And, off to the side, the aquarium will be linked to downtown and the piers by a promenade that provides views of the fishing fleet but leaves the working piers undisturbed by pedestrian traffic. A redesigned Route 18 will reestablish a pedestrian connection to the downtown.

Mixing uses in this way creates significant challenges. Aquarium developers initially worried that odors from seafood processing businesses or fishing boats would drive off tourists. Fishermen worried that tourists swarming to a new waterfront aquarium would overrun their docks and make daily tasks of vessel maintenance and gear repair all but impossible. But with careful planning, many potential problems have been avoided. On the waterfront, National Park Service rangers tell tourists the story of whaling within the gritty real-world setting of an active contemporary fishing fleet. The visitors already may be familiar with the vibrancy of the New Bedford working aterfront, first immortalized in Herman Melville's *Moby-Dick*. John Pilzecher, superintendent of the New Bedford Whaling National Historical Park, believes that this setting provides "an ideal backdrop for telling the story of the city's history and cultural heritage."

The $90 million New Bedford Aquarium will occupy the vast ComElectric power plant, which sits on a 37-acre waterfront property adjacent to the downtown. The evolution of the project, initially conceived as a blockbuster visitor attraction, increasingly has been influenced by New Bedford's unique characteristics as a seaport community. Annual economic impacts of $34 million are projected. Weathering early fundraising difficulties, the not-for-profit Aquarium Corporation recently secured a long-term lease on the site. Aquarium developers also have formed strategic alliances with Boston's New England aquarium 60 miles to the north. Although some initially questioned the marketability of two similar attractions, this cooperative effort is bringing substantial expertise to the aquarium development process and creating the basis for complementary products. The aquarium's potential to contribute to the New Bedford community is further enhanced by strong links with the Marine Sciences Department at the University of Massachusetts at Dartmouth, located five miles from the waterfront.

While projects like the aquarium could represent daunting fundraising challenges for most waterfront communities, Frank Mahady, president of FXM Associates, a Mattapoisett, Massachusetts-based economic consulting firm that focuses on waterfronts, suggests that lower-budget projects sometimes are more feasible and similarly profitable. "The potential eco-nomic benefit of other more modest projects is often severely underestimated." With very limited investment, New Bedford is expanding the use of its waterfront open areas on State Pier for seasonal events and festivals. This initiative will broaden an already successful program of festivals — the most significant of which is Summerfest, an annual event that attracts more than 100,000 visitors. This past August, an estimated 50,000 people came to State Pier to see the Russian tall ship *Kruzenshtern*.

Commercial fishing, charter, and excursion boats operating out of the waterfront make for picturesque scenery but even better economics, says Mahady, who notes that in the Cape Cod town of Provincetown, "Commercial whale-watch excursions have a greater economic impact than the entire cruise ship industry in all ports in the North Atlantic." Provincetown draws more than 200,000 visitors, who typically spend money on meals, gifts, and lodging, in addition to their water expedition. Mahady cites as another example the small waterfront community of Onset, Massachusetts, where "a 65-foot vessel doing Cape Cod Canal cruises draws 40,000 visitors, who spend more locally than would visitors to a typical 150-room hotel." The market for these services is largely untapped, he adds, and the potential for growth is substantial — particularly where vessel operators benefit from the critical mass associated with a central location and shared advertising costs.

While a focus on new uses attracts the most attention in public planning efforts, the needs of economically important traditional port industries can be inadvertently neglected. Fishermen, seafood processors, and other port industry groups often make effective advocates for their case when faced by perceived threats, but the strong individualism and competitive spirit that characterize these groups means that collaborative planning around future needs often is difficult.

Another problem in working with these industries is the absence of basic data on industry conditions. As the master plan process began in New Bedford, little data existed about the formal contribution of the fishing and seafood industry to the city's economy. Concerns were openly expressed about the future viability of the fishing and processing industries. But the facts, gleaned through in-depth interviews with individual processors and business owners, were illuminating. Despite a reduction in the local fishing catch associated with federally mandated restrictions aimed at fisheries conservation, processors were working at full capacity, and many were seeking expanded premises and had active reinvestment plans. Processors increasingly saw themselves as wholesalers and distributors, meeting the needs of individual corporate customers and supermarket chains. Over the years, processors had successfully diversified their sources for fish and many had agreements in place with South American, European, and Asian suppliers. The New Bedford seafood industry now has annual sales estimated at an impressive $900 million. The real challenge to the industry was not the supply of fish, but the supply of developable land needed to fuel the industry's growth and expansion.

With data in hand justifying the economic need to secure expansion space for harbor industries, the city acted quickly to acquire and subdivide Standard Times Field, an undeveloped 25-acre waterfront parcel, for seafood processing and other associated waterfront industrial uses. Because processors who required 10,000- to 40,000-square-foot structures were not in a position to acquire and subdivide such a large parcel, the city purchased the property to ensure that it would be dedicated to these strategically important harbor industries.

Resolving issues associated with environmental contamination is a constant challenge in urban waterfront development. In the strongest real estate markets, environ-

mental remediation often can be absorbed as part of the overall development cost, but in communities such as New Bedford, public funding is essential. When used creatively, public funding for remediation can facilitate reuse, as in the case of New Bedford's harbor cleanup.

The harbor was designated a federal Superfund site in 1983. As a result of settlements with state and federal governments in 1991 and 1992, manufacturers responsible for contaminating the harbor paid $100 million into a fund for its remediation and restoration. Of the $100 million settlement, $21 million has been dedicated to restoring the harbor environment. While many of the projects have focused on harbor habitat restoration, $3.3 million has been set aside for the New Bedford Aquarium and other University of Massachusetts marine science and technology proposals.

Cleanup dredging now progressing under the jurisdiction of the EPA and ACOE will remove approximately 440,000 cubic yards of contaminated sediments from the harbor and pave the way — literally — for developing a new harbor marine terminal. The sediments will be encapsulated and paved over to create new harbor land for a new marine terminal. The terminal will be developed at a modest incremental cost over the actual cleanup cost and will substantially increase the harbor's capacity to support waterside activity.

New Bedford has worked closely with state officials to ensure that its master plan is consistent with state regulations governing waterfront development, especially the stringent regulations that are applicable to port projects. State officials have supported the planning effort and have offered creative ideas on how best to advance port development through the complex regulatory process.

Outside of major cities or strong real estate markets, the high infrastructure costs associated with waterfront development projects rarely are justifiable to developers on a project-by-project basis. Consequently, renewal projects in smaller communities generally can succeed only with public support. These public costs can be justified through the significant off-site community and economic benefits derived from waterfront redevelopment. New Bedford's success in reshaping its waterfront is based on a strategy of targeting projects that can take advantage of state and federal funding and of making creative use of environmental cleanup funding to serve multiple goals. Waterfront tourism and recreation are being promoted to trigger revitalization of the adjacent downtown as the community continues to invest in its traditional port industries. Strategic public investments have repositioned the waterfront and adjacent downtown so that they now are experiencing renewed investment interest from the private sector.

CHAPTER 29

NEWARK'S PERFORMING ARTS CENTER CREATES REBIRTH OF DOWNTOWN

Marilyn J. Taylor

The much anticipated $180 million New Jersey Performing Arts Center (NJPAC) opened in downtown Newark last October. The red-brick complex is "an ambitious symbol of Newark's pride," proclaimed the *New York Times*, which described its 2,750-seat Prudential Hall as "breathtakingly gorgeous." Other facilities include the 514-seat Victoria Theater, rehearsal space, restaurants and bars, and community rooms.

NJPAC, however, is more than a much-applauded cultural center that hosts opera, symphony orchestras, dance troupes, and jazz performances. Unlike some stand-alone, megalithic cultural centers, NJPAC both merges into and enlivens the surrounding cityscape. The front facade includes a three-story-tall glass wall that allows pedestrians to look into the gleaming lobby and offers concert goers a view out onto historic Military Park (the city's original commons) and the downtown skyline, forging a strong visual connection to the rest of the city.

Of equal importance, NJPAC does not have the subterranean garage typical of many urban performing arts centers, which turns concert going into a drive-in/drive-out experience and does little to support the surrounding neighborhood. Instead, concert goers park their cars in the city-renovated, 1,100-car garage beneath Military Park, take an escalator or elevator to street level, and then cross Centre Street to NJPAC, adding crowds, movement, and energy to the immediate neighborhood.

While NJPAC's design is one factor in downtown Newark's rebirth, its location is another. The center occupies a strategic downtown site at the northern end of Military Park, one block east of once-bustling Broad Street and one block west of the Passaic River waterfront. The city has designated a 20-square-block area along the Broad Street corridor (from NJPAC and Military Park to the Newark Museum and Newark Public Library on Washington Park) as a downtown arts district.

The city also hopes that NJPAC will draw attention and provide a strong link to the redevelopment of the nearby Passaic River waterfront, where a motley collection of warehouses and industrial buildings recently was cleared for a planned riverfront es-

Originally published as "Newark Turns the Corner," *Urban Land*, Vol. 57, No. 2, February, 1998. Published by the Urban Land Institute, Washington, D.C. Reprinted with permission of the publisher.

planade and hoped-for mixed-use development, including a festival marketplace.

Newark civic leaders firmly believe that NJPAC will help lead downtown and the entire city to a more prosperous future. Mayor Sharpe James has called the NJPAC "a proud beginning" that will have a "ripple effect on development." NJPAC president Lawrence P. Goldman declared, "We mean to be the atom that starts the chain reaction."

The Tarnished Crown

Because of its troubles in recent decades, many people have forgotten that Newark was New Jersey's crown jewel from the 18th century into the mid–20th century. At the end of World War II, Newark was a dynamic city of more than 450,000 residents. Its then-thriving economy was solidly based on banking, insurance, shipbuilding, and particularly manufacturing. The crossroads of Market and Broad streets, the center of the downtown shopping district, reportedly was the third-busiest intersection in the world.

In the 1950s and 1960s, Newark began a several-decades-long decline. Middle-class residents moved to newer homes in nearby suburbs. One by one the downtown department stores, beset by competition from suburban shopping malls, closed their doors forever. Most seriously, the city's employment base was ravaged. Between 1960 and 1995, Newark lost three-quarters of its manufacturing jobs and half its private sector employment.

Poverty, despair, and an often-corrupt municipal government helped fuel the infamous 1967 riots, which left 26 people dead and hundreds of buildings destroyed by fire. Afterward, Newark became a national symbol of the country's urban problems, which only accelerated its decline. In 1977, then-Mayor Kenneth Gibson told a *New York Times* reporter: "Wherever America's cities are going, Newark will get there first."

A number of well-intentioned but ill-planned redevelopment programs in the 1970s and 1980s failed to turn downtown Newark around. For example, the four-building, high-rise Gateway Center, which totals more than two million square feet of office space, features a network of pedestrian bridges that connect the buildings to each other and nearby Pennsylvania Station. Designed to offer white-collar workers a sense of security in a supposedly hostile downtown, these bridges perpetuate a harmful separation of office and street life. Thousands of people who commute to downtown Newark every day rarely (if ever) "touch" the streets, thereby diminishing downtown retail activity, movement, and vibrance.

Enviable Assets

Newark also enjoys some important strengths, which are facilitating its turnaround. They include:

Accessibility. Newark is accessible by virtually all modes of travel — airplane, ship, train, bus, trolley, truck, and car. Newark Airport, just one mile from downtown, is the ninth-busiest airport in the United States, having served an estimated 30 million passengers last year. The port of Newark is the second-largest shipping container port in the country and the center of the nation's largest free-trade zone.

Corporate and Institutional Commitment. A number of Newark-based corporations and government agencies — such as Bell Atlantic, Blue Cross and Blue Shield of New Jersey, New Jersey Transit, Prudential Insurance, and Public Service Electric & Gas — have kept the downtown core alive with jobs, economic development initiatives, and generous charitable contributions. Public Service Electric & Gas (PSE&G)

maintains an active economic development office, staffed by relocation specialists who provide information about vacant land and buildings, current commercial lease rates, and incentive programs to companies interested in relocating to or expanding in Newark. Prudential Insurance, which has been headquartered in Newark since its founding in 1875, contributed $6.5 million to NJPAC, its largest charitable gift ever.

College Town. Just north and west of downtown are four rapidly growing institutions of higher learning: Essex Community College, the New Jersey Institute of Technology, the New Jersey School of Medicine and Dentistry, and Rutgers University's Newark campus. The Seton Hall Law School has its own downtown tower. Together, these five institutions serve approximately 40,000 part-time and full-time students, the equivalent of a major state university. To accommodate growing numbers of students and programs, they are building new facilities. Last year, for example, Rutgers University started construction on a $49 million law school in downtown Newark.

Stable, Growing Neighborhoods. The heavily Portuguese Ironbound district, two blocks east of downtown's busy Pennsylvania Station, is widely known for its restaurants, bakeries, and shops. More significant, this district is a thriving big-city community that is growing in population and expanding in size. Every year, dozens of new homes, ranging in size from one- to four-family units, are built on former industrial land at the neighborhood's edges. The homes, which are privately financed and built, benefit from various government measures, such as partial tax abatements.

A Pedestrian-Scale Downtown Core. Although the big department stores have closed, their massive buildings still stand along Market and Broad streets, waiting for imaginative adaptive use projects that will contribute to Newark's community, commercial, and cultural life; moreover, the downtown streetscape, though frayed and rundown in many places, largely escaped ill-conceived redevelopment initiatives. Gateway Center, with its isolating pedestrian bridges, was not duplicated elsewhere. The blocks around Military Park and Washington Park, which contain some extraordinary pre–World War II buildings and the new NJPAC, have the potential, many believe, to become one of the handsomest and most successful downtown districts on the East Coast.

Rediscovering Newark

In recent years more and more New Jerseyans, corporations, and real estate investors have recognized Newark's assets and its potential for recovery. Although NJPAC was built as a catalyst for redevelopment, downtown Newark had actually turned the corner *before* the center's opening.

"Newark suffers from a perception that's two years behind the reality," says Arthur R. Stern, chairman and CEO of Cogswell Realty Group LLC of New York, which recently acquired several of Newark's pre–World War II office towers. "If people don't work there, they just don't understand the vitality — and particularly the potential vitality — of Newark's central business district."

Newark boosters point to several encouraging events and trends as solid evidence of the city's turnaround. More than a decade ago, Blue Cross and Blue Shield of New Jersey relocated its corporate headquarters from downtown Newark to suburban Florham Park. In 1993, the insurer left Florham Park and moved into downtown Newark's 18-story Three Penn Plaza, bringing 2,500 jobs back to the city. Other well-known companies that have offices in downtown Newark are increasing their employment in the city. Prudential Insurance has moved several thousand suburban employees to its downtown buildings. By the end of 1997, more than 6,700 Prudential employees worked in downtown Newark, more than double the total a few years ago.

Between 1990 and 1992, three new high-rise office buildings totaling 1.8 million square feet were completed near Pennsylvania Station. Today, the vacancy rate for the cluster of Class A office space around Pennsylvania Station is an extraordinary three percent. In addition, renovation projects have transformed some long-empty or decrepit downtown buildings. Following a $6.25 million renovation, the New Jersey Historical Society moved into the former Essex Club, which was built in 1926 on Park Place, overlooks Military Park, and is one block from NJPAC. The elegant Firemen's Insurance Company building, built in 1922 on Park Place, has been renovated by the Berger Organization into what are now fully leased modern offices. In 1996, the Essex County Improvement Authority helped transform the former Gibraltar Building, built in 1926 on Halsey Street, into the Wilentz Justice Complex, which provides courtroom space and offices for Essex County.

Housing construction has been another key element in Newark's recovery. Hundreds of apartments for low-income residents have been constructed with public assistance. A sizable number of these are townhouse-style units, which have replaced some of Newark's notorious highrise public housing projects. Privately financed moderate- to middle-income apartments, condominiums, and townhouses make up more than 1,000 additional new residential units.

Newark's largest residential project is the 1,150-unit Society Hill community, built in the late 1980s and early 1990s on a 45-acre University Heights site that was the epicenter of the 1967 riots. Throughout the 1970s and early 1980s, this neighborhood consisted of trash-strewn vacant lots and run-down or boarded-up buildings blighting the hill between the central business district and University Heights. In the mid-1980s, K. Hovnanian Companies, located in Red Bank, New Jersey, entered into a public/private partnership with the city to build 1,150 townhouse-style units. Approximately 175 units, to be scattered throughout the development, were to be sold to qualified low- and moderate-income buyers.

Offering affordably priced new housing convenient to jobs in downtown Newark and the educational institutions at University Heights, Society Hill sold its first 40 homes from 1986 to 1987 without advertising. In August 1988, the next section of 168 homes opened for sale from plans and sold out within eight hours. As more phases of Society Hill sold out, increasingly affluent buyers, many of whom had abandoned Newark for the suburbs, were attracted to Society Hill. To accommodate these buyers, larger, amenity-filled homes were built in the later phases. Today, all 1,150 units have been completed and sold.

Property values have risen in the area surrounding Society Hill for the first time in decades. The project helped create a "critical consumer mass" that led to the opening nearby of Newark's first full-service supermarket in more than 25 years and a Hovnanian-built 110,000-square-foot shopping center with a second supermarket. Honored by the U.S. Department of Housing and Urban Development, the National Association of Home Builders, Harvard University, and others, Society Hill has become an inner-city laboratory for civic leaders, academics, and real estate developers who want to rejuvenate their older cities.

Turnaround Time

The 1990s may well be remembered as Newark's turnaround decade. At the new 40-acre, $270 million University Heights

Science Park just outside downtown, university-based high-tech research and development will be conducted and applied in the Newark business community. One large research lab and the New Jersey Institute of Technology's Enterprise Development Center for start-up companies already are open there, and construction of a third facility will begin shortly. Late last year, the state of New Jersey announced funding for a $78 million International Center for Public Health, which is scheduled to open at Science Park in 2000.

In the heart of downtown Newark, the former Macy's department store, a 1.2 million-square-foot building that anchored the southern end of the Broad and Haley streets retail corridor, is being converted into a mixed-use complex with a small department store, offices, warehouse space, and parking. An investment group headed by Samuel J. Jemal in New York City is putting $1.5 million into the project, while the state and several banks are making $3.3 million in low-interest loans.

At Military Park, the Berger Organizations is renovating the long-empty, 400,000-square-foot Hahnes department store, built in 1901 on Broad Street, which anchored the northern end of the Broad Street retail corridor, only four blocks from Macy's. The first phase, due to be completed in May, includes an 1,100-car garage, first-floor retail, office space, and a restored facade. The second phase of renovation will involve space that has 18- to 22-foot ceilings and will become offices, loft-style apartments, or both. While the building's lower three floors, which formerly contained a piano store, concert hall, and piano factory, are quite large, its fourth to 16th floors are each only 3,000 square feet. "We haven't formulated any specific plans for reuse yet, although the tower floors lend themselves to small-footprint offices or apartments," says chairman Miles Berger.

Of critical importance to Newark's future is the late Harry Helmsley's $5 billion real estate empire, which now is being liquidated. Its four downtown Newark office towers were put up for sale last year. Throughout the 1950s and 1960s, these four buildings, particularly the 34-story National Newark & Essex Building, built in 1930 on Broad Street, were some of Newark's proudest office towers. By last year the buildings, which are largely vacant, had "fallen into disrepair, victims of age and neglect," reported Newark's *Star-Ledger*. Now, bold investors are buying what the newspaper described as "Helmsley's tattered real estate jewels."

Last October, a trio of investors purchased 24 Commerce Street, which was built in 1926. They plan to invest more than $4 million in upgrading the 21-story tower. "We had an opportunity to buy a building very inexpensively and put a lot of sweat equity into it," partner Christian Benedetto told the *Star-Ledger* shortly after the sale. "The building was neglected for a number of years. Our plan is to modernize."

In December, Cogswell Realty Group purchased 744 Broad Street which was built in 1930 for an estimated $6 million, with the backing of an affiliate of Lehman Brothers, the Wall Street investment banking firm. "We believe that after many false starts, Newark finally has turned the corner, said Peter Marsh, chief operating officer of the investment group, shortly after the sale. Cogswell will spend an additional $45 million to renovate the 34-story, 650,000-square-foot building into B-plus or A-minus space. The renovation program includes all-new electrical and HVAC systems, new elevators, the repointing and refinishing of the facade, new windows, the construction of a new loading dock and freight entrance, the restoration of the lobby to its original art deco appearance, and floodlights. "The building will be a Newark landmark again," says Stern.

Upon completion of the renovation,

Cogswell Realty will target three different markets to fill the structure, according to Stern. The ground floor will be retail and restaurant space. The building's third to 13th floors, which have 29,000-square-foot floor plates, and the 14th to 22nd floors, which have 16,000-square-foot floor plates, will be marketed to corporate users. Finally, the 23rd to 34th floors, which have 6,000-square-foot floor plates, will be marketed to law firms that want a full-floor identity and proximity to the courts.

Last month, Cogswell Realty purchased 1180 Raymond Boulevard, built in 1930, from the Helmsley estate. This now-vacant, 35-story, 400,000-square-foot building, which stands diagonally across Broad Street from the 744 Broad Street tower, overlooks Military Park. The city owns the underlying land, and Cogswell intends to negotiate an extension of ground lease. "We don't foresee a renovation into office space, like the nearby 744 Broad Street building, or a market for one million square feet of high-end office product in this area right now," says Stern. "Instead, we foresee a complementary use such as a hotel or some type of residential use, possibly connected with one of the nearby hospitals or universities. We also want a large retail component on the ground floor."

Newark boosters and other downtown property owners are pleased with the quick sale of these important but long-neglected office buildings. "These are buildings that we thought would be written off," says Alfred Faiella, executive director of the Newark Economic Development Corporation. Now, it is believed that these renovated buildings will generate new jobs, tax revenues, and excitement for the city.

A number of proposed developments also are in the works. Last December, a partnership of the city of Newark, Essex County, and the Essex County Improvement Authority announced plans to build a $22 million baseball and multipurpose stadium on a riverfront site just north of NJPAC. Located on an 11-acre parcel, this complex will serve the Newark Bears minor-league baseball team, and it will be accessible by rail, public transit, and highway. In addition, this year work will begin on the $75 million Joseph G. Minish Riverfront Park, which runs along the western side of the Passaic River in Newark. This two-mile-long park, which will include a 40-foot-wide riverfront promenade, will link the new stadium and NJPAC at the northern end of downtown Newark with Pennsylvania Station and the Ironbound District.

Ongoing Challenges

Despite the renewed optimism about Newark's future, the city struggles with some serious liabilities: a declining but still intimidating crime rate, a public school system that had to be taken over by the state, real estate tax assessments that have not been updated in four decades, and a shortage of entry-level jobs for young people, among others.

Equally troubling, the city is not attracting large-scale commercial real estate development, even with the tight occupancy rate in Class A office buildings near Pennsylvania Station. "Nobody is building anything new," reported the December 7, 1997 *Star-Ledger.* "No one builds on spec in Newark." Samuel Crane, head of the Newark-based Regional Business Partnership, concurs: "You are going to see investments in Newark, but they will be specific, not speculative."

Perhaps the greatest impediment to revitalizing Newark is the lack of connection between important but isolated clusters of activity. NJPAC is a step in the right direction because it provides a critical link among Military Park, Broad Street, and the Passaic River waterfront. Other clusters must be connected to create a more unified city, however. The four large colleges at University Heights, for example, must forge stronger physical links (including safe, accessible pedestrian routes and new buildings to fill now-vacant lots) to become a single academic community. At the same time, these colleges must forge stronger physical connections with the nearby downtown. At present, there are several blocks of vacant lots, half-empty buildings, and ill-maintained stores that separate what should be two mutually supporting and enlivening activity centers.

Like most U.S. cities, Newark has experienced dramatic ups and downs throughout the 20th century. Now, like many once-depressed cities across the nation, Newark is on the upswing again. "There are indeed more signs of hope for the future in Newark than there have been for the last 30 years," declared the *Washington Post* last year.

CHAPTER 30

OAKLAND USES TRANSIT IMPROVEMENTS TO REVIVE INNER-CITY NEIGHBORHOOD

Ernesto M. Vasquez

In the Fruitvale District of Oakland, California, plans are afoot to transform the worn-out, overlooked neighborhood into a vibrant, bustling, mixed-use multicultural center. Now underway and set for completion next year, the revitalization of Fruitvale is being spearheaded by Arabella Martinez, CEO of the Unity Council, a local community development corporation. "I want to infuse Fruitvale's established ethnic identity with a new social and economic vitality," she says. "I envision a complete connection among transportation and land use strategies and economic development for this community." To that end, the private/public partnership formed to revitalize Fruitvale has developed a plan that celebrates Fruitvale's ethnic diversity in a contemporary setting that connects community, retail, commercial, residential, and transit uses — despite the many obstacles.

At first glance, the Fruitvale neighborhood seems riddled with near-empty streets, vacant and ruined buildings, and dark, uninviting sidewalks that connect the community to the Bay Area Rapid Transit system (BART). It is surprising to note that more

than 30,000 commuters a day travel on BART to and from work at the Fruitvale station; however, they do not stroll into the uninviting neighborhood for a bite to eat or to pick up last-minute groceries from the market.

Almost a century ago, the Fruitvale District, considered Oakland's second downtown, was renowned for its extensive orchards, mansions, and convenient streetcar transportation. The business sector thrived in Fruitvale, even attracting retail giant Montgomery Ward in 1923. During World War II, thousands of jobs were created in the district, attracting an influx of African American and Hispanic workers, but when the war ended, the factories shut down and local businesses suffered. At the same time, new freeways and subsidized mortgages encouraged more affluent residents to move out of Fruitvale into the suburbs.

By the 1960s, the district's malaise was undeniable. What few residents remained lived in deteriorating houses or apartments while community parks and facilities went unattended. Concerned residents wanted

Originally published as "Bearing Fruit," *Urban Land*, Vol. 59, No. 7, July, 2000. Published by the Urban Land Institute, Washington, D.C. Reprinted with permission of the publisher.

change. In 1989, Martinez began to explore ways to revitalize Fruitvale in an effort to regain some of its past luster.

In 1993, a team of graduate students from the University of California at Berkeley's Oakland Metropolitan Forum performed a study of water use in Fruitvale. The students also devised various ideas for improvements in Fruitvale, including creating a pedestrian link from the BART station to the area's primary shopping/business district on International Boulevard, implementing a building improvement program, increasing signage, and replacing store awnings. Martinez credits the students' report with being the initial template for Fruitvale's redevelopment strategy.

Although funding to complete the changes was not available at the time, the Unity Council began to devise a strategy for forming a new neighborhood. When BART proposed building a stand-alone parking structure on a ten-acre site in Fruitvale that, as proposed, would further separate commuters from the district, the Unity Council took action. Many residents were already dissatisfied because the BART station produced so little pedestrian traffic in the neighborhood, and the community did not want another parking lot. The Unity Council quickly informed local residents of BART's plan, encouraging them to work together to propose other options. Community discussions prompted a number of alternative ideas for the ten-acre parcel, and recognizing the need for community-friendly transportation, BART joined in the efforts. According to Manuela Silva, executive director of Fruitvale Transit Corporation, the implementation arm of the Unity Council, the Unity Council, in partnership with BART, began to develop a plan that included a community center, a shopping area, and a public plaza, linking pedestrians and commuters to the surrounding shopping and business district.

The Benefits of Smart Growth

Fruitvale's redevelopment plan includes 33,000 square feet of retail/restaurant space, 40,000 square feet for a health clinic, 40,000 square feet for offices, a 12,000-square-foot community resource center, a 5,550-square-foot library, and 47 residential lofts. A number of smart growth design and land use concepts have been adopted in designing the project, including infill, mixed-use, and high-density development; concentration of development along rail transit corridors; and pedestrian-oriented retail development. Reducing pollution, traffic congestion, and reliance on automobiles while elaborating on those elements of the city grid that are applicable to development is central to these concepts. Redeveloping an urban infill location will effectively increase density within the neighborhood. The challenge is to use the underused and undervalued land in an adequate and cost-effective manner.

While the project is planned to include commercial, residential, and retail uses, it also will include community facilities such as a health care center, a child-care center, a seniors' center, and a library. The placement of these community facilities within the main plaza should encourage residents of all ages to interact while providing much-needed services. Buildings will house retail stores on the first level, community facilities on the second level, and loft housing on the third level. A central element of the project is a seniors' housing facility called Las Bougainvilleas. Located on land donated by the city of Oakland, the 68-unit housing complex funded by the U.S. Department of Housing and Urban Development (HUD) provides much-needed seniors' and affordable housing in Oakland. The three- and four-story buildings surrounded by fountains, benches, gardens, and landscaping are a welcome addition to the neighborhood. Underground parking and balconies, not generally seen in low-income facilities, optimize use of space. Another key component of Fruitvale will be La Clinica de la Raza's new headquarters, a 40,000-square-foot, state-of-the-art health facility. Serving more than 70,000 patients a year, the facility will have the space to serve a growing public, and it will benefit from its proximity to the BART station and nine bus lines. Fruitvale also will feature 47 live/work loft units. The affordable units are subsidized by a below-market-rate loan from the city of Oakland and will rent for $750 to $950. Market units will rent for approximately $1,150 to $1,550.

One of the early steps in reinventing Fruitvale's image was changing the area's name to Fruitvale Transit Village. According to Silva, the transit village moniker denotes opportunities to link transit to communities and to promote integrated neighborhoods that meet consumer needs for retail stores, housing, and child care. If clusters are designed to complement one another, residents and commuters can benefit from the convenience of Fruitvale's multiple services.

Initially, however, not even the new name convinced shopowners on International Boulevard — most of whom perceived the redevelopment as a hindrance to their businesses — of the project's advantages. Several community forums ensued with the Unity Council, architects, builders, and other members of the redevelopment team to discuss proposed plans and to incorporate the community's recommendations. The forums were crucial in delivering the message to residents and shopowners that their input was important to the planning of Fruitvale Transit Village and that the project needed their participation to be successful.

"When you bring people together, they start talking about their dreams and fears," notes Silva." We started forming neighborhood associations, offering leadership training, and just getting people involved. Residents started coming out of their homes and shopping on International Boulevard and investing in their community," she explains. "Both the residents and the shopowners felt included and considered themselves stakeholders in the project. They now have a sense of belonging and a sense of place. And they can't wait for the work to be completed."

Investor Support

Today, Fruitvale has raised nearly $50 million in federal grants and private investments toward its $100 million goal; however, raising the money has not been easy. Private investors initially feared the Fruitvale redevelopment project because there was no money in Fruitvale to support it. Martinez has used her political muscle to secure more than $43 million in federal grants to date. "It takes a tremendous amount of time to make these inner-city redevelopment projects economically feasible and to receive the funding," Martinez notes. "After we secured the first $7.65 million grant, private investors began to support us. When they began to see improvements to the streets, even the shopowners on International Boulevard started to support the project, and they have invested $2.3 million in their own community for redevelopment."

One of Fruitvale's biggest supporters is the city of Oakland. According to Ignacio de la Fuente, president of Oakland's city council, "Our role has been to aid in financially supporting Fruitvale's improvement and facilitating the Unity Council's efforts, especially with land use." With federal and private dollars being raised for Fruitvale, Martinez felt a weight lifted off her shoulders. "The private sector finally appreciated Fruitvale's unique vision," she says. The Unity Council's money-raising efforts are not over yet, however. It currently is trying to fund a bike station at BART.

One of the greatest challenges for a

public/private partnership project is the amount of time the development process can take. "Public agencies have their own internal processes, which inevitably take longer than those of a private developer who just wants to get the job done," notes Silva. "On the other hand, one of the great achievements of this project has been that each public agency — knowing its constraints — has assigned a team to facilitate the process and move forward, while the development teams have met to discuss issues and come up with solutions to get the job done. Will this ultimately speed things up? Probably not, but at least we are all working together," she adds.

Another unforeseen obstacle is the economic prosperity the nation is experiencing. The Bay Area, especially Oakland, is pro union, and labor costs have been increasing with the duration of the project. Alternative ways to reduce costs are being researched. Even though some costs are increasing, Martinez praises the builder and the architect for their efficiency and cost-containment efforts.

Mingling Cultures

The inspiration for redesigning Fruitvale came from the idea of increasing interaction between younger and older generations. By intermingling jurisdictions and public agencies, no particular side has full control of the development, and land and facility usage is maximized. Fruitvale's mixed-use design, reminiscent of old town centers where communities gathered and met, is intended to create environments for socializing. Since Fruitvale is a highly multicultural area with Latino, Cambodian, Vietnamese, and African American residents, it was important to represent this ethnic mix in the redesign, and Fruitvale has created its own identity — a contemporary expression of the character of Oakland, with

its blend of nationalities and colors and its history — in the urban landscape theme. Everything in Fruitvale will have its own character — down to the signage. "By capitalizing on the area's strong past and incorporating expectations for the future, the design will capture what makes us feel good about Fruitvale," explains Martinez. In turn, it was important to focus on creating an international theme, through paving patterns, graphics, and signage, to encourage residents and BART commuters to come to the community.

According to Martinez, since redevelopment started, Fruitvale has blossomed. Ten years ago there was a 50 percent vacancy rate on International Boulevard, a high rate of crime and violence, and dirty streets. Today there is less than a one percent vacancy rate, less crime, less graffiti, cleaner streets, more than 110 new jobs, and a premium for property. With the area looking better because of the facade improvement program, shopowners continue to invest in upgrading their properties. The results of the long-awaited improvements can be seen in residents' and shopowners' attitudes: there is a sense of pride within the neighborhood.

"To me Fruitvale is already a success," comments Martinez. "With the obstacles we've had to go through, I am satisfied with the positive community involvement and the main street enhancements." Besides the number of Class A tenants signed to a building, the success of Fruitvale can be measured by the level of public acceptance. The hope is that the 30,000 BART commuters will feel safe and comfortable enough to pause in Fruitvale's new shopping and dining district before they travel on to their final destination and that Fruitvale residents will be encouraged to explore the area's heritage. With community stakeholders expressing trust and pride in the Fruitvale redevelopment project, notes Martinez, a special feeling of achievement already is present.

CHAPTER 31

ORLANDO USES FREE RAPID TRANSIT TO IMPROVE DOWNTOWN TRANSPORTATION

Craig Amundsen

Bus Rapid Transit (BRT) is growing more popular as a mode of public transportation. Pittsburgh and Orlando, Fla., are successfully operating what could be considered forerunners of today's more complex BRT systems, which are in various stages of development in Cleveland; St. Paul, Minn.; Charlotte, N.C.; Eugene, Ore.; and Boston.

BRT systems are as distinct from conventional bus transit as heavy rail is from light rail. BRT is, at a minimum, faster than conventional local bus service and, at a maximum, includes grade-separated bus operations. The essential features of a BRT system are bus priority, fast passenger boarding and fare collection, and an image that is unique from other locally available modes of public transportation. For local governments that want to increase bus ridership and public transportation passenger satisfaction, BRT offers an alternative to traditional bus and light rail transit in the form of electronically guided, rubber-tired vehicles that operate on exclusive transitways with the same quality of ride, safety and reliability as rail-guided vehicles.

The Components

BRT systems can range from the simple to the complex. A simple system could be totally on-street with reserved lanes marked with painted diamonds and signs, "super" bus stops and limited stop/express service during peak hours. Over time, a simple system could be improved incrementally by permanently separating BRT lanes with a rumble strip and special pavement; constructing larger, more elaborate stations with interactive information kiosks; purchasing low-floor buses of a special color/livery; using an honor fare system to allow for multi-door boarding; and increasing vehicle stop frequencies to permit random passenger arrivals.

A complex system could have a dedicated BRT facility in the median of a boulevard or on an abandoned or underused railroad right-of-way. The system could have stations equipped with a full complement of mode-change facilities, information resources and high-platform boarding for single- or double-articulated, hybrid vehicles.

Additionally, a dedicated right of way, all-stops service could be operated all day on a 10-minute-or-better headway, with fares collected off-board with smart cards. A complex BRT service could be complemented by market-driven peak express and combined collection/distribution services.

Either system could be implemented with the capital costs of purchasing buses and constructing roadways. Operating costs — dictated by speed of operation and work rules — are relatively low. BRT costs much less than rail transit because it uses multiple vehicles, which is more efficient than using a few rail cars, and the system costs less to operate and maintain than a rail system.

The ingredients of a successful BRT system are:

- **Modern, rail-like vehicles.** The vehicles must offer an attractive exterior and modern interior with large windows.
- **Exclusive rights-of-way.** Signal priority helps, but it is usually not sufficient to achieve the speeds needed to attract riders. The exclusive rights-of-way can be underground, elevated or grade-separated.
- **Attractive infrastructure.** To a large extent, the aesthetic quality of the system's environment, including landscaping, public art and stations, should distinguish BRT from traditional busways.
- **Streamlined fare collection.** Fare collection can be via free-fare zones, self-serve media at stations or even on board vehicles. Pay-as-you-go fare collection inhibits the rapid pace needed for BRT to compete with other forms of transportation.
- **Strong "brand identity."** BRT must be marketed as a fixed guideway line to gain acceptance among residents. The same marketing message will interest real estate developers who are drawn to investing near traditional rail systems.
- **Fast "dwell" times.** Guidance technologies speed docking times and help BRT compete with light-rail transit. Level boarding is essential, whether accomplished with low-floor vehicles or high platforms.

Orlando's Head Start

Orlando's no-fare BRT system, named Lymmo, has been operating downtown since 1996, and it has been gaining popularity among residents and city leaders. Lymmo is a free bus in the central business district that runs on exclusive lanes for its entire 2.3-mile, circular route.

The lanes are identified with distinctive pavers and are separated from general traffic lanes either with a raised median or with a double row of raised, reflective ceramic pavement markers embedded in the asphalt. In the middle of the route, which has loop sections at each end, the two directions of Lymmo service are on the same street, with one running opposite the flow of traffic.

Because Lymmo operates in places and directions that are counter to other traffic, all bus movements at intersections are controlled by special bus signals. To prevent confusion with regular traffic signals, the bus signals use lines instead of standard red, yellow and green lights. When a bus approaches an intersection, a loop detector in the bus lane triggers the signal in the intersection to allow the bus to proceed.

In addition to dedicated lanes and signal pre-emption, Lymmo includes stations with large shelters and route information; automatic vehicle location; next-bus arrival information at kiosks; low-floor compressed natural gas buses; and a unique brand, which is communicated with vehicle graphics, advertisements and business tie-ins. The Lymmo route replaced an earlier downtown loop circulator, Freebee, and was a substitute for the proposed use of historic trolleys.

In its first year of operation, Lymmo averaged about twice the ridership of Freebee. Its total capital cost, $21 million, was at least half the cost of the trolley proposal. The design of Lymmo's facilities and the quality of the system have made the BRT competitive with other modes of transportation.

Going a Step Further

While Orlando's Lymmo represents a forerunner of the true BRT system, other cities are taking the concept quite a bit further. Cleveland, for example, is designing one of the most sophisticated BRT systems in the country.

The Cleveland BRT is part of a broad redevelopment program for the Euclid Avenue corridor, one of the city's oldest areas. The redevelopment includes a building-to-building reconstruction of Euclid Avenue with enhanced pedestrian zones, sidewalk and center median landscaping, new street and sidewalk lighting, new center median platform stations with distinctive shelter architecture, and exclusive bus and auto lanes. Designated the Euclid Corridor Transportation Project, the construction of the BRT line will connect the region's largest employment center (the central business district) with the second largest employment center (the University Circle area) approximately 4.5 miles away.

The goal of the project is to improve the operational constraints of the existing downtown street network and increase the flow of bus service during peak periods. Motorcoach bus traffic will be directed into and out of the corridor on two north-south streets with auto traffic directed to a third north-south street. The main east-west street of the corridor will have exclusive curbside bus lanes, which will allow better distribution of bus riders to destinations within the central business district.

The project includes construction of an intermodal transfer facility at Public Square in downtown to integrate Euclid Avenue bus service and other suburban bus routes with the rail rapid transit line, which connects to the central business district and, from there, to the airport. A significant percentage of the new ridership in the corridor is expected to come from the bus/rail transfers at that facility.

The system will consist of an exclusive center median busway on Euclid Avenue and median lanes and center platform stations along most of the length of the street. The city plans to purchase 24 hybrid-electric trolley buses and six spares for the system. The buses are low-floor; 60-foot-long articulated, rubber-tired vehicles with left- and right-side doors. Fare collection will occur onboard the transit vehicles. Reduced-fare and free-fare zones are being considered to encourage ridership.

The project also includes the creation of a new radio communications system to incorporate wide-area coverage, automatic vehicle location (AVL) and emergency alerting. Thirteen of 16 channels will be dedicated to voice communication, and the other three will be data channels, which will provide automated passenger count information and fare collection monitoring. In addition to onboard emergency alerting, the AVL system will include a traffic signal/bus priority system, passenger on-board schedule information, bus stop passenger information displays and a passenger transfer management system.

The city is installing new traffic control striping to conform to the busway design and a new traffic signal system to give priority to buses on Euclid Avenue. A two-foot utility chase will be constructed on both sides of the avenue for traffic signal wiring, street lighting, pedestrian lighting, signs and spare conduit for future growth.

The project involves removing the Euclid Avenue roadway and reconstructing it with a busway and landscape median, bus stop platforms and a rumble strip to separate the bus and automobile lanes. Sidewalks will be replaced with upgraded treatments, including backfilling and/or reconstruction of underground vaults. Construction of the $220 million Cleveland BRT is expected to start in 2003, with completion scheduled for 2005 or 2006.

Getting on Board

When considering BRT, cities must weigh all the benefits and challenges of rapid transit. Besides costing less than constructing a rail system, BRT is easier to expand than rail. A BRT system can be constructed in successive phases, adding scope and features, such as additional stations, grade separations and electric power, when conditions warrant.

However, changing the image of bus transit to one that lures people out of their cars the way light-rail transit has over the past 20 years is not easy. Opposition to BRT comes from many sources. The public often perceives anything associated with buses as being second-rate — a transportation option to be used only when no other option exists. As a result, municipal officials sometimes discourage consideration of bus options for fear of losing public support for a rail transit investment.

Also, many planners do not know the capabilities of BRT and incorrectly attribute the high performance and customer acceptance of rail rapid transit to rail characteristics, such as tracks. In reality, exclusive guideways, stations and service quality are the features of rail rapid transit that attract most riders, and those features are offered by BRT. As BRT systems increase in number and sophistication, they will continue to gain wider acceptance as an effective mode of public transportation.

CHAPTER 32

PETALUMA PROVIDES TRANSIT OPTIONS TO REVIVE DOWNTOWN RIVER AREA

Charles Lockwood

Petaluma, California, is used to making planning history. A quarter century ago, it became the second American city (after Ramapo, New York) to enact growth controls. Later, those controls were the first to be tested in the courts — and upheld as a legitimate use of municipal authority.

Located 40 miles north of San Francisco, Petaluma began jumping after U.S. Highway 101 was widened in 1956. The city's population almost doubled — from 14,000 to nearly 25,000 — in the 1960s, schools began double shifts, and city services were strained. In 1972, in an effort to contain growth, Petaluma began limiting residential development to 500 new housing units a year.

That 500-unit ceiling — called the Residential Growth Management System — is still in effect and still popular. "It allows us to plan all of our community facilities and our capital improvements at a pace that is manageable and financeable," says Pamela Tuft, Petaluma's planning director.

Regulations have their limits, however. Despite its growth controls, Petaluma now has 50,000 residents and is plagued by

sprawl — with fringe residential and commercial development devouring surrounding farmland and traffic snarling streets and highways. The city is now close to its urban limit line, unchanged since 1969. Next month, a 20-year urban growth boundary plan will appear on the city ballot. The measure is expected to pass easily.

Meanwhile, about a quarter of the city's central area remains vacant or underused. But now that picture is changing with a new plan that could once again put Petaluma on the map.

A River Runs Through It

When it comes to redevelopment of the central area, Petaluma has many advantages, including the Petaluma River, which has been the focus for commercial and industrial development since the town's founding in 1833. It also has an active rail corridor, historic commercial buildings, a circa-1910 train station, and progressive residents willing to try new things.

However, the central area is cut in half

Originally published as "Pioneering Petaluma," *Urban Land*, Vol. 59, No. 7, July, 2000. Published by the Urban Land Institute, Washington, D.C. Reprinted with permission of the publisher.

by the Petaluma River, and each side of the river has a distinct identity. The west side — used by director George Lucas as the setting for his classic 1973 movie, *American Graffiti* — is a healthy pre–World War II district with a mix of housing, industry, and commerce. The east side, which has developed less densely in recent decades, consists largely of residential subdivisions.

The problem is what lies between. Central Petaluma is a sparsely developed district of nearly 400 acres at the geographical heart of the city. With its scattering of residential properties and low-density strip commercial, industrial, and institutional uses, Central Petaluma lacks a clear identity.

What to Do

Recent development proposals haven't helped matters. "We were getting piecemeal proposals for projects, like a drugstore in the middle of a parking lot, that were not conducive to a true downtown environment," says planning director Pamela Tuft. "So we decided to get more proactive, to create a plan, and to offer the community the opportunity to participate in developing the plan."

The city council began the process in 1996 by appointing a 26-member advisory committee that includes two city council members, two planning commissioners, a representative of the Petaluma Downtown Association, the executive director of the Chamber of Commerce, property owners, developers, and interested residents. The group met monthly in 1996, and that summer the committee helped to write an RFP for the Central Petaluma specific plan.

In 1997, the advisory committee chose the ROMA Design Group of San Francisco to prepare the new plan, noting that the document would have to support and complement an existing river enhancement and

access plan and the city's 1986 general plan. Among other things, the general plan directs growth to the city center and the river. Refinements to the specific plan are now in the works, and it is expected to be adopted within the next few months. "Our approach," says Bonnie Fisher, a principal at ROMA, "is to provide the structure to knit downtown Petaluma together and complete the urban fabric."

River and Rail

The specific plan makes the Petaluma River downtown's major organizing element. Thus the plan supports riverbound industrial uses while also orienting new development projects to the river. Entertainment and leisure-based businesses will be sought for the turning basin, where big ships turn around to sail back to San Francisco Bay.

In addition, "the specific plan is very pedestrian-oriented," says city councilman David Keller, "with a wide range of, and connections to, transit facilities, including the railroad, boats, cars, bicycles, buses, and transit." The city's historic train depot will provide rail service as well as local and regional bus service, and the station will serve as a gateway to the pedestrian-oriented downtown. Two light rail transit stops have been included in the plan in the hope that Sonoma County voters will approve a light rail line in next month's election.

Other projects outlined in the plan include tree-planting, a fourth river crossing, and a traffic circle to relieve congestion and create a gateway into Central Petaluma. In addition, the city is buying the 32-acre McNear Peninsula, adjacent to the turning basin, for a regional park with pedestrian, car, and transit connections to Central Petaluma sites.

New commercial and entertainment uses are to be introduced to Central

Petaluma on both sides of the river. And because the west side-based Downtown Association is concerned that new development on the east side of the river will steal away their cachet and customers, the advisory committee has worked hard to allay that fear.

To prevent the development of a new, rival downtown, the specific plan calls for integrating redevelopment into the existing downtown through pedestrian and view orientation, architectural design guidelines, parking, and transportation connections. The specific plan also encourages recycling Central Petaluma's many underused properties by developing mixed-use projects that complement the west side's commercial district.

Where It Stands

Central Petaluma is about to bloom with restaurants, a small cineplex, specialty shops, and food marketplaces showcasing Sonoma County's various specialty crops. The cornerstone for redevelopment in the area, says city councilman David Keller, is a "wasted resource" called the Golden Eagle, a seven-acre shopping center dating from the 1960s that backs onto the river. Keller says the Golden Eagle is fully leased and its owner has no financial incentive to redevelop it, but "he is very amenable to redoing the shopping center if other owners and developers begin implementing the specific plan."

High-density housing will also help to create a vibrant downtown core. The specific plan calls for a mix of live/work studios and apartments, low-income units, and elderly housing. A total of 400 housing units is anticipated.

"The plan tries to do away with regimented zoning" by accommodating a combination of housing, office, and commercial uses, says Vincent Smith, a planner with the city.

Public hearings on the specific plan are scheduled to begin this fall. Members of the planning department and the advisory committee say they expect easy adoption. Officially, implementation is likely to begin in early 1999, but privately driven redevelopment activity has already begun. Several property transactions for major downtown blocks are under way.

In addition, the city's advisory committee has already endorsed the preservation and renovation of the historic downtown rail station and continued use of the existing rail lines — key elements in the specific plan. Roadways and circulation, open space, and bicycle access plans have also been approved.

"Any city can be a sprawling, freeway-centered community," says David Keller. "We are trying to steer Petaluma in another direction. If we do it right, we can have a thriving downtown that will last for generations and preserve Petaluma's character and rich sense of community."

CHAPTER 33

PORTLAND GUIDES URBAN GROWTH THROUGH PUBLIC TRANSPORTATION

Gordon Oliver

Perched in his seventh floor office in the heart of downtown Portland, Fred Hansen, director of Oregon's Department of Environmental Quality, enjoys an excellent view of the city's past successes and current challenges. He can look down on the tree-covered transit mall, symbol of Portland's efforts to pump up what had been a flagging downtown. But he can also see the suburbs spreading out all around the city.

"We've got a rare opportunity to make this city livable," Hansen said during an interview in his office. "But if we continue the breakneck growth we've had for the last five years without basic changes, we'll really have problems."

Portland has a reputation as a place that works, partly because it has attempted regional solutions to regional problems. Portland's Downtown Plan, adopted in 1972 under former Mayor Neil Goldschmidt, helped revive a struggling core and gave Portland the reputation of a city that knows how to plan for its future. In the years that followed, Goldschmidt went on to become U.S. Secretary of Transportation in the Carter administration, and the Portland metropolitan region continued to attract attention for its success in both land-use and transportation planning.

The tree-shaded transit mall, which opened in 1978 along two downtown streets, is part of a three-county transit system. That system, including a light rail line that carries 25,000 riders every weekday, delivers 40 percent of the core area's workers to their jobs.

But the region of 1.1 million people cannot rest on its laurels. Steady growth is pushing jobs and housing to the edge of a regional urban growth boundary that encompasses 234,000 acres in 24 cities and parts of three counties. Development is also spreading out — even into small towns outside the urban growth boundary dozens of miles from downtown Portland.

Moreover, despite huge investments in transit, the automobile is becoming more — not less — important in the region. On average, Portland-area residents are increasing their travel by almost four percent a year, placing a burden on the transportation system and the airshed, Hansen notes. A population growth rate of about 1.4 percent a year compounds the challenge.

Originally published as "Portland Revs Up for Action," *Planning*, Vol. 60, No. 8, August, 1994. Published by the American Planning Association, Chicago, Illinois. Reprinted with permission of the publisher.

Hansen is among the regional leaders seeking new approaches in a region that has shown it is open to them. His agency has broad authority under Oregon and federal law to restrict automobile use and impose industrial restrictions in order to preserve air quality. But Hansen hopes the region can avoid punishing industry and the public by gradually developing a strong transit system while establishing land-use patterns that give residents a choice in how to get around.

Hansen is optimistic. He notes that the area has a history of finding regional solutions through an obscure but powerful group called the Joint Policy Advisory Committee on Transportation — JPACT for short — which represents major political and transportation constituencies. Technically an advisory committee to the elected council of the regional government, known as Metro, JPACT calls the shots in all major transportation issues.

"Things that are very tough fights in other regions are worked out by consensus here," says Hansen, a JPACT member. "There is more of a regional ability to try to set goals."

The Clean Air Hook

Reshaping growth will be a tough battle even here, but Hansen is hoping that the federal clean air mandate will give a boost to regional planning efforts.

The Portland region is now listed as a marginal nonattainment area for ozone, although it has met federal standards every year since 1990. It's also listed as a moderate nonattainment area for carbon monoxide, although that problem has almost entirely disappeared, and downtown Portland has not violated the carbon monoxide standard since 1985.

The environmental quality department is now preparing plans to submit to the U.S. Environmental Protection Agency early next year requesting clean air status for both ozone and carbon monoxide. Those plans will include a strategy for meeting federal standards for the next decade.

The strategy will call for expanding the motor vehicle inspection program into areas outside the regional urban growth boundary, combined with implementation of a more sophisticated vehicle emission test. The environmental quality department is also preparing an "employee commute options rule" that will require companies with 50 to 100 workers to submit plans for reducing single-occupancy vehicle trips by 10 percent. The figure jumps to 20 percent for larger employers. Both programs would start next year.

Neither of these programs has aroused much opposition. Even the employee commuting rule seems likely to glide through without controversy because it is far less demanding than a similar program in neighboring Washington State.

Parking Changes Ahead

What could be controversial is the department's recommendation to lift Portland's 20-year-old downtown parking lid, which allows no more than 44,322 parking spaces in the core area. Hansen says his agency is convinced that it can keep carbon monoxide to acceptable levels without the current lid, and the city has promised to maintain a strict parking ratio downtown.

The main reason that lifting the downtown parking lid hasn't caused a furor is DEQ's proposal to impose what would be the nation's first regional parking restrictions on the Portland area. The agency's "parking ratio rule" would reduce the number of new parking spaces by requiring local governments to establish *maximum* parking ratios for new development. Its goal is a 10 percent reduction in vehicle trips generated by new retail, commercial, and industrial projects.

The parking rule, which was authorized by the state legislature in 1993 and is now being developed for implementation in 1995, parallels the statewide Transportation Planning Rule, which was adopted in 1991 by Oregon's Land Conservation and Development Commission and is being implemented in phases by local governments.

The transportation planning rule calls for a 10 percent reduction in parking spaces over the next 20 years. It also calls for a 10 percent reduction in vehicle miles traveled per capita over 20 years, and a 20 percent reduction in 30 years. The region's residents now average 12.8 miles of travel per day.

The transportation rule, which only this summer is beginning to be reflected in city and county planning codes, requires all commercial developments to be oriented to transit, bicycles, and pedestrians. In practice, that could mean that supermarkets could no longer be set back behind parking lots. And builders of fast-food restaurants would have to make them accessible by pedestrians and cyclists. Subdivision streets and bike paths would have to hook up to schools and stores.

Case Study

Portland's Lloyd District, just across the Willamette River from downtown, will be a test site for the new parking rule. In the 1960s, the former residential and warehouse district started to take shape as a suburban-style shopping and office district. In addition to the office towers, it includes the huge Lloyd Center shopping mall, the Oregon Convention Center, Memorial Coliseum, and a new arena under construction by the Portland Trail Blazers.

Many of the district's 17,000 workers commute by car, although the opening of a light-rail line in 1986 and expansion of bus service have allowed for job growth without an increase in parking spaces. Today, there are 17,600 parking spaces, but nearly half in shopping mall lots. The environmental quality department clean air strategy calls for expanding the free bus service now provided downtown by the Tri-County Metropolitan Transit District to the Lloyd District, perhaps before the end of this year.

But the biggest change will be the establishment for the first time of a maximum parking ratio. The new rule will allow two parking spaces per 1,000 square feet of office space in the district. In contrast, the city allows between 0.7 and one parking space for every 1,000 feet of office space downtown.

"In downtown," says Elsa Coleman, deputy director of Portland's Office of Transportation, "we've always had four goals: air quality, transit ridership, traffic flow, and accommodating development. By expanding to the Lloyd District, we're expanding that combination."

The LUTRAQ Approach

In the 1980s, a nonprofit land-use watchdog group called 1000 Friends of Oregon challenged a highway bypass proposed for suburban Washington County, outside Portland. That challenge raised issues about the link between land-use and transportation policies that led the state to adopt its Transportation Planning Rule.

While the bypass question is still not resolved, 1000 Friends of Oregon has broadened its effort. It is leading a $1 million study, financed by grants and federal funds, of the links between suburban land-use patterns and transportation demands. The study is called "Making the Land Use/Transportation/Air Quality Connection"—LUTRAQ for short.

A key finding so far is that vehicle miles traveled could be reduced by 10 percent in the suburbs by creating a pedestrian-oriented environment similar to what already exists in old Portland neighborhoods.

The study has also concluded that a market demand exists for 1,150 multi-family and 1,400 single-family housing units annually in transit-oriented developments in Washington County.

"When we began the study in 1989, many people were incredulous," says Keith Bartholomew, a 1000 Friends attorney who heads the study. "Nobody had thought of changing traffic by changing land-use." Today, the project is attracting attention regionally and nationally. This spring, several hundred planning professionals from all over the U.S. attended a Portland conference sponsored by 1000 Friends and the Lincoln Institute of Land Policy to consider its implications.

Metro's Take

Simultaneously, Metro, the Portland-area regional government, is working on its own long-range plan known as "Region 2040." Agency planners are examining the implications of three scenarios: continued sprawl, tightly contained development within the urban growth boundary, and controlled development of satellite cities centered around existing small towns. This fall, the Metro council is expected to make key decisions about whether to move or hold the present urban growth boundary.

Eventually, Metro will develop the nation's first regional framework plan with authority to override local plans. Over time, the huge planning effort should slowly transform the region's transportation system.

"The land-use pattern changes won't be too great in the next 10 years," says Andrew Cotugno, Metro's planning director. "In 20 to 40 years it will be more noticeable, and people will see more transit and there will be more willingness to fund more bike and pedestrian projects."

Light Rail Works

Public support is high for the region's light rail system, called MAX — the Metropolitan Area Express. The first 15-mile-long line, which opened in 1986, runs east from the downtown through the Lloyd District to suburban Gresham. A second 12-mile line to the west side suburbs is now under construction. The first phase of the project is expected to be completed in September 1997, with a six-mile extension to be finished a year later. The entire project will cost nearly $1 billion.

The Tri-County Metropolitan Transit District, which runs the light rail and bus service, expects to draw 18,900 riders in the west side line's first year of operation, increasing to 27,100 in 2005. A third line, which would run from suburban Clackamas County on the south through Portland and north into Clark County, Washington, is now under study. The transit district may ask voters this fall to approve $475 million in bonds to help pay the estimated $2 billion construction costs. The money will be collected only if the federal government approves the project in 1996.

Although light rail has helped focus development on the transit spine running east through the downtown and the Lloyd District, the transit-oriented housing developments and shopping centers visualized east of the central city haven't materialized. Still, Tri-Met has found that 36 percent of the region's residents ride transit at least once a month, double the number of occasional riders before light rail. MAX has almost as many riders on Saturdays as the 25,000 it averages on weekdays.

"Light rail, for good or evil, has been perceived as different than transit," Fred Hansen says. "People who would never get on a bus will get on MAX."

Hoping to take advantage of light rail's popularity, Tri-Met, local governments, and the Department of Environmental Quality are engaged in an unusual public-private venture. They want to create transit-oriented developments on large undeveloped parcels near planned west side light rail stops.

They're starting with a 124-acre wooded site in suburban Beaverton. The city of Beaverton, Tri-Met, Metro, and DEQ are working with several property owners to develop a master plan, which is expected to be completed this month. Portland architect George Crandall is leading the planning effort, and Peter Calthorpe of San Francisco is a participant.

Tom Walsh, general manager of Tri-Met, is convinced that elected officials will no longer be able to sell Congress or local voters on funding light rail solely because of its value as a mode of transportation. Development patterns will also be an issue.

"The principal value of light rail is as an organizing tool," says Walsh. "It won't ever be good enough just to keep believing in it. We need to galvanize public support for what the region should look like."

Model City?

Planners and public officials from around the nation will be watching eagerly as Portland tries to strike a balance between transit and automobiles.

"Generally speaking, on land-use and parking management issues, Portland is at the top of the list," says Grace Crunican, a former official of Portland's Office of Transportation who is now the deputy administrator of the Federal Transit Administration. "People around the country have been talking about doing things that Portland takes for granted."

In the 1970s, for example, the city killed a project known as the Mount Hood Freeway — which was to run from downtown Portland through the city's east side, ending at another freeway — and instead spent the money on arterial improvements

and light rail. Later in the same decade, a waterfront expressway disappeared and was replaced by the Tom McCall Waterfront Park, named for the state's environmentally crusading governor, who died in 1973.

Portland tackled its air pollution problems by imposing the downtown parking lid in 1972 and beginning a gradual phase-out of surface parking. Now, there are 11,639 spaces in surface lots, down from an estimated 15,800 two decades ago. The downtown has added over 30,000 jobs since the early 1970s while adding fewer than 5,000 parking spaces, and the percentage of downtown workers riding transit to work has doubled in that period.

Now there seems to be some slippage. Car pooling has declined by 20 percent in two years. Transit ridership has held steady for almost two years at about 200,000 trips a day, but the percentage of transit commuters has also dropped by 20 percent since 1980, according to U.S. Census figures.

In the region, less than four percent of all travel is by transit, and the percentage is declining. According to U.S. Department of Transportation 1990 statistics, Portland residents take 47 transit trips a year. That's double Houston's rate of 25 trips but less than half the San Francisco Bay Area's 109.

"Many double-wage households and single-parent households don't have alternatives to the car," says Keith Lawton, a Metro transportation planner who is leading a federally funded study of travel habits. "I don't care how good transit is; they don't have time to use it." Metro is asking 6,000 Portland-area residents and 6,000 elsewhere in the state to keep two-day diaries of all their activities, including transportation.

So far, Metro's Region 2040 plan doesn't offer a way to meet state goals for reducing vehicle miles traveled. Even if all growth were to be contained within the urban growth boundary, Metro projects just a 12 percent drop in vehicle miles traveled, far short of the state's 20 percent goal.

No one can ignore the sense of looming crisis. "There's enough evidence from everyplace else that things do get worse in a hurry," says Walsh. "We don't have the luxury of a lot of time."

Last year, however, a legislature preoccupied by a school finance crisis killed the transportation package that would have increased funding for roads and transit. JPACT members are searching for an alternative, but this summer they're busy looking for future light rail money.

Nervousness

For now, regional leaders are hoping that the U.S. EPA will approve clean air maintenance plans for both ozone and carbon monoxide. "If we can implement a plan now, we can get through until 2005," says John Kowalczyk, manager of DEQ's air planning section. "If we go over the limit, we might have to limit industrial growth."

The next step is to carry out the long-range transportation and land-use policies that are now being put on the books. But even in Portland, new ideas like the transportation planning rule won't come without controversy. "It's one thing to write rules," says Roger Millar, a consultant who represents industrial associations in discussions about the new rule. "It's another thing to change hearts and minds."

Yet Hansen believes that the region's residents will rise to the challenge. He is convinced that Portlanders place a high value on the clean air that gives them a clear view of snow-capped Mt. Hood 50 miles east of the city.

"If parking ratios become too burdensome, then people will have to come forward with alternatives," he says. "The choice we don't have is to do nothing."

CHAPTER 34

SAINT PAUL USES "NEW URBANISM" TO REVITALIZE DOWNTOWN RIVERFRONT AREA

Frank Edgerton Martin

In the late 1980s, Saint Paul's Mississippi riverfront exhibited the decline evident in many Midwestern river cities. Office towers and retail areas turned their backs on the river, and waterfront industries that had flourished for decades became increasingly stagnant, even though Minnesota's service economy was booming.

Following the flight to the suburbs of downtown's primary anchor, West Publishing, in 1992, Saint Paul's leaders recognized that something had to be done. They hired architect Benjamin Thompson, a Saint Paul native son who had gone on to serve as design architect for the revitalization of Boston's Fanueil Hall Market and Baltimore's waterfront, to create a new vision for downtown, expecting him to produce a massive report detailing economic and urban design strategies. Instead, Thompson came back a few months later with a simple but daring panoramic sketch of a reforested stretch of the Mississippi Valley that transformed the city's sense of possibility. The broad river valley, with the tops of houses and steeples showing through the tree canopy, suddenly seemed like a place where people could live again, a network of neighborhoods replacing old industrial facilities and empty lots.

Thompson's image appeared on television and newspapers throughout Minnesota, generating genuine enthusiasm for the idea that the forgotten river might hold the key to Saint Paul's future. In 1995, the Saint Paul foundation created a nonprofit organization, Greening the Great River Park, to oversee replanting the valley forest. Although Thompson did not specify tree types, the involvement early on of ecologists and landscape architects led to a focus on restoration of the native ecological community. But the real story of the rescue of Saint Paul's riverfront began when this vision of trees was turned into a public/private partnership between the city and the developers to create new houses, jobs, and cultural attractions in the valley.

Creating a Frame for Thompson's Picture

To begin the transition from a watercolor landscape painting to urban develop-

Originally published as "Saint Paul's New Riverfront Urban Villages," *Urban Land*, Vol. 60, No. 4, April, 2001. Published by the Urban Land Institute, Washington, D.C. Reprinted with permission of the publisher.

ment, the city hired architect Ken Greenberg of the Toronto-based architecture and planning firm Urban Strategies, who had overseen development in the mid-1990s of a new master plan for the Twin Cities campus of the University of Minnesota. City officials were impressed with the common-sense urbanism of the design, which called for making the campus more pedestrian friendly and reopening connections between Northrop Mall and the Mississippi River. Working with Close Landscape Architecture of Saint Paul and Applied Ecological Services of Brodhead, Wisconsin, Urban Strategies completed its plan, the Saint Paul on the Mississippi Development Framework, in June 1997.

As stated at the beginning, the "Development Framework is based on an implicit understanding that quality of life — the ability of a city to effectively balance economy, environment, and society — provides a primary competitive advantage in an increasingly globalized world." The framework specifically called for formation of an agency to steward riverfront projects over the long term, and in 1997, with significant grant money from regional foundations, the Saint Paul Riverfront Corporation was created to fulfill that role. Working closely with the Riverfront Corporation is the Saint Paul on the Mississippi Design Center, which includes staff from nearly all city departments who meet regularly to discuss new projects with developers and architects.

The framework has served as the philosophical touchstone for every development project that has gotten underway in downtown Saint Paul and along the river since its completion. The city government's ongoing, interdepartmental agreement to follow the policies outlined in the framework is one of the most significant factors in Saint Paul's success. Ten basic framework principles (see Figure 1) that have served as the basis for building the urban environment now are being refined as site-specific guidelines for

---

FIGURE 1
Saint Paul on the Mississippi Development

Framework Principles
- Evoke a sense of place
- Restore and establish the unique urban ecology
- Invest in the public realm
- Broaden the mix of uses
- Improve connectivity
- Ensure that buildings support city building goals
- Build on existing strengths
- Preserve and enhance heritage resources
- Provide a balanced network for movement
- Foster public safety

---

developing new urban villages along both sides of the river.

Activity Day and Night

With the emphasis on supporting and working with developers, rather than simply responding to individual proposals, the Saint Paul Riverfront Corporation now is stewarding projects ranging from housing, to new banking and software company facilities, to museums and other cultural attractions that draw evening and weekend activity. The Science Museum of Minnesota is a major addition to the downtown side of the river that draws thousands of visitors and school groups each year. Following Thompson's early sketch, the building, designed by Ellerbe Becket of Minneapolis, steps down the limestone bluff from the uplands on which downtown is built to lowlands near the river's edge. The museum building, with its terraces overlooking the valley, can be thought of as a metaphorical "staircase" that connects the city to the river. Around the base of the museum, Great River Greening (formerly Greening the Great River Park) has planted hundreds of native trees that eventually will extend to the adjacent Upper Landing Park.

Upper Landing Park, whose concept was designed by Close Landscape Architecture, will include a limestone riverside amphitheater shaded by a soaring canopy and exhibits from the Science Museum. A large commons will accommodate festivals, and a river balcony and promenade are planned, along which permanently moored boats will provide concessions, rentals, and educational and restroom facilities to minimize the impact on the fragile floodplain site. One of the most unusual Upper Landing projects will be the restoration of the headhouse of the former Harvest States grain elevators for commercial uses such as cafés, waterfront taverns, and galleries.

The Upper Landing Urban Village

Just to the west of Upper Landing Park, a new mixed-use neighborhood will front a new regional trail along the north bank of the river. The 17-acre project, which is being developed by Dallas-based Centex Corporation, will include open space and seven blocks of condominiums, townhouses, and apartments. The Saint Paul city council made the surprising decision in 1997 to reserve the highly contaminated site — once slated for a plastics plant — to create one of the urban villages envisioned by the development framework. Centex will coordinate site cleanup with $4 million in financing from the Metropolitan Council — the Twin Cities' regional government — and $11 million in tax increment financing. Centex will invest an additional $3 million for site landscape architecture and another $2.5 million to bury power lines on the site.

The $140 million project will include for-sale housing ranging from condominiums costing $200,000 to two-story townhouses in the $600,000 range to be devel-

oped by Rottlund Homes. Rental units will range from $800 to $2,100 a month. One of the project's most innovative components is a mixed-use city block that includes housing and 23,000 square feet of mostly on-grade retail and restaurant space facing the river at the Upper Landing's front door to downtown. Construction is estimated to take three years, with completion expected before 2005.

Bridging the River

For decades, the area south of the Mississippi known as Harriet Island and the West Side Flats languished, beset by flooding problems that stymied development. In the early 1990s, the Army Corps of Engineers began a massive project to protect the floodplain area, developing a linear dike that offered an ideal opportunity to create a new promenade extending from Harriet Island to the Lafayette bridge, located near downtown's eastern edge. Upriver, directly linking downtown to Harriet Island, the Wabasha Bridge recently was rebuilt with new railing, paving, and lighting to draw pedestrians from downtown across the river to Harriet Island and the neighborhoods that Saint Paulites call the "West Side."

Now designated a regional park, Harriet Island serves as the centerpiece of a 3,000-acre riverfront park system that stretches from the University of Minnesota to the city's southern boundary. This citywide network of parkways and recreational trails is a boon for city residents because, with its sinuous route, no neighborhood is more than three miles from the river.

The West Side Flats: A Model for New Urban Villages

A second urban village is planned directly east of Harriet Island in the West Side

Flats to complement the Upper Landing project. Working to translate the framework plan into real-world development, Hammel, Green and Abrahamson, Inc. (HGA), a Minneapolis architecture/engineering firm, is creating an overall plan for housing, open space, and a hydrological system on the sensitive Flats site. Ultimately, developers Sherman & Associates, Jerry Troyen, and KKE Architecture will implement these ideas for the 45-acre area.

A market analysis conducted by Zimmerman/Volk Associates, Inc., of Clinton, New Jersey, looks beyond local comparables to encourage a mix of high-density housing for the West Side Flats: "Given the potential nonresidential uses — ranging from retail to entertainment — that may occur on the site, an overall residential density of approximately 20 to 25 units to the acre should be achievable." The report goes on to say that a target mix of approximately 1,000 housing units could be broken down into multifamily rental units (58 percent), multifamily for-sale units (24 percent), and single-family, attached, for-sale units (17 percent).

Zimmerman/Volk envisions target households for the West Side Flats as a mix of urban and suburban, older and younger families with an affinity for urban life. A majority of these households might include professionals, small business owners, software and computer specialists, and office workers.

Serving as consultant to HGA, urban designer Rich McLaughlin has been involved with the southern bank of the river, where the West Side Flats is located, since 1995. He recalls the early conflicts between landowners who wanted a themed entertainment complex built on the site and the city, which, following the framework plan, wanted an urban neighborhood with multiple uses and a variety of owners. Five years later, no theme park plan has surfaced, leaving open the opportunity for the urban alternative.

"I see it as an opportunity to reactivate the riverfront with restaurants and nightclubs, hot dog and ice cream stands, that reflect a traditional urban neighborhood scenario," says McLaughlin. HGA's urban planner, Nick Koch, takes a broader view of the potential new neighborhood: "West Side Flats is really becoming a rich blending of corporate employment, housing density, and significant investment in the public realm of parks, streets, and even stormwater retention," he argues. "It's an unprecedented multiuse project for our region … and it makes sense both physically and economically."

The West Side Flats and much of Harriet Island lie in lowlands protected by the Army Corps of Engineers' recently completed levee, which also serves as a riverfront esplanade linking the two districts and offering views of downtown. Future residents of West Side Flats will be able to make use of riverfront trails and Harriet Island's improved open space.

The Saint Paul River Corridor Urban Design Plan, developed by Close Landscape Architecture, calls for extending the adjacent grid of streets through the new development rather than creating superblocks divorced from the city. An existing rail corridor that snakes through the neighborhood and over the river will be treated as an opportunity to frame a central park and accommodate a new trail. To establish a strong urban streetscape, mansion-style apartment buildings and condominiums, along with other types of housing, will be built with clear setback requirements to guarantee consistent street edges. Regular setbacks and relatively consistent housing massings are seen throughout Saint Paul neighborhoods, part of the urban fabric that the city's new urban designers see as worth emulating.

Because the West Side Flats was once floodplains, the site-specific guidelines now being developed encourage the preservation of native riparian landscapes and the integration of stormwater management elements with "green fingers" of open space that channel and filter runoff. HGA and Sherman & Associates currently are gathering market research on "comparable" three- to four-story urban housing projects to show interested developers that low-rise, mixed-price housing has been successful in other cities.

When he presented the Saint Paul on the Mississippi Development Framework to residents in 1997, Mayor Norm Coleman, with an instinct for ecological as well as political benefit, spoke of the riverfront and its connection to every neighborhood in the city. The Saint Paul River Corridor Urban Design Plan argues that the river and its reaches are more than a "thin ribbon through the city." Instead, it says, the "river corridor should be viewed as a watershed model, an entity that incorporates elements, communities, and patterns from well beyond the river itself." These elements include both ecological and culturally significant elements such as sacred Native American sites and historic riverboat landings and commercial areas. Several projects have been undertaken to preserve the city's riparian resources and integrate them into the built environment.

The Lower Phalen Creek Watershed Restoration Project is a neighborhood-driven effort to enhance the habitat along this small creek, improve trails, and reconnect the neglected strand of green space with surrounding neighborhoods. Further to the north, the Phalen Corridor Initiative is a large-scale strategy to bring new industries to deteriorated East Side neighborhoods. One unusual component of the initiative was the replacement of the declining Phalen Shopping Center with a wetland intended to filter and improve the quality of runoff water headed for the Mississippi.

The Saint Paul Riverfront Corporation is supporting the Renaissance Project, a network of greenways, streetscape improvements, and parks that will extend the river valley's reach into downtown and older neighborhoods. The project is envisioned as flexible, changing as necessary to meet new market needs and take advantage of development opportunities. To date, the project has supported 92 acres of new or improved parks, five miles of new trails, and eight miles of improved streetscapes, along with overlook terraces and viewpoints. Heeding the development framework plan's call for connected infrastructure and integrated transportation modes, the Renaissance Project is funding two new stair towers that will link the new Wabasha Bridge to parklands below.

Taking a Long-Term View

When riverfront work began in 1994, Patrick Seeb, then deputy mayor, and Mayor Coleman realized that they would have to be patient, setting ten years as a benchmark for tangible progress. Although Coleman has announced that he will not run for a third term, advocates such as the Saint Paul Riverfront Corporation will continue to raise money from the private sector and foundations for riverfront planning.

To celebrate the tenth anniversary of work along the river, the Riverfront Corporation is staging the Grand Excursion 2004, a steamboat flotilla that will bring passengers from Rock Island, Illinois, to Saint Paul. The event marks the sesquicentennial of an earlier expedition, the 1854 steamboat journey of 1,200 people from Rock Island to Saint Paul. The excursionists, one of whom was former President Millard Fillmore, were considered by the *Chicago Tribune* to be "the most brilliant ever assembled in the West, statesmen, historians, diplomats, poets, and the best editorial talent in the country."

As a result of the publicity generated by the 1854 junket, millions of dollars were invested in the region and Minnesota was catapulted into statehood. A century and a half later, Mississippi River towns ranging from Dubuque, Iowa, to Wabasha, Minnesota, have passed resolutions supporting the 2004 excursion. The Mississippi River — which urban visionary William Morish once described as "America's fourth coast" — is poised for rediscovery.

When the river towns were founded in the 19th century, the Mississippi meant everything to the mining, manufacturing, and milling industries, which depended on the river to transport raw materials and finished products. Today, the historic and cultural landscapes left behind by these industries are being integrated with restored upland and floodplain forests. The excursionists of 2004 will not see a purely "native" river valley in Saint Paul. What they will see is the beauty of a working river where shipping and service industries thrive, thousands of people live, and the complex river ecology that existed in President Fillmore's time is coming back to life.

CHAPTER 35

SANTA MONICA USES PROMENADE AND PUBLIC TRANSIT TO REVITALIZE OLD MAIN STREET

Charles Lockwood

Downtown Santa Monica is a hodge-podge. The area includes some of Southern California's most popular destinations, including the recently rejuvenated Santa Monica Pier; the two-mile-long Palisades Park; and the Third Street Promenade, a re-vamped and highly successful pedestrian mall. At the same time, some sections of the downtown are run-down and deserted at night and on weekends.

That picture could soon change. In late July, the Santa Monica city council approved a five-phase, $18.7 million downtown streetscape plan prepared by the ROMA Design Group of San Francisco. The plan is aimed at improving traffic and transit patterns, creating stronger pedestrian and transit linkages, and luring new shops and restaurants to the 28-block downtown core. It envisions wider sidewalks on several key streets, improved landscaping, and new street furniture and lighting.

City officials say work is scheduled to start this month on the plan's $500,000 first phase.

Inspiration

If Santa Monicans want proof that change is possible, they need only look at the Third Street Promenade.

Once a thriving main street, the old Third Street had seriously declined by the mid-1960s as shopping malls in other communities drew customers away. In 1965, in an effort to compete, the city followed the prevailing planning wisdom and converted three blocks of Third Street into a pedestrian mall.

For a while, the strategy worked. The problem was that adjacent blocks kept declining, pulling the Third Street mall down with them. The mall also had some serious design flaws, including its 600-foot-long blocks and 80-foot-wide pavement.

The final blow came with the opening in 1980 of a new enclosed shopping center, Santa Monica Place, at the south end of Third Street. The center became one of the nation's most successful downtown shopping centers, while the Third Street mall became a concrete wasteland.

Originally published as "Onward and Upward in Downtown Santa Monica," *Planning*, Vol. 63, No. 9, September, 1997. Published by the American Planning Association, 122 South Michigan Avenue, Suite 1600, Chicago, Illinois 60603-6107. Reprinted with permission of the publisher.

The Promenade

In 1986, the city commissioned the ROMA Design Group to come up with a revitalization plan for the pedestrian mall. "Our design for Third Street Promenade was based on the premise that a city's public spaces — its streets, parks, plazas, and other gathering places — are the principal stages on which the life of the city is acted out," says Boris Dramov, the design principal for the project.

Following the plan, the city installed new 30-foot-wide sidewalks to encourage strolling while lessening the impact of the mall's excessive width. New sidewalk cafes soon followed. The city also planted dozens of trees and hung banners from poles. And it created a new "mixed-use zone" down the center of Third Street, a place for kiosks, newsstands, art displays, seating areas, and even topiary dinosaurs. The mixed-use zone broke up the long blocks into smaller, more welcoming activity areas.

To complement — not compete with — the popular Santa Monica Place, the 1986 plan gave priority to entertainment and food rather than retail, says former mayor Dennis Zane. At the same time, the city put zoning controls on commercial development in other areas. Among other things, the new zoning forbade the construction of new movie theaters anywhere but on Third Street.

Success came quickly. The first new occupants — several multiplex theaters and a group of moderately priced restaurants — became magnets for other new businesses, including a number of specialty shops. Thanks to a zoning incentive — an increase in floor area ratio — apartments were built atop a new restaurant and entertainment complex. Retail sales have risen every year since 1989, even during the recession years of the early 1990s. In 1992, ROMA's plan for the mall won a national urban design award from the American Institute of Architects.

This summer, the promenade had a 100 percent occupancy rate, reports Kathleen Rawson, executive director of the Bayside District Corporation, the management entity created by the city. Shops, restaurants, and movie theaters generated more than $1.3 million in local sales taxes in 1996. Some 20,000 shoppers and visitors flock to the mall on a good weekend, Rawson says.

The makeover is not without its critics. One target of their complaints is national retail chains such as Disney and Banana Republic, which moved in several years ago, displacing some of the locally owned businesses that gave the Third Street Promenade a distinctive character.

Another often-heard complaint is that Third Street caters to tourists at the expense of Santa Monicans. A particularly irksome feature, critics say, is the increasing number of noisy street performers. "What started out as a very innovative and cute feature that attracted people has gotten overloaded, almost chaotic," says Paul Rosenstein, city council member and chair of the downtown urban design plan steering committee.

Moving On

Now the city hopes to capitalize on Third Street's success and solve some of its problems at the same time. "One of the key goals of the new streetscape plan," says ROMA's Boris Dramov, "is to transfer some of Third Street Promenade's energy and crowds onto nearby streets." The hope is that lower-rent Second and Fourth streets will attract local merchants and the unusual stores and cafes that many residents and visitors look for.

The plan also seeks to create strong pedestrian activity on streets like Santa Monica Boulevard to balance the crowds that gather on the Third Street Promenade.

A second goal, Dramov says, is to restore downtown streets to their original role as public meeting places. Parades, farmers' markets, street fairs, and sidewalk sales are all part of the picture.

To improve traffic circulation and reduce congestion, the plan calls for making two one-way streets, Fifth and Broadway, two way; redirecting traffic onto other underused streets; and ensuring slow-speed vehicular access throughout the downtown. The idea, says Dramov, is to make sure that pedestrians, not drivers, get top priority on downtown streets.

In an effort to define the downtown core, the plan recommends that a richly landscaped formal gateway be created at the Fifth Street exit ramp from the Santa Monica Freeway. The plan also recommends that palms and flowering trees be planted along Ocean, Colorado, Lincoln and Wilshire boulevards, streets that define the core.

Finally, street furniture — including specially designed transit shelters — should be installed to bolster the impression of a community-oriented space, Dramov says. For instance, benches would be placed in clusters facing away from street traffic. The plan also includes design guidelines for elements that open to and interact with the street — entries, courtyards, gardens, windows, and signs, for instance.

Getting Into Gear

Phase one, which includes restriping Fifth Street and Broadway to make them two-way, and adding curbside parking on Fourth Street as a traffic calming measure, is expected to be complete by Thanksgiving. The city will use already budgeted general funds for this work, according to planning department sources.

The $5 million for phase two, which is likely to begin in mid-1998, is also budgeted. This phase involves more extensive streetscape improvements, with big changes for Santa Monica Boulevard between Ocean Avenue and Fifth Street.

"We will take a lane of traffic out of Santa Monica Boulevard, and all curbside parking will be eliminated in these four blocks," Rosenstein explains. "We will widen the sidewalks on each side by 12 feet to create a pedestrian promenade with plenty of space for sidewalk cafes. The center of the roadway will have one lane of traffic in each direction. One curbside lane will be designated for transit. The other curbside lane will be set aside for cabs, valet parking for restaurants, and loading activities."

The redesigned boulevard will lead people past the Third Street Promenade intersection, two blocks down to Ocean Avenue and Palisades Park, and then over to the Santa Monica Pier, which boasts a new Ferris wheel and roller coaster.

Uncertainties

Funding for subsequent projects could prove more difficult, particularly since last year's passage of Proposition 218, which requires California municipalities to win the approval of affected property owners before they can impose special assessments.

Nonetheless, the outlook for implementation of the downtown streetscape plan is good, given Santa Monica's excellent fiscal condition and good planning and development track record. According to the city finance department, Santa Monica is the only California municipality with an AAA bond rating.

"Most cities are so economically strapped that they will do anything to get new development," says Rosenstein. "They can't be choosy about developers or design issues. Sometimes, they're not even aware of the best thinking on urban design. So they take whatever happens."

In contrast, he says, Santa Monica has a clear vision of what it wants to be. "We have a dream of what our downtown could be like — a vibrant place where all kinds of people can live, shop, work, and recreate — and do it safely, without having to dodge traffic at every step."

CHAPTER 36

SEATTLE USES BRANCH LIBRARY AS A TOOL FOR COMMUNITY RENEWAL

Anne Jordan

Seattle has long cultivated its reputation as a progressive and literate city. So it was quite a civic embarrassment when, in 1994, a $155 million bond measure — to finance a new central library as well as improvements to some of the system's 22 branches — fell three points short of the 60 percent needed for approval.

This defeat came at a time when library referenda were experiencing great success around the country, and major cities from San Francisco and Denver to Chicago and Cleveland were opening bold new main libraries.

Soon, however, Seattle had a new mayor, Paul Schell, and a new library director, Deborah L. Jacobs, who quickly pushed libraries to the top of the administration's agenda. For months, Jacobs spent as many as four evenings a week attending meetings in all of Seattle's neighborhoods, listening to residents express their library-related hopes and dreams. The concerns turned out to be less about the cost to taxpayers than about how the spending would be allocated: People felt that the emphasis on erecting an impressive central library would shortchange the existing branches out in the neighborhoods.

In 1998, a retooled "Libraries for All" initiative went on the ballot with a price tag of $196.4 million — at that time, the largest single bond issue for libraries in U.S. history. This time, $66.8 million was set aside for the branch libraries, nearly double the amount in the earlier proposal. The second measure passed with 72 percent of the vote.

The commitment is being kept. This fall, when Seattle breaks ground for its new central library, it already will have celebrated the grand re-opening of two branches in low-income neighborhoods. Altogether, 26 new or upgraded libraries are slated for completion by 2006.

Seattle isn't the only city where branch libraries are turning out to have surprising political appeal. Contrary to predictions of their demise in an era of electronic media and mega-bookstores, libraries in almost every metropolitan area are thriving on the changes of the past decade: a huge influx of immigrants; networked technology that gives even the tiniest storefront libraries access to materials from around the world; and the disappearance of other community integrators — groceries, banks, post offices and schools — from the urban landscape. Branch libraries are becoming hybrid institutions

Originally published as "Branching Out," *Governing*, Vol. 14, No. 13, October, 2001. Published by Congressional Quarterly Inc., Washington, D.C. Reprinted with permission of the publisher.

that not only offer books and information but foster the social, cultural and even economic vitality of neighborhoods.

The image of the library as a quiet, scholarly place has given way to that of a "neighborhood living room or front porch — a place where everybody in the community can get together and connect with each other," says Wayne Disher, a branch manager in San Jose and past chairman of the Public Library Association's branch libraries committee. In a growing number of places, it's a literal living room as well as a figurative one. The new 29,000-square-foot Glendale branch in Indianapolis, for example, has a lounge area with a big-screen TV, overstuffed chairs and a fireplace — not to mention a coffee shop.

While libraries have always tried to be welcoming places for all ages and races, they are moving toward "a little bit more comfortable environment conducive to today's lifestyles," Disher notes. "That may even include food and drink, or a space where kids are being as loud and wild and crazy as can be." Not everyone is happy about such changes, but its clear that branch libraries are responding to their customers' interests and demands in order to remain relevant. Many of them are paying as much attention to the number of people who come in their doors — for whatever reason — as they are to the number of books and other materials that go out.

For more than a decade, the Queens Borough Public Library in New York, with its 62 branches, has had the highest annual circulation of any library system in the country. Last year, 17.2 million items were checked out to 16.9 million customers, and more than half a million people participated in nearly 28,000 programs there. The standard library fare — poetry readings, computer training and puppet shows — is only the beginning in Queens. The 30- to 40-page monthly schedule of programs for adults and children includes jewelry-making, yoga, de-

fensive-driving courses, science experiments, cooking demonstrations and asthma screenings, to name just a few.

"We really try to use the branches as a community focal point and a place of destination," says Gary E. Strong, the Queens library director. "So much of what we're trying to do is create neighborhood dialogue." That's no small task in the most ethnically diverse county in the United States. Indeed, the question these days isn't whether people are talking in the Queens library, but rather how many languages are being spoken there.

While Queens operates on a larger scale than most library systems, services similar in scope are being implemented all over the country. Indeed, as their programming has broadened to include art exhibits, concerts, film festivals and Scrabble clubs, more and more branch libraries are becoming full-fledged community centers. One of their most sought-after assets is the free meeting space that they provide for local chambers of commerce, neighborhood associations and other civic groups.

The growth in programs — along with the need to become technologically sophisticated and handicapped-accessible — has fueled a boom in the construction, renovation and expansion of both central libraries and neighborhood branches. Between 1994 and the end of 2000, *Library Journal* estimates, some 1,200 new libraries were built or expanded in the United States — at a cost of $3 billion.

A number of cities that focused on the downtown flagship library in the early 1990s have followed up with comprehensive capital improvements to branches. Since cutting the ribbon on the Harold Washington Library Center a decade ago, Chicago has spent $200 million on 39 new or renovated branch libraries; 25 more are scheduled for completion by 2005, at a cost of $100 million.

The Los Angeles Public Library, which has the largest population base of any system in the nation at 3.8 million, is also in the midst of a huge branch-construction program. In 1989, a $53 million bond issue was approved for 26 new or expanded libraries, and then in 1998, an additional $178.3 million to upgrade 32 more. The master plan calls for nine new libraries citywide for a total of 72 built, renovated and expanded by late 2004.

And last November, by a 75 percent vote, San Francisco approved a $106 million bond measure to make seismic and other structural improvements to 19 neighborhood branches, build a new branch in the Mission Bay neighborhood, and replace four old storefront libraries between 2003 and 2009.

Other cities have decided for political or logistical reasons to refurbish their branches before tackling their central library. Philadelphia is one of those. In the early 1990s, that city was having extraordinary financial difficulties. "We looked at how we could be part of the solution, rather than part of the problem," says Elliot L. Shelkrot, director of the Free Library of Philadelphia. "We knew it was important to do something in these neighborhoods. This is where the quality of life in the city could be affected the most."

So, in 1995, the library launched a fund-raising campaign called "Big Change," with a goal of renovating all 52 branches. The city chipped in $25 million and an additional $35 million was raised from private individuals and corporations. Then-Mayor Edward Rendell allowed the money to be turned over to the Free Library Foundation, which oversaw a fast-tracked construction process. All but four of the branches are finished, and the system is just shy of breaking its all-time circulation record set in the 1960s, when Philadelphia had half a million more people than it does today.

Philadelphia's attention is now shifting to rehabilitation of the central library. That's also the case in Indianapolis, which is moving forward with a $103 million downtown library expansion following a $50 million effort to rebuild or renovate more than a dozen of its 21 neighborhood branches.

San Diego has been wrangling for decades over plans to build a new central library. Meanwhile, as the city sprawled, new branches were constructed in fast-growing areas, but little was done to update facilities in the older neighborhoods. Finally, this summer, the city council settled on a site for the $145 million downtown library, but also decided that the plans should include improvements to the entire system.

Seattle's Deborah Jacobs warns that any library debate about downtown versus the neighborhoods is counterproductive. "I wasn't going to allow myself to get into that," she says. Other recent recruits to the library renaissance, such as Minneapolis and Jacksonville, are taking the same approach and tackling both central and branch library projects simultaneously.

When it comes to building new libraries, "it's the opposite of NIMBY," says Los Angeles City Librarian Susan Kent. Every council member wants to have one in his or her ward, and every citizen wants one within easy walking distance.

The sense of pride and ownership that residents feel toward their branch library is something of a double-edged sword for local government. Deep reservoirs of grassroots support can quickly turn into protests against plans to relocate or consolidate facilities in an effort to operate a library system more efficiently.

In a few cities, tight finances and shifting demographics are forcing officials to make those difficult choices. Last year, the Buffalo and Erie County Public Library system explored a consultant's proposal that advocated reducing the total number of branch libraries in the county from 52 to 39. Within the city of Buffalo itself, branches would have dropped from 15 to 8. The idea was to move to fewer but bigger branches that would be open longer hours. In 22 public meetings over four months, residents resoundingly decried the consolidation proposal. In response to intense opposition from the community and its elected representatives, the library board scrapped the plan last fall.

Carla D. Hayden, director of the Enoch Pratt Free Library in Baltimore, unveiled a master plan four years ago to build a regional branch in each quadrant of the city, in addition to the 26 existing branch libraries. Shortly afterward, however, the city found itself with serious budget problems, and this summer, a frustrated Hayden announced that five branches would be shuttered on September 1. They were chosen on the basis of usage, size, condition, renovation cost, proximity to other branches and the library's ability to maintain a presence in the community.

Mayor Martin O'Malley backed Hayden's decision, but in a city where only half of the schools offer any library service at all, and where several schools and fire stations have recently been shut down, residents were outraged. The libraries "are the last sign of government" in these neighborhoods, says state Senator George W. Della Jr., who represents a part of the city not far from the ill-fated Hollins-Payson branch library. "In this less-than-affluent neighborhood, people cherish that library. They may not have taken out many books, but they used the facility. It's a safe haven for children and seniors."

Della believes that if the library had reached out to the corporate community, some or all of the branches might have been saved. Hayden doesn't think so. "The private sector wants to do public-private partnerships to supplement and enhance services," she says, "but they do not want to replace city dollars just to keep the doors open."

Given the dire fiscal situation, Hayden says she'll be lucky to build two of the four regional libraries in the next decade. Nevertheless, construction is under way on an $8 million, 45,000-square-foot branch in Highlandtown. Supporters believe it will breathe new life into a moribund commercial district. Others are skeptical. "I never have seen a library work as a magnet for business," city council member Nicholas C. D'Adamo Jr. wrote in a letter to the Baltimore *Sun*.

Other cities, however, have seen libraries serve exactly that purpose. In Chicago, Mayor Richard M. Daley refers to them as the "heartbeat of communities" and has been championing them as people-intensive anchors in a larger, holistic approach to the redevelopment of housing, retail, offices, schools and parks in the city's 78 neighborhoods. "The Chicago Public Library," says Eleanor Jo Rodger, president of the Urban Libraries Council, "is in the Chicago business."

The city's library system has all but abandoned the practice of using leased, storefront branches — which tend to be very small and poorly suited — in favor of what Library Commissioner Mary A. Dempsey calls "freestanding 'monumental' buildings that make a bold statement about the city's commitment to these neighborhoods."

Just as Chicago's Harold Washington library spurred revitalization of the South Loop, the city's Near North branch has served as a catalyst for public- and private-sector investment in the long-blighted area around the Cabrini-Green housing project. The library's opening in 1997 has been followed by construction of a new high school, police station, park, several thousand mixed-income housing units and a shopping center that includes a large supermarket and a Starbucks. A diverse mix of people from both Cabrini-Green and the affluent lakeshore area nearby can be found in the checkout lines of both the library and the stores.

In Indianapolis, the College Avenue

branch library also bridges two worlds: the Meridian-Kessler neighborhood, an affluent community with large homes on the National Register of Historic Places, and a low-income area with a history of crime and racial tension that culminated in a "mini riot" between police and the black community in 1995. At its opening, Caroline J. Farrar, executive director of the Meridian-Kessler Neighborhood Association, described the branch library as "the most outstanding asset that has come into this neighborhood in a decade."

Several miles away, on Indianapolis' North Side, is the new Glendale branch, which anchors a retail mall. In 1999, the local library was overcrowded but had no room to expand. At the same time, the owner of the city's oldest enclosed shopping center was looking for an infusion of tenants with drawing power and proposed that the library relocate there.

As library officials pondered the six-block move, 1,300 people signed a petition opposing the plan. "It would have been easy to say no. There were people who felt strongly on both sides of the issue," says Edward M. Szynaka, chief executive officer of the Indianapolis-Marion County Public Library system. "But by the time we opened, some of the very citizens who had been the most vociferous critics were saying it had worked out so much better than anything they could have imagined." With some 3,000 daily visitors to the library, he adds, "I know the owner is delighted with the foot traffic."

While Indianapolis' library-in-a-mall is unique, Seattle is emerging as a national leader when it comes to co-location and collaboration, despite the logistical headaches of such an approach.

Seattle opened its NewHolly branch library in 1999 as part of a neighborhood campus/learning center that also houses a branch of South Seattle Community College, a child care center and a youth tutoring program. The surrounding "urban village" mixes 900 low-income housing units with 200 market-rate homes.

Another branch library, Wallingford, is a $400,000 project in a $5 million building that also houses a family-support center, food bank, meeting hall and social services for the homeless. Plans call for the new $6.5 million Ballard branch to be the centerpiece of a six-block stretch with a park, store and housing for seniors. And the International District library will be part of a complex developed by the Seattle Chinatown/International District Preservation and Development Authority. It will include 57 units of low-income housing, a community center, retail space and underground parking.

"We developed a policy that says we prefer a stand-alone library," Jacobs says. "But what we've discovered is that neighborhood by neighborhood there are different needs. Some absolutely demand freestanding libraries. But in lower-income neighborhoods, in order to achieve other goals, they are developing mixed-use buildings and want us to be part of it."

Philadelphia's Shelkrot says the evidence is indisputable that libraries "can change the look and vitality of an area." The role they have to play now, he insists, "is not one of bricks and mortar, but programs, services and technology."

CHAPTER 37

TORONTO UPDATES ZONING CODE FAVORING MIXED-USE DEVELOPMENT TO REVIVE OLD WATERFRONT AREA

Albert Warson

The city of Toronto's chief planner is an unabashed fan of the intense street activity in Manhattan — people walking, biking, shopping, eating, strolling in parks and near open water while surrounded by crushing traffic, a constant din, and overall congestion. This same kind of street vitality and urban spontaneity is about to wash over Toronto's central waterfront with a diverse mix of commercial, entertainment, sports, residential, infrastructure, and institutional development in all stages — projects recently completed, under construction, poised to start, in the approvals pipeline, or actively planned.

"It's an unusual mix," says planner Paul Bedford, "but natural in a Toronto context because we're evolving slowly. It isn't pre-planned as it is in other cities and that is what cities are about — evolution and diversity, not traditional land use controls. Our waterfront will replicate an evolving city over the next five to ten years. We deliberately took most of the zoning control out of two former industrial neighborhoods down-

town, for example." Over the past 20 months, that dezoning has produced about $660 million worth of development, notably factory building conversions to residential, graphic arts, film, small office, and other uses.

"The reality is that we're coming out of the recession," notes Bedford. Virtually no waterfront development has taken place since the early 1990s for that reason and partly because of a government-imposed freeze to sort out issues of ownership, financing, and future development. The city of Toronto has wound up with what was originally federal government real estate, with, he notes, the provincial government's blessing.

Architect Eberhard Zeidler's firm, Zeidler Roberts Partnership, Toronto, designed the new National Trade Center; Ontario Place, a park/entertainment complex on a manmade island in the city's harbor; the waterfront retail/office/condo complex known as Queen's Quay Terminal; and the World Trade Centre condominium complex.

Originally published as "Toronto's Waterfront Revival," *Urban Land*, Vol. 57, No. 1, January, 1998. Published by the Urban Land Institute, Washington, D.C. Reprinted with permission of the publisher.

Ziedler says he hopes "the public has access and that new development won't block views to the lake. The waterfront," he continues, "is one of Toronto's great treasures." Zeidler applauds the city's unification of waterfront development, although he harbors a greater fondness for Chicago's parklike waterfront. What Toronto is doing, he explains, is "a second-best solution." Forty acres of federal government-owned parkland recently deeded to the city, he adds, is fine "as long as it isn't just statistics."

Trade/Convention Centers

The $120 million National Trade Centre opened last March on the Canadian National Exhibition grounds, with 750,000 square feet of new and 250,000 square feet of renovated space under one soaring roof. A $124 million, 1.1 million-square-foot expansion of the Metropolitan Toronto Convention Centre, a stone's throw from the CN Tower, opened last June. Except for an 11,000-square-foot entrance and a few skylights, all of the multipurpose space is buried under a 15-acre park. Together with what is available in the old above-grade facility, the expanded center encompasses about two million square feet of space, and includes 1,700 underground parking spaces. "It is the first major project in Toronto that links the downtown core with the waterfront through the transitional element of an urban park," says Dan McAlister of Bregman + Hamann Architects, Toronto, the partner in charge of the expansion design. "We also addressed the lake from the entrance, as well as north/south pedestrian and east/west park linkages along the rail corridor."

Residential

Roughly 2,000 residential units are on the central waterfront. With another 1,750

suites in the offing, the waterfront community's population, based on 2.5 persons per suite, could balloon from about 5,000 to about 9,375 by the millennium. The most recent additions are a 16-story atrium on Queen's Quay condominium, two-thirds of whose 289 suites, priced from $55,000 to $94,000, were sold within the first month of marketing, and the Yacht Club, a project with 640 suites priced from $80,000 to $235,000. The Yacht Club, a collaboration of Urbancorp, a Toronto-based developer, and Monarch Development Corporation, a Canadian homebuilder and developer, is by far the largest of the waterfront condominium buildings. Marketing began in late October, with construction expected to be underway next summer.

In the more immediate future, the Beach, a residential development, is under construction on an 82-acre former racetrack site, a few hundred yards from the beaches and legendary boardwalks on the Lake Ontario waterfront. Nearly 1,000 homes will be built, and when it is completed in four or five years, the Beach will be reminiscent of the original model across the street — a historic, tightly knit community informally called "the Beach." Fraser Nelson, general manager of Metrus Development Inc., Toronto, the developer, says once their interests and the ratepayers' were brought close together, they were able to proceed to "duplicate the look, feel, and texture of the existing Beach with a park and open space."

The Beach includes some 50,000 square feet of retail development along a main street boundary and another 45,000 square feet adjacent to a 43,000-square-foot tele-theater (off-track betting by simulcast broadcasts of races at international tracks) under construction in a 28-acre park (out of a total 40 acres) at the western boundary, which is toward the eastern end of Toronto's waterfront. At the opposite end are three highrise condominium projects on Queen's Quay West, a four-lane road with a dedicated light rapid transit line parallel and close to the shoreline.

In addition, the Riviera, a $55 million development with 328 condo suites in twin 18-story towers, was developed by the Kimble Group, Toronto. A $1.2 million marketing budget helped sell 270 of those suites within about ten weeks in the spring, out of a 48,000-square-foot sales center that can be disassembled, reconfigured, and wheeled off to another site with little fuss. The rest of the suites have since been sold, priced from $76,000 to $127,000. The project includes 10,000 square feet of retail, a 15,000-square-foot health club with a 60-foot-long indoor/outdoor pool overlooking the waterfront, and underground parking for 400 cars. Fiber-optic cable will connect each owner to the Internet and provide access to video telephone calling and conferencing, 100-channel cable TV, online security services, and E-mail. Occupancy is scheduled for next December.

500 Queen's Quay West — which, at $87 million, is the most costly condo project on the waterfront — will consist of four interconnected towers. Though construction will not start until this fall, roughly half of the 180 suites in the first two 12-story towers — some of them equipped with fireplaces and whirlpool tubs — have been sold. The two ground-floor levels will include restaurants and retail and service establishments, a fitness club, and a fiber-optic network that also provides Internet access to each suite. The range includes one-bedroom units, which are priced from $87,000, to penthouses, which start at $472,000. The developer is Pacific Century Limited Partnership, a subsidiary of Hong Kong-based Pacific Century Group.

"Queen's Harbour," also being developed by Monarch Development Corporation and Urbancorp, is a $23.5 million, 229-unit condominium project housed in ten-story twin towers, positioned far away from the busiest parts of the waterfront.

"We've tried to orient the building so that most units have a view of the lake, even from the back of the building, where it is wider, with a wraparound view," says David A. George, Monarch's vice president and general counsel. The suites are priced from about $80,000 to $251,000, and more than half have been sold.

CityPlace, a $665 million development by Grand Adex Developments, a Vancouver-based partnership of companies, will be built on a 41-acre site known as Railway Lands West near the CN Tower. Capping 30 years of wrangling over zoning issues and failed proposals for the vacant site near the waterfront, Toronto's city council approved the project unanimously in early October. Construction of 5.2 million square feet of residential development will begin in the middle of this year. Another 200,000 square feet has been set aside for retail, office, and hotel uses. Over the next ten to 12 years, up to 5,200 condo units, in towers ranging from 23 to 46 stores and a 56-story landmark tower, will be built. Grand Adex will devote 18 acres of the site to parks, schools, a community center, two daycare centers, a library, public art, and pedestrian bridges.

Gooderham & Worts Historic District, a well-preserved example of Victorian-era industrial architecture in Canada, is a 19th-century distillery warehouse complex in what once was the world's largest distillery. The 14-acre site is located near the eastern end of the waterfront in a still-functioning industrial neighborhood that includes 95 brick and stone buildings built between 1859 and 1927. The first 95-suite condominium building — already sold out — is being built; construction on another 175-suite tower will likely begin this spring. Prices in the second phase range from $43,000-plus for a 392-square-foot studio to $116,000-plus for a 1,176-square-foot, three-bedroom unit. When Allied-Lyons Pension Funds Limited (Bristol, U.K.), which owns the property, sells it to another pension fund group early this year, a $200 million, mixed-use development that is to accommodate 2,500 residents in 900 residential units will begin. Approvals and financing are in hand for 200,000 square feet of retail; 175,000 square feet of industrial space and 67,500 square feet for a museum, arts center, and interpretive center are planned.

Commercial

FedEx Centre, a $2.6 million, 65,000-square-foot Federal Express regional courier distribution center opened in May and replaced several inadequate, scattered offices downtown. Redpath Sugars completed a $26.8 million expansion and renovation of its sugar refinery on the waterfront last September. Loblaws Supermarkets Limited, one of Canada's largest supermarket chains, is constructing a 70,000-square-foot store scheduled to open this spring.

The most significant commercial developments are those with mixed office and sports uses, or entertainment and retail. Air Canada Centre, a $139 million office and basketball stadium near the lakefront at the foot of Bay Street (the Canadian equivalent of Wall Street), for example, is under construction within the historic facade of a former main post office. The 200,000-square-foot, 15-story office tower will be occupied primarily by a Canadian airline. Its greatest public attraction, however, will be the 22,500-seat Raptors Stadium. The first game at the stadium is scheduled to be played on the opening of the dual-purpose facility in February 1999.

Schools and Cultural Centers

A $7.7 million, 85,000-square-foot school designed to accommodate 350 elementary school pupils opened in the water-

front area last September enabling children to attend school in their own neighborhood. The school includes a gymnasium and meeting and activity rooms for use by the resident adult population as well. An existing elementary school for 200 children living on the Toronto Islands was expanded last fall and accommodates 80 mainland students who spend a week at a time in a nature-study preserve.

The Walter Carsen Centre opened late in 1996 within a 95,000-square-foot unused space in a 13-year-old, upscale lakefront condominium. The $6.7 million center houses the administrative and rehearsal facility of the National Ballet of Canada. A marine interpretive center will be moved, along with a historic steam tug, from a heritage building surrounded by vast parking lots to a 1920s-era warehouse on the water, where the marine museum's tug can be floated once again, at a cost of $1 million.

Parks

The park on top of the convention center expansion, which will someday incorporate a demothballed railway roundhouse museum, and Spadina Gardens, opposite the 500 Queen's Quay West condominium, accounted for about $2 million worth of landscaping recently. An agreement that essentially removed federal and provincial government ownership or financial interest in the waterfront lands, specifically ones controlled by a nonprofit entity called Harbourfront, was negotiated in late 1996. Some 40 acres on the lakeshore side of Queen's Quay were deeded at that time to the city as parkland.

Infrastructure

With the removal of a railway bridge over the street between the convention center expansion and Air Canada Centre, pedestrians can now walk within a covered, climate-controlled passage between Union Station, the main transportation terminal downtown, and the waterfront. This project was accompanied by streetscape improvements — widened sidewalks, street planters, and sidewalk furniture added on Queen's Quay. Retail opportunities along the passageway are being considered. In late July, a $70 million light rapid transit (LRT) — basically a dedicated, dual streetcar line — started running on a 2.3-mile line from a downtown subway terminal to connect with an existing LRT along Queen's Quay. Two streets connecting the convention center expansion and SkyDome to other main streets and the lakeshore expressway will be extended as part of other road and traffic improvements, at a cost of about $9 million.

A two-lane bridge — which will cross a 366-foot channel to the Toronto Island Airport and replace an aging, unprofitable ferry service — has been approved, and the $80 million budget has been allocated by the city council. The project has been deferred, however, to allow for final consultation with residents in the immediate area, but should be under construction by spring. Six bridges are being constructed over the Humber River at a cost of $60 million. A $1.6 million fire station that will adjoin an existing waterfront marine police facility is also under construction.

Entertainment

A $13.4 million reconstruction of 25,000 square feet of food outlets and game-type attractions in the CN Tower entrance is underway. A 300,000-square-foot, $167.5 million second phase — described as an entertainment/sports/retail center with a parking garage connected underground to the Toronto Convention centre expansion —

is expected to start late this year and be completed in 1999, according to Bud Purves, vice president for development for TrizecHahn Corporation, Toronto.

The ten-story, 470,000-square-foot, $33.5 million Festival Hall entertainment/retail complex downtown will be anchored by a 4,300-seat, 14-screen Famous Players theater and Imax 3-D facility, along with restaurants, coffee bars, booksellers, and 415 underground parking spaces. The entire complex is expected to open late this year or early 1999. A three-story Second City Theatre and restaurant costing nearly $2 million was opened a few months ago near the Sky Dome.

At the extreme end of the waterfront is the Docks, a complex offering a dance floor in a converted warehouse, a 41,000-square-foot patio, a nightclub, a 13-acre sports facility, fast food outlets, live entertainment, and special events. Nearby, and also relatively new, is a 160-seat pub.

Near-Term Projects

The city is actively reviewing a number of other waterfront development proposals, such as a 130,000-square-foot Home Depot store; 1,400 residential units on a ten-acre site; a nonprofit Canadian music facility that includes a business center, a hall of fame, an 800-seat theater, and retail outlets in city-owned, renovated silos, at a cost of $32.6 million; and three residential towers on property owned by Canada's largest daily newspaper, located across the street. The Toronto Economic Development Corporation also has made a proposal to attract Price Club and other discount, warehouse-type enterprises to sites on the 420 waterfront acres it manages on behalf of the city. A $53.6 million aquarium at Ontario Place will be funded and built by Ripley Entertainment Inc., owned by Vancouver businessman Jim Pattison. A smaller version opened at Myrtle Beach, South Carolina, in May. The Port Lands, consisting of 1,000 acres of mainly vacant land, could well become the last frontier of development on the central waterfront.

Commenting on how central waterfront development will evolve in the near future, Jeff Evenson, director of central waterfront projects for Waterfront Regeneration Trust, notes "we've made the connection with the downtown core. The challenge now," he says, "is to return this area to a human scale and circulation. After 200 years of being defined by a singularity of use, the waterfront is being defined by a diversity of use. We can once again look at opportunities, at least variations on ones that existed ten years ago." Adds Evenson, "a year ago we were saying we had a billion-dollar waterfront; now it's a $3 billion waterfront. It's at a point unprecedented in the last 30 years in terms of urban development."

CHAPTER 38

Washington, D.C., Stimulates Development by Linking Suburbs to the Inner-City Using Public Transit

Libby Howland

Development markets on the east side of downtown Washington are picking up steam. The opening in December of the MCI Center, the new multipurpose sports and entertainment arena, and the launching of a downtown business improvement district (BID) last summer are two examples of this trend. Mixed-use developments, destination entertainment attractions, and centralized management are the leitmotifs of the area's resurgence.

Though commercial real estate brokers may refer to the 120-block area — roughly bounded by 15th Street, Massachusetts Avenue, 2nd Street, and Constitution Avenue — as the East End, other real estate and civic interests are calling it Washington's "new downtown." Most of the office development now taking place in the District of Columbia is occurring here, where the vacancy rate for Class A space stands at around six percent and average Class A rents — at almost $37 per square foot — are high.

Metrorail subway access was a main reason cited by Abe Pollin, owner of the Wizards basketball team and the Capitals hockey team, for choosing a downtown Washington location for the $200 million, one million-square-foot state-of-the-art arena and destination retail/entertainment complex that many say already has sparked the revival of its down-at-the-heels neighborhood. The MCI Center is built over the Gallery Place-Chinatown Metro station, through which three lines pass — a situation that complicated construction — and it is near four other Metro stations.

According to Pollin, 70 percent of fans in the first weeks of the MCI Center arrived by Metro. Attendance at Wizards games was strong in the five weeks following the arena's opening but less so at Capitals games; however, Capitals games were not selling well earlier in the season when they were held at the US Airways Arena in suburban Landover, Maryland. Seating capacity is close to 20,000 for basketball games and slightly less for hockey. Approximately 100 Wizards, Capitals, and Georgetown University Hoyas games are scheduled annually, and it

Originally published as "Resurgence in Downtown Washington," *Urban Land*, Vol. 57, No. 3, March, 1998. Published by the Urban Land Institute, Washington, D.C. Reprinted with permission of the publisher.

is expected that another 170 concerts and other events will be booked each year.

Crews can accomplish changeovers from one sport to another or to other events in a matter of hours by taking up or installing floors that fit over the ice and rearranging the retractable seats. Also providing flexibility for quick transitions are ample equipment storage and staging areas, truck and bus access to the building interior, and an extensive backstage area that contains dressing rooms for performers, a special super-star suite, locker rooms, a fitness room, a family lounge for players' relatives, and production offices.

In some corporate circles, access to professional sports facilities increasingly is considered an amenity. The MCI Center therefore should have some influence on the market for office development in the neighborhood, and corporations should provide a primary market for the arena's luxury suite and club seat sales. The arena has 110 private suites, which are located at the 19th, 25th, and 31st rows and cost $100,000 to $175,000 a year, with minimum five-year leases. They are well appointed, with 12 theater-style seats, televisions, private restrooms, phones, wet bars, and refrigerators. Associated services include catering, underground parking, and access to a full-service business center that is still under development. Another 3,045 extrawide club seats are located between rows 20 and 31, and their ticket holders enjoy access to the Capital Club, a full-service restaurant and lounge; in-seat foodservice; specialty food concessions; and the business services center. The Capital Club is open to the public for private events. The arena's premium-seating food services are operated by Chicago-based Levy Restaurants.

Perhaps the most unusual aspect of the new MCI Center is its operation as a destination retail/entertainment complex. Plans call for the center to remain open from 9:00 a.m. to 11:00 p.m. daily for nonarena uses.

Among the attractions are Discovery Channel's Destination: DC; the National Sports Gallery, the Velocity Grill, and Modell's Sporting Goods Team Store:

- Destination: DC, Discovery Channel's flagship store, is a 30,000-square-foot, $20 million interactive multimedia complex that opened early this month. Owned by the Bethesda, Maryland-based cable television network, the Discovery Channel store is expected to attract a million customers during its first year. Aptly tagged a cross between a museum and an entertainment center, the store features four themed floors where visitors "explore the universe" through Discovery Channel exhibits — and retail items — in paleo world (level 1), including a 42-foot cast of a Tyrannosaurus Rex skeleton; ocean planet (mezzanine); world cultures and animal habitats (level 2); and outer space (level 3). A state-of-the-art, high-definition theater is on the top level.

- Velocity Grill, a 20,000-square-foot, upscale sports-theme restaurant on three levels, can be entered from the street or from the arena's main and club concourses. It overlooks the Wizards' practice court, which also is used by local recreational basketball leagues. It features on-site video production capabilities and ubiquitous television screens and video monitors.

- The National Sports Gallery — codeveloped by TeamWorks-Sports Consulting Group, the American Sportscasters Association, and the MCI Center — is a 25,000-square-foot sports museum and participatory activities zone. It houses the American Sportscasters Association Hall of Fame and also showcases treasured sports memorabilia. Among the activities that can be enjoyed there are pitching to on-screen major league hitters, putting at the 18th hole of the MCI Heritage Classic in Hilton Head, or tossing the football to on-screen receivers at rookie training camp.

- The 2,500-square-foot Modell's Sporting Goods Team Store features a full line of NBA, NHL, MLB, and NFL team apparel and merchandise, as well as 12 television monitors that show satellite transmissions of on-the-road Wizards and Capitals games and other sporting events.

Another draw for visitors is a behind-the-scenes, one-hour tour offered throughout the day for groups and individuals. Tour stops include team locker rooms; star dressing room; the television control room; the Zamboni ice resurfacing machine; a luxury suite; and *An Insider's View*—a film about the nation's capital that is shown at Destination: DC's theater.

The MCI Center features a number of other advanced technology applications. A high-speed fiber-optic network called arena Net provides tenants with Internet access, intranet capability, LAN/WAN systems, E-mail, and point-of-sales and office systems support. Seventeen interactive arena Net stations around the facility provide visitors with local tourist and MCI Center events information and also entertain them with features such as replays of great moments in sports history or digital postcards in which they appear in scenes with star athletes. A 15-ton suspended scoreboard with 12-by-16-foot video screens using LED (light-emitting diode) technology provides spectators with bright, clear images of the action on the event floor.

One clear impact that the MCI Center already has had is on development activity in Chinatown, a small area north of the arena. After years of what many consider a stagnant existence, Chinatown, with its restaurants and small shops, has become what many characterize as a boom town. Few regret the loss of some of its Chinese character as a price of transformation, although some Chinese residents and business owners fear that the area may change and drive some of them out of business as a result of high rents, huge crowds, and increasing traffic.

Downtown DC BID

Efforts to establish a downtown business improvement district began in the late 1980s, and in 1996 enabling legislation was passed. The imminent arrival of the arena provided the final push, according to Richard Bradley, the BID's executive director. Part of a burgeoning national trend, Washington's downtown BID was approved by the city last August and became operational shortly thereafter.

Directly north of the Mall, Washington's primary tourist draw, the downtown BID encompasses an area that contains 67 million square feet of office space. Fifty million square feet is in private ownership; 14 million square feet belongs to the government; and three million square feet is owned by tax-exempt organizations. There are 6,500 hotel rooms, and a slowly growing residential sector. All Metro subway lines serve the area.

More than a dozen new restaurants opened last year, and more are in the pipeline. Major attractions in the area include a number of theaters — National Theatre, Ford's Theater, Shakespeare Theatre, and Warner Theatre; museums, among them the Museum of American Art, National Building Museum, National Museum of Women in the Arts, and National Portrait Gallery; a concentration of art galleries; the J. Edgar Hoover FBI Building; the Washington Convention Center; and now the MCI Center. The Washington Opera also has tentative plans to build an opera house in the new downtown area, possibly converting the vacant Woodward & Lothrop department store on F Street.

In addition, the city plans to construct

a new, two million-square-foot, $650 million convention center on the north edge of downtown at Mount Vernon Square along New York Avenue by the year 2001. A consortium of developers has put forth a proposal to redevelop the city's current 800,000-square-foot convention center — built 15 years ago and already seen as too small to meet current demand — as an "American entertainment center" containing restaurants, retail venues, and up to 20 movie screens. The location is just three blocks away from the MCI Center.

A recently announced office project speaks to the entertainment focus of new development in the downtown district. The U.S. Mint has signed a 20-year lease with Development Resources Inc. (DRI) for a 232,000-square-foot building that DRI will develop at 801 9th Street. It is scheduled for completion at the end of next year and will occupy 140,000 square feet and lease out the remaining space. The agency is contemplating retail and entertainment uses for the first-floor space, including a historical exhibit about the U.S. Mint.

The downtown BID is a private nonprofit corporation that is run by and accountable to the area's business sector. Its stated purpose is to stabilize and improve the district's environment; retain, expand, and attract businesses and investment; and create a positive identity for the downtown. The BID's organizing effort was overseen by a coalition of area property owners, business owners, and civic and cultural organizations led by Robert Gladstone, president of Quadrangle Development and of the BID planning committee, and by Robert Carr, chairman of Carr Real Estate Development Corporation and the committee's vice president. Its business plan includes six main elements:

Public Safety. Uniformed, unarmed public safety officers have begun patrolling the area as adjuncts to regular metropolitan police patrols. They monitor street activity, provide security escorts and assistance in personal emergencies, and give directions. Together with special street and sidewalk maintenance personnel, they are known as downtown SAM (safety and maintenance) personnel.

Maintenance. Downtown SAM personnel also provide street and sidewalk cleaning services, remove graffiti, maintain street furniture and signs, and provide landscaping services.

Transportation. The BID works with other organizations to improve the district's accessibility by all modes of transportation and to improve directional signage and maps and other visitor guides. Some effort will be made to persuade Metro to extend its operating hours past midnight, especially on weekends.

Marketing. The BID is undertaking a campaign to market downtown Washington to a variety of target audiences and plans to work with local businesses to support activities to bring people downtown.

Physical Improvements. The BID plans to work with the city to implement a multiyear physical improvements program involving street lights, signage, street furniture and landscaping, and visitor-attracting uses like sidewalk cafés.

Homeless Services. Downtown SAM personnel seek to provide helpful information to homeless individuals in the area and to homeless service providers. The BID helps coordinate communication among the providers and works to find support programs for the homeless, including employment in the SAM force.

The downtown BID's budget for its first full year of normalized operations is $7.7 million, distributed as follows:

• Security Programs	$2,400,000
• Maintenance Programs	1,340,000
• Transportation Programs	270,000
• Marketing	910,000
• Physical Improvements	1,150,000

- Homeless Programs   340,000
- BID Operations, including
  program overhead   1,000,000
- Contingency (four percent)   290,000

Its funds come from a BID assessment on taxable commercial real properties within the BID area and from voluntary contributions and contracts for services from tax-exempt properties. First-year assessments are $50 per room for hotels and $0.12 per square foot on net rentable square footage (calculated as 90 percent of gross building area for properties for which net rentable area is not available) and on unimproved land and parking lots. The first-year budget of $7.7 million is expected to be raised from the BID assessment ($6.1 million from 51 million square feet of commercial space); an anticipated contract with the U.S. General Services Administration to sell BID services to government-owned properties in the BID area ($1.2 million); and voluntary contributions from tax-exempt properties ($400,000).

Proceeding by fits and starts, the resurgence of Washington's new downtown has been a long time in the making. With the coming of the MCI Center, the downtown appears to have chosen mixed-use development with an emphasis on entertainment to propel itself into the future.

CHAPTER 39

WASHINGTON, D.C., PROMOTES DEVELOPMENT NEAR TRANSIT STATIONS TO SPUR NEIGHBORHOOD RENEWAL

Alvin R. McNeal and *Rosalyn P. Doggett*

The Washington Metropolitan Area Transit Authority's (WMATA's) chief mission is to provide safe, clean, and reliable public transportation for the nearly four million people in its service region. However, WMATA recognized from the outset that it could recoup part of its public transportation investment by sharing in the value added to land by transit. WMATA has aggressively sought private partners to develop the real property it purchased to accommodate transit stations and related facilities. The authority's public/private land development program has spurred high-density private office, retail, and residential concentrations in many station areas. These improvements, in turn, enhance the quality of life for transit patrons as well as for persons who live, work, and shop in nearby neighborhoods. WMATA's development program is attracting new riders to the transit system, rejuvenating and creating neighborhoods, and augmenting federal, state, and local tax revenues. And it is bringing WMATA significant income, which the authority pours back into the transit system's operating and capital programs.

WMATA was organized in 1968 by the Washington Metropolitan Area Transit Authority Compact among the states of Maryland and Virginia and the District of Columbia. The authority's governing board comprises six voting members and six alternates representing all members of the compact. One of only a few Washington regional agencies with the authority to implement programs, WMATA is charged with providing metropolitanwide public transportation service. The authority operates a rail system that will encompass 103 miles and 84 stations, when current projects are completed, and a bus system with more than 1,300 vehicles. Approximately 6.5 rail miles and five rail stations are under construction and scheduled for completion by 2001. WMATA's combined rail and bus system carries nearly one million riders per day and is the fourth-largest system in the United States; its rail service is the second busiest in the country. In 1997, Metrobus operated 73

Originally published as "Metro Makes Its Mark," *Urban Land*, Vol. 58, No. 9, September, 1999. Published by the Urban Land Institute, Washington, D.C. Reprinted with permission of the publisher.

percent of the total bus service in the Washington region. With increasing pressure to become more consumer oriented and cost efficient, WMATA is energizing its resources to compete with the private sector. To date, it has won contracts to furnish bus and related services in the region's outlying jurisdictions.

Long before the rail system became operational, WMATA's board adopted policies and procedures that formed the basis of the authority's public/private land development program. The first private development project, Rosslyn (Virginia) Metro Center, was initiated in 1973, three years before the Metrorail system opened. To date, WMATA has approved 29 projects; 24 have been completed, providing the authority with nearly $6 million in annual revenue from four million square feet of office space, 0.5 million square feet of retail space, 1,000 hotel rooms, and 300 residences. Since the inception of the land development program, WMATA has realized more than $60 million in real estate income. The yield has also included more than one million new rail trips per year, more than $20 million in annual taxes to localities, and 25,000 primary jobs.

WMATA receives program revenue from two types of projects: private development on property owned by the authority and private development on non-WMATA-owned sites with direct connections into Metrorail stations. On WMATA-owned land, the authority generally executes a long-term, unsubordinated ground lease with private developers. In a few cases, it makes fee simple sales. Ground leases not only provide for a base rent but also for a percentage rent that allows WMATA participation in the success of a project. In several cases, the authority has participated in the refinance or sale proceeds of improvements. Connection agreements usually provide for a simple annual rental fee with periodic escalations.

Success Stories

Situated in the heart of Washington's central business district, McPherson Square had been a deteriorating section of downtown, notorious for its concentration of adult bookstores and entertainment. Today, the immediate area over the station is home to a first-class, 153,000-square-foot, 12-story office building and 11,000 square feet of quality retail space — all on a WMATA-owned 18,000-square-foot site. The project generates $450,000 annually for WMATA and has had a remarkable impact on the immediate surrounding area, which is now home to some of the most prestigious office buildings in the Washington region. The area has come a long way since the McPherson Square Metrorail station opened in 1977.

Constructed on 18,000 square feet in downtown Washington on upscale Connecticut Avenue, Farragut North embraces 144,000 square feet of office space and 42,000 square feet of retail space both at grade and in a below-grade food court. The food court has a direct connection to the Metrorail station and is an early example of this now-popular food service concept. Constructed in 1978, the development provides more than $600,000 in base ground rent and an annual percentage rent after revenues reach a certain level. In 2000, as part of an adjustment every decade, the project also will pay $1 million to the authority in premium rent. Though Connecticut Avenue has reemerged as a sought-after address, the avenue was losing ground to trendier parts of downtown at the time the station opened.

Bethesda Metro Center is one of a number of examples in metropolitan Washington of how the introduction of rail transit has helped revive a decaying inner-suburban retail district. Situated in Montgomery County, Maryland, at the center of the commercial spine of Bethesda, Bethesda Metro Center contains 378,000 square feet of office space, a 380-room Hyatt Hotel, 60,000 square feet of retail space, and more than 1,140 parking spaces. WMATA receives an annual rent of $1.6 million. In addition to its enormous success, Bethesda Metro Center has spurred a host of major private office, retail, and residential developments — all within immediate walking distance of the Metrorail station. Today, downtown Bethesda has more than tripled the development of its pre–Metrorail days. Montgomery County is home to several major corporations and is recognized nationally for the quality of its land use planning.

WMATA's public/private project at the Ballston Metrorail station encompasses 283,000 square feet of office space, 6,200 square feet of retail space, a health club, a Hilton Hotel, and more than 200 residential condominiums. Situated in Arlington County, Virginia, at the terminus of the Rosslyn/Ballston corridor, the project generates a yearly rent of more than $600,000 for WMATA. An outstanding example of how a community can use transit for economic development purposes, the Rosslyn/Ballston corridor, located along an older commercial boulevard, is punctated by five Metrorail stations. Arlington County targeted the corridor and its station areas for intensive, transit-oriented growth and, to that end, provided planning incentives such as density/height bonuses. Rosslyn/Ballston is probably the most successful public/private development corridor in the United States. Since Ballston station opened in late 1978, the corridor has seen more than 12 million square feet of new office development in addition to the development of significant multifamily residential, university, and hotel facilities.

Even after all its successes, WMATA still controls more than 1,000 acres of land that are deemed to have development potential. Much of the acreage is used for surface parking that can be incorporated into parking structures as land values increase around stations, thus freeing up the remainder of the authority's property for development.

Efforts to attract development have required a combination of vigorous entrepreneurship and an improving business climate. During the late 1980s and early 1990s, a regional real estate recession caused development to languish. Recognizing that intensive station-area development was pivotal to greater transit ridership in a time of reduced local and national subsidies, the WMATA board of directors reevaluated its non-fare-box revenue programs — such as advertising, parking, and joint use of rights-of-way for fiber-optic cables — and decided to enhance its public/private redevelopment program to make it more active, credible, responsive, and reliable.

The New and Improved WMATA

More Educational Outreach. The purpose of WMATA's educational outreach program is to inform both developers and communities of the advantages of transit-oriented development. Activities have included a highly successful two-day, transit-oriented development conference cosponsored by the Urban Land Institute (ULI), the Federal Transportation Administration, and other organizations. The conference attracted more than 400 participants. Outreach also extends to frequent presentations to real estate industry and civic organizations.

Active Site Marketing. The authority widely disseminated and advertised a comprehensive solicitation for 33 sites in 1996 and two solicitations for 25 sites in 1999. Each year, WMATA markets remaining sites that become available upon completion of portions of the rail system. It also makes consistent use of an upgraded WMATA Web site and other advertising.

A Clear Procurement Process. To encourage the participation of private entrepreneurs, WMATA has clarified its proposal requirements. In particular, it streamlined its procurement process by reducing the number of review and approval steps to ensure a rapid and flexible response to proposals submitted by the development community. The authority also has spelled out each step so that developers can readily envision the full process. And it has incorporated standard commercial tools, such as business term sheets, into its negotiations.

Local Involvement. Local development officials now play a greater role in the selection of WMATA sites to be marketed for development. Officials help market the sites and provide advice during the developer selection process. Consequently, they are inclined to support developer proposals as well as requests for density bonuses at Metrorail station sites.

Clear Selection Criteria. Criteria for selecting projects take the form of project impacts on ridership, fare-box receipts, rental income to help operate the transit system, and local tax revenues. The viability of the proposed development team is also subjected to scrutiny.

WMATA now operated the most active public/private transit program in the United States. As a result of solicitations issued since 1996, the authority has received 31 proposals for 20 sites and is in varying stages of evaluation and negotiation. In all, the proposals include plans for more than 10 million square feet of office space, more than three million square feet of retail space, and more than 8,000 residences. Six of the projects, for which preferred developers have already been approved by the WMATA board of directors, would generate $88 million in sales and rental revenue over their first ten years. In terms of rental revenue alone, both old and new projects are expected to generate the equivalent of $12 to $15 million of income per year. WMATA also projects the addition of 105,000 new daily trips with the concomitant increases in annual fare-box revenue.

On Tap for the Future

In the heart of downtown Washington, the proposed Gallery Place project will occupy 1.71 acres that abut the city's new 20,000-seat MCI Center and H Street, which is the retail spine of Washington's Chinatown. The project calls for a 22-screen movie theater, 300,000 square feet of retail space, 180 residences, and 90 parking spaces. WHATA's board recently approved the $26 million sale of the property; construction will begin in fall 1999.

The office/retail/residential project at White Flint will locate on 32 open acres in one of Washington's most prosperous suburbs — Montgomery County, Maryland. The site is the county's last large developable parcel at a well-established commercial destination. Though business terms are still under negotiation, it is likely that WMATA will receive substantial rental payment as the White Flint site is developed in stages over the next ten years. Payments will far exceed those from existing public/private development projects. A Montgomery County conference center on an additional 13 acres of WMATA-owned land is also slated for White Flint.

Located within the city of Greenbelt, a Roosevelt-era town in Prince George's County, Maryland, the Greenbelt project would reconfigure station facilities and a 3,600-space surface parking lot within 78 acres at the Greenbelt Metrorail station. The required WMATA parking will be relocated to a structure pursuant to WMATA's policy that the developer must replace at cost any WMATA facilities that need to be moved. The authority will, however, adjust rental/sales rates in accordance with the facility replacement requirement. The newly proposed suburban development will combine WMATA property and an adjacent, privately owned parcel. Project plans include a 1.8 million-square-foot upscale shopping mall, two 200-room hotels, 1.5 million square feet of office space, more than 2,000 apartments, and 300,000 square feet of entertainment retail space. Greenbelt is the largest WMATA project approved to date.

WMATA's development activity is the product of a renewed interest in both suburban infill locations and previously unmarketable inner-city sites. The authority is moving expeditiously to capitalize on a healthy real estate market and to adopt creative approaches, which will likely include special financial incentives that will spur development on certain remaining sites. Without doubt, suburban traffic problems (Washington is second only to the Los Angeles area in traffic congestion) have helped spark an interest in concentrating development near Metrorail stations.

Getting Results

The benefit to WMATA of an additional $15 million in annual real estate rental income cannot be underestimated. Each year, WMATA Compact members must subsidize WMATA transit system operations by approximately $300 million. The equivalent of five percent of that amount earned from real estate revenues is a boon to WMATA operations. Indeed, real estate revenues, including parking and fiber-optic fees, are the single largest source of non-fare-box revenue for WMATA. Further, development earnings can be used at the board's discretion to provide incentives for additional real estate development on sites

that are not as readily marketable as those already developed. In fact, WMATA has established a Transit Infrastructure Investment Fund for less promising sites.

Public/private land development revenue will most certainly pay back the estimated $400 million invested since 1968 by the federal, state, and local governments in WMATA rail system property acquisition. Of that amount, state and local government provided 20 percent, or $80 million. By 2003, WMATA's receipts from the public/private land development program will total almost double that amount, a nearly 200 percent return on local investment.

Metrorail's role as a catalyst for transit-oriented development goes beyond Metro-owned station sites. The Urban Land Institute estimates that Metrorail has generated $15 billion in additional development within the Washington region, and that figure is expected to grow to $20 billion with completion of the 103-mile system. The international accounting firm of KPMG Peat Marwick has estimated that the state of Virginia is receiving a 19 percent annual rate of return on its investment in Metrorail as a result of additional development attracted by the rail transit system.

WMATA's proactive management of its real estate assets has produced the desired results for all parties — the authority, developers, the public, and local jurisdictions — showing that transit agencies can be creative asset managers as well as outstanding mobility managers and that, in fact, the two activities are mutually reinforcing.

CHAPTER 40

THE FUTURE OF MUNICIPAL SELF-INVESTMENT

Roger L. Kemp

The case studies in this volume reveal that cities and towns throughout the country are investing in themselves in a number of different ways. The goal of these efforts is generally twofold: to improve the quality of life in our inner-cities and their neighborhoods, and to attract private investment to these aging downtown areas. Many of these municipal investments go hand-in-hand with private investment. That is, a new downtown library or museum not only improves the quality of life for residents, but may also help clean up an undesirable area, as well as stimulate local commercial activity. Many public improvements bring people back downtown and help jump-start the local economy because people have purchasing power, and commercial activity and small businesses will follow. For these reasons, municipal self-investment projects serve a number of different and worthwhile purposes.

It would not be appropriate for communities to demand federal or state aid to revive their inner-cities and improve the quality of their neighborhoods until they invested in themselves. The first step in any revitalization project, or neighborhood improvement program, is self-help. That is, public officials must invest first in their own city or town before seeking help from others. It also goes without saying that initial

municipal investments should be for basic public infrastructure purposes. If roadways, walkways, streetscapes, and/or transit systems are undesirable or outdated, this serves as a major drawback to community revitalization. After these "basics" have been taken care of, numerous investment options exist to improve the quality of life and stimulate commercial activity in our inner-city areas and their adjacent neighborhoods. The types of incentives available are numerous, diverse, and limited only by one's imagination. Many public improvements bring long-term economic returns that far exceed their initial investment cost.

Figure 1 provides an analysis of these case studies by municipality and type of investment. The many communities examined in this volume used numerous types of incentives. These incentives ranged from arts districts, to building or restoring inner-city parks, to creating open spaces and linear trails, to building such things as museums, libraries, and ports, to name a few. It should be noted that many cities and towns undertake projects simultaneously. They are shown in this figure to describe the major types of investments made by public officials to improve their community. While traditional economic development incentives include financial incentives such as tax rebates, the correct types of municipal investments

FIGURE 1
Analysis of Case Studies in Municipal Investment
(Shown by Name of City and Type of Investment)

Listed in Alphabetical Order by Name of City

Name of City	*Type of Investment*
Atlanta, GA	Low-Density Public Housing New Inner-City Parks
Baltimore, MD	Building Linear Trails Redeveloped Inner-City Harbor Area Restoring and Protecting Public Open Space
Baton Route, LA	Community Involvement in Master Planning Revisions to Existing Master Plans
Berkeley, CA	Community Involvement in Master Planning Creation of Inner-City Arts District Making Downtown Public Improvements
Boulder, CO	Community Involvement in Master Planning Creation of New Transportation Plan Redesign Street Patterns to Restore Neighborhoods and Cluster Commercial Development
Cambridge, MA	Approving Public Art for Community Open Spaces Creating Public Open Spaces Interconnecting Public Open Space with Parks
Charleston, SC	Construction of New Downtown Public Library
Chattanooga, TN	Community Involvement in Master Planning Realignment of Traditional Street Patterns Redevelopment of a New Town Center
Chesterfield County, VA	Building New Library to Anchor Commercial Core Changes to Zoning and Subdivision Regulations Community Involvement in Master Planning Modified Public Roadways with Pedestrian Path Preserving & Maintaining Community Open Spaces
Chicago, IL	Involving Civic Leaders in Downtown Master Planning Process
Cleveland, OH	Involving Civic Leaders in Downtown Master Planning Process Revisions to General Plan and Zoning Regulations
Denver, CO	Protecting Historic Buildings in Downtown Area Providing Downtown Access Using Shuttle Buses and Light-Rail Transit System Raising Revenues for Scientific and Cultural Facilities
DuPont, WA	Changing Traditional Municipal Street Patterns Permitting More Transit-Sensitive Development

Grand Forks, ND	Creating Public Open Space and Walkways Involving Outside Experts in Community Master Planning Process Revitalization of Old River Waterfront Area
Hampton, VA	Creation of Downtown Business Improvement District Creation of Public Streetscapes and Walkways Protection of Sensitive Public Open Spaces & River
Hartford, CT	Building Streetscapes and Walkways Creating Public Parks and Public Open Spaces Restoring Old Downtown Riverfront Area
Hayward, CA	Approving Light-Rail Rapid Transit System Stimulating Downtown Redevelopment
Houston, TX	Building Public Parks and Open Spaces Creation of Public Light-Rail Rapid Transit System Creation of Streetscapes and Walkways
Kansas City, MO	Redevelopment of Aging Train Station to Create Downtown Science Center Revitalization of Old Inner-City Area
Lake Worth, FL	Involving Civic Leaders and Residents in Planning Process Restoration of Municipal Beachfront Property Revitalization of Adjacent Downtown Area
Little Rock, AR	Municipal Investment in Inner-City Area Restoration of Downtown Riverfront Area Revitalization of Aging Capitol Facilities/Area
Madison, WI	Fighting Sprawl to Preserve a Lifestyle Integrating Transportation and Land-Use Planning Involving Public in Planning Process Major New Street and Roadway Improvements
Minneapolis, MN	Involving Citizens in Planning Process Permitting More Flexible Development Standards Revising Old Zoning Laws

Nashville, TN	Involving Stakeholders and Citizens in the
	  Planning Process
	Municipal Investment in Riverfront Area
	Stimulating Private Investment through Public
	  Improvements

New Bedford, MA	Involving Stakeholders and Citizens in the Planning Process Preservation of Cultural and Historical Amenities Restoration of Old Waterfront Port/Whaling Area Revising Existing Street Patterns

Newark, NJ	Creation of an Inner-City Arts District Construction of New Streetscapes and Walkways Making Downtown Public Improvements Involving Stakeholders and Citizens in the Planning Process
Orlando, FL	Improvement of Downtown Public Transportation Investment in Bus Rapid-Transit System
Petaluma, CA	Improving Public Transportation Investing in Parks and Public Open Spaces Involving Civic Leaders and Citizens in the Planning Process Preservation of Old Downtown Area Restoration of Old Train Station Revision of Zoning Regulations Traffic Circulation and Roadway Improvements

Portland, OR	Guiding Urban Growth through Public Transit
	Investment in Public Mass-Transit System
	Involving Public Stakeholders in the
	    Transportation Planning Process
	Protecting and Restoring Nature by Reducing
	    Auto Emissions

Saint Paul, MN	Involving Development Stakeholders in the Planning Process Preserving Downtown Historical Buildings Restoration and Preservation of Riverfront Area Restoration of Urban Ecology in Inner-City Area
Santa Monica, CA	Improvements to Pedestrian and Transit Linkages Improvements to Traffic and Transit Patterns Investment in Downtown Public Landscaping Investment in Streetscapes and Walkways
Seattle, WA	Investment in Public Libraries (Main and Branch) Neighborhood Revival through Public Investment
Toronto, ON, Canada	Public Investment in Infrastructure Improvements Restoration and Preservation of Riverfront Area Revisions of Existing Zoning Regulations Stimulate Inner-City Waterfront Development

Washington, DC	Creation of Business Improvement District
	Promoting Development Near Light-Rail Public
	    Transit Stations
	Stimulating Downtown Development through
	    Citizen Access Provided by Public Mass-Transit
	Using Public Mass-Transit to Connect Inner-City
	    with the Suburbs

may attract private investment, frequently without this type of financial assistance.

In order to make sense out of the numerous types of municipal investments that can be made, they are shown by investment grouping, number of communities using each group of investments, and the actual names of the cities and towns that fall into each of these grouping categories. Nine investment groups are used for this analysis. They include business improvement districts, cultural and historical amenities, protecting and restoring nature, parks and open spaces, planning process and codes, general public improvements, revised street patterns, streetscape and walkways, and public transit system. Figure 2 sets forth this information in order to show the popularity of individual investment groupings.

The popularity of these municipal investment groupings reveals a lot about state-of-the-art practices in this particular aspect of economic development. Figure 3 lists these groups in hierarchical order, starting with the most popular type of investment. This information reveals that many communities have initiated citizen-oriented planning processes that involve major downtown and neighborhood stakeholders. The construction and restoration of cultural and historical public amenities came in second, followed by parks and open spaces, and the protection and restoration of nature. The next four categories included public transit systems, general public improvements, streetscapes and walkways, and changing dysfunctional street patterns. Two communities formed business improvements districts. Under this plan, cities and towns turn over management of downtown areas to stakeholders, who typically levy an additional tax to enhance the level of services provided within the district.

These municipal investment groupings, as well as the types of specific projects being invested in, reveal the evolution of America's cities and towns. Transportation

infrastructure helped to shape the evolution of our cities and towns in many ways. In the U.S., our first major cities were developed around seaports. The second phase of urban growth took place along the networks of rivers and canals during the Industrial Revolution. The railroads generated the third phase of urban development as they opened up inland areas to manufacturing and commercial trade. Major goods processing and distribution centers emerged at rail hubs and terminal points throughout the country. The next phase of urban growth was brought about by the transportation shift to cars and trucks to move people and goods. New highways, freeways, and expressways led to a massive dispersion of housing and commercial activity along these roadways. Shopping malls and office complexes are a part of this trend that continues today.

Many of the types of investments made depend upon the age of a community. For older communities, railroad stations are being restored, as well as port and harbor areas, and aging components of the public infrastructure. There is also a definite trend to bring back nature to our aging cities and towns. This has taken the form of new or restored civic plazas and parks, and to create more open spaces and linear trails. In many cases transportation needed to be improved in the oldest areas of our cities and towns. The antiquated roadways and automobile congestion has given way to a concern for new forms of public mass-transportation, such as bus rapid transit and light-rail transit. Nowadays, when transit investments are made, the areas along these routes, and the transportation hubs they create, sow the seeds of further economic development activities. It is also important to note that public planning, unlike times in the past, is now a more open process, involving major business and neighborhood stakeholders.

As mentioned in the beginning of this volume, the 35 communities examined in these case studies represent 22 states, the

FIGURE 2
Analysis of Case Studies in Municipal Investment
(Shown by Investment Groupings, Number of Cities, and Name of City)

Listed in Alphabetical Order by Investment Grouping

Investment Groupings/Number of Cities	*Name of Cities*
Business Improvement Districts (2)	Hampton, VA Washington, D.C.
Cultural and Historical Amenities (16)	Baltimore, MD Berkeley, CA Cambridge, MA Charleston, SC Chesterfield County, VA Denver, CO Grand Forks, ND Hartford, CT Kansas City, MO Little Rock, AR Nashville, TN New Bedford, MA Newark, NJ Petaluma, CA Saint Paul, MN Seattle, WA
Nature, Protecting and Restoration (10)	Baltimore, MD Chesterfield County, VA Hampton, VA Hartford, CT Lake Worth, FL Little Rock, AR New Bedford, MA Portland, OR Saint Paul, MN Toronto, ON, Canada
Parks and Open Spaces (12)	Atlanta, GA Baltimore, MD Cambridge, MA Chattanooga, TN Chesterfield County, VA Grand Forks, ND Hartford, CT Houston, TX

	Newark, NJ Oakland, CA Petaluma, CA Toronto, ON, Canada
Planning Process and Codes (18)	Baton Rouge, LA Berkeley, CA Boulder, CO Chattanooga, TN Chesterfield County, VA Chicago, IL Cleveland, OH Grand Forks, ND Lake Worth, FL Madison, WI Minneapolis, MN Nashville, TN New Bedford, MA Oakland, CA Petaluma, CA Portland, OR Saint Paul, MN Toronto, ON, Canada
Public Improvements, General (10)	Atlanta, GA Berkeley, CA Kansas City, MO Lake Worth, FL Little Rock, AR Nashville, TN Newark, NJ Oakland, CA Petaluma, CA Toronto, ON, Canada
Street Patterns, Revised (7)	Boulder, CO Chattanooga, TN DuPont, WA Madison, WI New Bedford, MA Petaluma, CA Toronto, ON, Canada
Streetscapes and Walkways (8)	Baltimore, MD Grand Forks, ND Hampton, VA Hartford, CT Houston, TX

	Newark, NJ
	Santa Monica, CA
	Toronto, ON, Canada
Transit Systems, Public (10)	Chesterfield County, VA
	Denver, CO
	Hayward, CA
	Houston, TX
	Oakland, CA
	Orlando, FL
	Petaluma, CA
	Portland, OR
	Santa Monica, CA
	Washington, DC

District of Columbia, and one municipality in Canada. These communities represent all major geographic areas of the U.S. The geographic areas represented include the Four Corners, Great Lakes, New England, Middle Atlantic, North Central, Northeastern, Northwestern, South Central, Southeastern, and Southwestern regions of America. Also, the communities selected for inclusion in this case study book represent various population sizes, different forms and types of municipal government, diverse personal and family income levels, and a variety of political persuasions.

As previously mentioned, the use of municipal investment tools and strategies has evolved primarily over the past few decades. They have typically been applied in a piecemeal and incremental fashion by public officials. Since the efforts of public officials are usually limited to the confines of their own communities, the need exists to codify the available information concerning the best practices for downtown renewal, and neighborhood revitalization. This information must be made available to our local elected leaders, our appointed municipal officials and, most importantly, to the citizens they represent and serve. It has been the goal of this volume to provide the best available case studies in this field, featuring the best practices that can be used in other cities and towns throughout the country in the coming years.

The reader's attention is also directed to the following three appendices contained in this volume. These include a *Regional Resource Directory*, a *National Resource Directory*, and a *Bibliography*. The *Regional Resource Directory* contains a listing of local government organizations and special district agencies included in the case studies in

---

FIGURE 3
Analysis of Case Studies in Municipal Investment (Shown by Investment Groupings and Usage)

Listed in Priority Order Based on Usage

Investment Groupings	Usage
Planning Process and Codes	18
Cultural and Historical Amenities	16
Parks and Open Spaces	12
Nature, Protection and Restoration	10
Transit Systems, Public	10
Public Improvements, General	10
Streetscapes and Walkways	8
Street Patterns, Revised	7
Business Improvements Districts	2

this book. In many cases the specific public agencies involved in making the important economic development decisions in these case studies may be contacted directly. The *National Resource Directory* includes a listing of major professional associations and research organizations serving municipal government in the field of development and redevelopment. Lastly, and possibly most importantly, the *Bibliography* is made up of a listing of books, monographs, articles, and other sources from the fields of development and redevelopment. The editor hopes that these appendices serve as valuable resources for those readers wishing to pursue additional information about case studies in specific, or the field of economic development in general.

REGIONAL RESOURCE DIRECTORY

Local government organizations and special district agencies included in the case studies in this volume, alphabetized by city (county).

Atlanta Housing Authority
Office of the Chief Executive Officer
230 John Wesley Dobbs Avenue, N.E.
Atlanta, GA 30303-2429
Telephone: (404) 817-7463
FAX: (404) 332-0100
Internet: *http://www.atlantahousingauth.org*

City of **Atlanta**, Georgia
Office of the Mayor
City Hall
55 Trinity Avenue
Atlanta, GA 30303
Telephone: (404) 330-6100
FAX: (404) 658-7361
Internet: *http://www.ci.atlanta.ga.us*

City of **Baltimore**, Maryland
Office of the Director
Department of Recreation and Parks
3001 East Drive
Druid Hill Park
Baltimore, MD 21217
Telephone: (410) 396-6690
FAX: (410) 576-9425
Internet: *http://www.ci.baltimore.md.us*

Baton Rouge Area Foundation, Baton
  Rouge, Louisiana
Office of the President and Chief Executive
  Officer
406 North Fourth Street
Baton Rouge, LA 70802

Telephone: (225) 387-6126
FAX: (225) 387-6153
Internet: *http://www.braf.org*

City of **Baton Rouge**, Louisiana
Office of the Mayor-President
City Hall
222 St. Louis Street
3rd Floor
Baton Rouge, LA 70802
Telephone: (225) 389-3100
FAX: (225) 389-3127
Internet: *http://www.ci.baton-rouge.la.us*

City of **Berkeley**, California
Office of the Director
Department of Economic Development
2118 Milvia Street
Suite 200
Berkeley, CA 94704
Telephone: (510) 705-8123
FAX: (510) 644-8830
Internet: *http://www.ci.berkeley.ca.us*

City of **Boulder**, Colorado
Office of the City Manager
Municipal Building
1777 Broadway
2nd Floor
Boulder, CO 80306
Telephone: (303) 441-3090
FAX: (303) 441-4478
Internet: *http://www.ci.boulder.co.us*

City of **Cambridge**, Massachusetts
Office of the City Manager
City Hall
795 Massachusetts Avenue
Cambridge, MA 02139
Telephone: (617) 349-4300
FAX: (617) 349-4307
Internet: *http://www.ci.cambridge.ma.us*

City of **Charleston**, South Carolina
Office of the Mayor
City Hall
80 Broad Street
Charleston, SC 29401
Telephone: (843) 724-3727
FAX: (843) 720-3959
Internet: *http://www.ci.charleston.sc.us*

Charleston County, Charleston, South
   Carolina
Office of the County Administrator
Public Services Building
4045 Bridge View Drive
Charleston, SC 29405-7464
Telephone: (843) 958-4000
FAX: (843) 958-4004
Internet: *http://www.charlestoncounty.org*

City of **Chattanooga**, Tennessee
Office of the Mayor
City Hall
100–11th Street
Chattanooga, TN 37402
Telephone: (423) 757-5200
FAX: (423) 757-5456
Internet: *http://www.chattanooga.gov*

Chesterfield County, Chesterfield,
   Virginia
Office of the Director
Planning Department
Main Administration Building
9901 Lori Road
Second Floor, Room 203
Chesterfield, VA 23832-0040
Telephone: (804) 748-1040
FAX: (804) 748-1502
Internet: *http://www.co.chesterfield.va.us*

City of **Chicago**, Illinois

Office of the Director
City Hall
121 North La Salle Street
Room 1000
Chicago, IL 60602
Telephone: (312) 744-2976
FAX: (312) 742-3738
Internet: *http://www.cityofchicago.org*

City of **Cleveland**, Ohio
Office of the Director
City Planning Commission
City Hall
601 Lakeside Avenue
Room 501
Cleveland, OH 44114
Telephone: (216) 664-2210
FAX: (216) 664-3281
Internet: *http://www.city.cleveland.oh.us*

City and County of **Denver**, Colorado
Office of the Mayor
City and County Building
1437 Bannock Street
Suite 350
Denver, CO 80202
Telephone: (720) 864-9000
FAX: (720) 865-9040
Internet: *http://www.co.denver.co.us*

Downtown **Denver** Partnership, Inc.,
   Denver, Colorado
Office of the President and Chief Executive
   Officer
511–16th Street
Suite 200
Denver, CO 80202-4250
Telephone: (303) 534-6161
FAX: (303) 534-2803
Internet: *http://www.downtowndenver.com*

Scientific & Cultural Facilities District,
   Denver, Colorado
District Administrative Officer
899 Logan Street
Suite 500
Denver, CO 80203
Telephone: (303) 860-0588
FAX: (303) 861-4315
Internet: *http://www.scfd.org*

City of **DuPont**, Washington
Office of the City Manager
City Hall
303 Barksdale Avenue
DuPont, WA 98327
Telephone: (253) 964-8121
FAX: (253) 964-4554
Internet: *http://www.ci.dupont.wa.us*

City of **Grand Forks**, North Dakota
Office of the Mayor
City Hall
255 North 4th Street
Room 109
Grand Forks, ND 58206
Telephone: (701) 746-4636
FAX: (701) 787-3725
Internet: *http://www.grandforksgov.com*

City of **Hampton**, Virginia
Office of the City Manager
City Hall
22 Lincoln Street
8th Floor
Hampton, VA 23669
Telephone: (757) 727-6392
FAX: (757) 729-3037
Internet: *http://www.hampton.va.us*

City of **Hartford**, Connecticut
Office of the City Manager
City Hall
550 Main Street
Hartford, CT 06103
Telephone: (860) 543-8520
FAX: (860) 722-6619
Internet: *http://www.ci.hartford.ct.us*

Riverfront Recapture, **Hartford**,
   Connecticut
Office of the President and Chief Executive
   Officer
One Hartford Square West
Suite 100
Hartford, CT 06106-1984
Telephone: (860) 713-3131
FAX: (860) 713-3138
Internet: *http://www.riverfront.org*

City of **Houston**, Texas

Office of the Mayor
City Hall Annex
900 Bagby
Houston, TX 77002
Telephone: (713) 247-2200
FAX: (713) 247-2710
Internet: *http://www.cityofhouston.gov*

Houston Downtown Management
   District, Houston, Texas
Office of the Director of Communications
1111 Bagby
Suite 2600
Houston, TX 77002-2546
Telephone: (713) 650-3022
FAX: (713) 650-1484
Internet: *http://www.downtowndistrict.org*

City of **Kansas City**, Missouri
Office of the City Manager
City Hall
414 East 12th Street
29th Floor
Kansas City, MO 64106
Telephone: (816) 513-1408
FAX: (816) 513-1363
Internet: *http://www.kcmo.org*

City of **Lake Worth**, Florida
Office of the City Manager
City Hall
7 North Dixie Highway
Lake Worth, FL 33460
Telephone: (561) 586-1600
FAX: (561) 586-1798
Internet: *http://www.lakeworth.org*

City of **Little Rock**, Arkansas
Office of the City Manager
City Hall
500 West Markham Street
Suite 203
Little Rock, AR 72201
Telephone: (501) 371-4510
FAX: (501) 371-4496
Internet: *http://www.accesslittlerock.org*

City of **Madison**, Wisconsin
Office of the Mayor
City Hall
210 Martin Luther King Jr. Blvd.

Room 403
Madison, WI 53703
Telephone: (608) 266-4611
FAX: (608) 267-8671
Internet: *http://www.ci.madison.wi.us*

City of **Minneapolis**, Minnesota
Office of the Director
Planning Department
City Hall
350 South Fifth Street
Room 210
Minneapolis, MN 55415-1385
Telephone: (612) 673-2597
FAX: (612) 673-2305
Internet: *http://www.ci.minneapolis.mn.us*

City of **Nashville**, Tennessee
Metropolitan Government of Nashville and
    Davidson County
Office of the Mayor
107 Metro Courthouse
Nashville, TN 37201
Telephone: (615) 862-6000
FAX: (615) 862-6040
Internet: *http://www.nashville.gov*

City of **New Bedford**, Massachusetts
Office of the Mayor
City Hall
133 William Street
New Bedford, MA 02740
Telephone: (508) 979-1410
FAX: (508) 991-6189
Internet: *http://www.ci.new-bedford.ma.us*

New Jersey Performing Arts Center,
    Newark, New Jersey
Office of the Executive Vice President
One Gateway Center
12th Floor
Newark, NJ 07102
Telephone: (201) 648-8989
FAX: (201) 648-6724
Internet: *http://www.njpac.org*

City of **Newark**, New Jersey
Office of the Mayor
City Hall
920 Broad Street

Newark, NJ 07102
Telephone: (201) 733-6400
FAX: (201) 733-5352
Internet: *http://www.ci.newark.nj.us*

City of **Oakland**, California
Office of the City Manager
City Hall
One City Hall Plaza
3rd Floor
Oakland, CA 94612
Telephone: (510) 238-3301
FAX: (510) 238-2223
Internet: *http://www.ci.oakland.ca.us*

City of **Orlando**, Florida
Office of the Chief Administrative Officer
City Hall
400 South Orange Avenue
P.O. Box 4990
Orlando, FL 32802-4990
Telephone: (407) 246-2226
FAX: (407) 246-3342
Internet: *http://www.cityoforlando.net*

City of **Petaluma**, California
Office of the City Manager
City Hall
11 English Street
Petaluma, CA 94952
Telephone: (707) 778-4345
FAX: (707) 778-4419
Internet: *http://www.ci.petaluma.ca.us*

City of **Portland**, Oregon
Office of the Director
Office of Transportation
1120 SW Fifth Avenue
Room 800
Portland, OR 97204
Telephone: (503) 823-5185
FAX: (503) 823-7576
Internet: *http://www.ci.portland.or.us*

Tri-County Metropolitan Transit District,
    Portland, Oregon
Office of the General Manager
Tri-Met Administration Building
4012 SE 17th Avenue
Portland, OR 97202

Telephone: (503) 962-4831
FAX: (503) 962-6451
Internet: *http://www.tri-met.org*

City of **St. Paul**, Minnesota
Office of the Mayor
City Hall
Room 390
15 West Kellogg Boulevard
Saint Paul, MN 55102
Telephone: (651) 266-8510
FAX: (651) 266-8513
Internet: *http://www.ci.stpaul.mn.us*

RiverCentre Authority, **St. Paul**,
  Minnesota
Office of the Executive Director
175 West Kellogg Boulevard
Suite 501
Saint Paul, MN 55102-1299
Telephone: (651) 265-4800
FAX: (651) 265-4899
Internet: *http://www.rivercentre.org*

San Francisco Bay Rapid Transit District
  (SFBART), San Francisco, California
Office of the Director
1330 Broadway
Suite 1800
Oakland, CA 94612
Telephone: (510) 464-7581
FAX: None Listed
Internet: *http://www.bart.gov*

City of **Santa Monica**, CA
Office of the City Manager
City Hall
1685 Main Street
Room 209
Santa Monica, CA 90401
Telephone: (310) 458-8301
FAX: (310) 458-1621

Internet: *http://pen.ci.santa-monica.ca.us*

City of **Seattle**, Washington
Office of the Mayor
City Hall
600–4th Avenue
12th Floor
Seattle, WA 98104
Telephone: (206) 684-4000
FAX: (206) 684-5360
Internet: *http://www.ci.seattle.wa.us*

City of **Toronto**, Ontario, Canada
Office of the Chief Administrative Officer
City Hall
100 Queen Street West
11th Floor East Tower
Toronto, Ontario M5H 2N2
Canada
Telephone: (416) 397-5707
FAX: (416) 395-6440
Internet: *http://www.city.toronto.on.ca*

Washington, District of Columbia
Office of the City Administrator
John A. Wilson Building
1350 Pennsylvania Avenue, NW
Suites 301 and 302
Washington, D.C. 20004
Telephone: (202) 727-6053
FAX: (202) 727-9878
Internet: *http://www.dc.gov*

Washington Metropolitan Area Transit
  Authority, Washington, D.C.
Office of the General Manager and Chief
  Executive Officer
600 Fifth Street, NW
Washington, D.C. 20001
Telephone: (202) 637-7000
FAX: (202) 962-1180
Internet: *http://www.wmata.com*

NATIONAL RESOURCE DIRECTORY

Major professional associations and research organizations serving municipal governments in the field of development and redevelopment.

Advisory Council on Historic Preservation
Old Post Office Building
1100 Pennsylvania Avenue, N.W.
Suite 809
Washington, D.C. 20004
Telephone: (202) 606-8503
FAX: (202) 606-8647 or 8672
Internet: *http://www.achp.gov*

American Economic Development Council
9801 West Higgins Road
Suite 540
Rosemont, IL 60018-4726
Telephone: (847) 692-9944
FAX: (847) 696-2990
Internet: *http://www.aedc.org*

American Planning Association
122 South Michigan Avenue
Suite 1600
Chicago, IL 60603-6107
Telephone: (312) 431-9100
FAX: (312) 431-9985
Internet: *http://www.planning.org*

American Real Estate and Urban Economics Association
Kelley School of Business
Indiana University
1309 East Tenth Street
Suite 738
Bloomington, IN 47405

Telephone: (812) 855-7794
FAX: (812) 855-8679
Internet: *http://www.areuea.org*

Asset-Based Community Development Institute
Institute for Policy Research
Northwestern University
2040 Sheridan Road
Evanston, IL 60208-4100
Telephone: (847) 491-3518
FAX: (847) 491-9916
Internet: *http://www.nwu.edu/IPR/abcd.html*

Association for Enterprise Opportunity
1601 North Kent Street
Suite 1120
Arlington, VA 22209
Telephone: (703) 841-7760
FAX: (703) 841-7748
Internet: *http://www.microenterpriseworks.org*

Brownfields Technology Support Center
U.S. Environmental Protection Agency
1200 Pennsylvania Avenue, N.W.
Washington, D.C. 20460
Telephone: 1-877-838-7220 (toll free)
Internet: *http://brownfieldstsc.org*

Building Officials and Code Administrators International
4051 Flossmoor Road
County Club Hills, IL 60478-5795

Telephone: (708) 799-2300
FAX: (708) 799-4981
Internet: *http://www.bocai.org*

Center for Compatible Economic Development
7 East Market Street
Suite 210
Leesburg, VA 20176
Telephone: (703) 779-1728
FAX: (703) 779-1746
Internet: *http://www.cced.org*

Center for Neighborhood Technology
2125 West North Avenue
Chicago, IL 60647
Telephone: (773) 278-4800
FAX: (773) 278-3840
Internet: *http://www.cnt.org*

Committee for Economic Development
477 Madison Avenue
New York, NY 10022
Telephone: (212) 688-2063
FAX: (212) 758-9068
Internet: *http://www.ced.org*

Community Associations Institute
225 Reinekers Lane
Suite 300
Alexandria, VA 22314
Telephone: (703) 548-8600
FAX: (703) 684-1581
Internet: *http://www.caionline.org*

Community Development Society International
1123 North Water Street
Milwaukee, WI 53202
Telephone: (414) 276-7106
FAX: (414) 276-7704
Internet: *http://comm-dev.org*

Corporation for Enterprise Development
777 North Capitol Street, N.E.
Suite 410
Washington, D.C. 20002
Telephone: (202) 408-9788
FAX: (202) 408-9793
Internet: *http://www.cfed.org*

Downtown Development and Research Center
215 Park Avenue South
Suite 1301
New York, NY 10003
Telephone: (212) 228-0246
FAX: (212) 228-0376
Internet: *http://www.DowntownDevelopment.com*

Habitat for Humanity International
Partner Service Center
121 Habitat Street
Americus, GA 31709
Telephone: (912) 924-6935, Ext. 2551 or 2552
FAX: (912) 924-6541
Internet: *http://www.habitat.org*

Interactive Economic Development Network
1730 "K" Street, N.W.
Suite 700
Washington, D.C. 20006
Telephone: (202) 223-4735
FAX: (202) 223-4745
Internet: *http://www.iedn.com*

International City/County Management Association
777 North Capitol Street, N.E.
Suite 500
Washington, D.C. 20002
Telephone: (202) 289-4262
FAX: (202) 962-3500
Internet: *http://www.icma.org*

International Conference of Building Officials
5360 South Workman Mill Road
Whittier, CA 90601-2258
Telephone: (310) 699-0541
FAX: (310) 692-3853
Internet: *http://www.icbo.org*

International Downtown Association
190–17th Street, N.W.
Suite 210
Washington, D.C. 20006
Telephone: (202) 293-4505
FAX: (202) 293-4509
Internet: *http://ida-downtown.org*

Local Government Commission
1414 "K" Street
Suite 250
Sacramento, CA 95814
Telephone: (916) 448-1198
FAX: (916) 448-8246
Internet: *http://www.lgc.org*

National Association of Counties
Joint Center for Sustainable Communities
440 First Street, N.W.
Washington, D.C. 20001-2080
Telephone: (202) 393-6226
FAX: (202) 393-2630
Internet: *http://www.naco.org*

National Association of Development Organizations
444 North Capitol Street, N.W.
Suite 630
Washington, D.C. 20001
Telephone: (202) 624-7806
FAX: (202) 624-8813
Internet: *http://www.nado.org*

National Association of Housing and Redevelopment Officials
630 Eye Street, N.W.
Washington, D.C. 20001
Telephone: (202) 289-3500
FAX: (202) 289-8181
Internet: *http://www.nahro.org*

National Association of Regional Councils
1700 "K" Street, N.W.
Suite 1300
Washington, D.C. 20006
Telephone: (202) 457-0710
FAX: (202) 296-9352
Internet: *http://www.narc.org/narc*

National Association of State Development Agencies
750 First Street, N.E.
Suite 710
Washington, D.C. 20002
Telephone: (202) 898-1302
FAX: (202) 898-1312
Internet: *http://www.ids.net/nasda*

National Business Incubation Association
20 East Circle Drive
Suite 190
Athens, OH 45701-3751
Telephone: (740) 593-4331
FAX: (740) 593-1996
Internet: *http://www.nbia.org*

National Center for the Revitalization of Central Cities
College of Urban and Public Affairs
University of New Orleans
New Orleans, LA 70148
Telephone: (504) 280-6519
FAX: (504) 280-6272
Internet: *http://www.uno.edu/~cupa/ncrcc*

National Civic League
1445 Market Street
Suite 300
Denver, CO 80202-1728
Telephone: (303) 571-4343
FAX: (303) 571-4404
Internet: *http://www.ncl.org*

National Council for Urban Economic Development
1730 "K" Street, N.W.
Suite 700
Washington, D.C. 20006
Telephone: (202) 223-4735
FAX: (202) 223-4745
Internet: *http://www.cued.org*

National Housing Conference
815 Fifteenth Street, N.W.
Suite 538
Washington, D.C. 20005
Telephone: (202) 393-5772
FAX: (202) 393-5656
Internet: *http://www.nhc.org*

National Housing Institute
439 Main Street
Suite 311
Orange, NJ 07050
Telephone: (973) 678-9060
FAX: (973) 678-8437
Internet: *http://www.nhi.org*

National League of Cities
1301 Pennsylvania Avenue, N.W.
Washington, D.C. 20004-1763
Telephone: (202) 626-3000
FAX: (202) 626-3043
Internet: *http://www.nlc.org*

National Trust for Historic Preservation
1785 Massachusetts Avenue, N.W.
Washington, D.C. 20036
Telephone: (202) 588-6219
FAX: (202) 588-6050
Internet: *http://www.mainst.org*

United States Conference of Mayors
1620 Eye Street, N.W.
Washington, D.C. 20006
Telephone: (202) 293-7330

FAX: (202) 293-2352
Internet: *http://www.usmayors.org*

Urban and Regional Information Systems Association
1460 Renaissance Drive
Suite 305
Park Ridge, IL 60068
Telephone: (847) 824-6300
FAX: (847) 824-6363
Internet: *http://www.urisa.org*

Urban Land Institute
1015 Thomas Jefferson Street, N.W.
Suite 500 West
Washington, D.C. 20007-5201
Telephone: (202) 624-7000
FAX: (202) 624-7140
Internet: *http://www.uli.org*

BIBLIOGRAPHY

Books

Aaron, Henry J., and Charles L. Schultze, eds. *Setting Domestic Priorities*. Washington, D.C.: The Brookings Institution, 1992.

Baily, John T. *Marketing Cities in the 1980's and Beyond*. Rosemont, IL: American Economic Development Council, 1989.

Barnett, Jonathan. *The Fractured Metropolis: Improving the New City, Restoring the Old City, Reshaping the Region*. New York, N.Y.: Icon Editions, 1995.

Bates, Timothy. *Banking on Black Enterprise: The Potential of Emerging Firms for Revitalizing Urban Economies*. Washington, D.C.: Joint Center for Political and Economic Studies, 1993.

Bawden, D.L., and Felicity Skidmore. Editors. *Rethinking Employment Policy*. Washington, D.C.: The Urban Institute Press, 1989.

Birch, David L. *Job Creation in America*. New York, NY: Free Press, 1987.

Blakely, Edward J. *Planning Local Economic Development: Theory and Practice*. Thousand Oaks, CA: Sage Publications, 1989.

Bleakly, Ken. *Economic Impact Analysis: Assessing a Project's Value to a Community*. Rosemont, IL: American Economic Development Council, 1993.

Burchell, Robert W., et al. *Development Impact Assessment Handbook*. Washington, D.C.: Urban Land Institute, 1994.

Cisneros, Henry G., ed. *Interwoven Destinies: Cities and the Nation*. New York, NY: The American Assembly, 1993.

Clemetson, Robert A., and Roger Coates. *Restoring Broken Places and Rebuilding Communities*. Washington, D.C.: National Congress for Community Development, 1992.

Cohen, Burt, Martha Cohen, and Barbara Cohen. *America's Homeless: Numbers, Characteristics, and Programs that Serve Them*. Washington, D.C.: The Urban Institute Press, 1989.

Downing, Paul B. *Local Service Pricing Policies and Their Impact on Urban Spatial Structures*. Vancouver, B.C.: University of British Columbia Press, 1977.

Dryfoos, Joy G. *Full-Service Schools: A Revolution in Health and Social Services for Children, Youth, and Families*. San Francisco, CA: Jossey-Bass Publishers, 1994.

Elwood, David T. *The Spatial Mismatch Hypothesis: Are There Teenage Jobs Missing in the Ghetto?* Chicago, IL: The University of Chicago Press, 1986.

Fosler, R. Scott. *Local Economic Development: Strategies for a Changing Economy*. Washington, D.C.: International City/County Management Association, 1991.

Harrell, Adele V., and George E. Peterson, eds. *Drugs, Crime, and Social Isolation*. Washington, D.C.: The Urban Institute Press, 1992.

Hatry, Harry, Mark Fall, Thomas Singer, and Blaine Liner. *Monitoring the Outcomes of Economic Development Programs*. Washington, D.C.: The Urban Institute, 1990.

Herzog, Henry W., Jr., and Alan M. Schlottmann, eds. *Industrial Location and Public Policy*. Knoxville, TN: The University of Tennessee Press, 1991.

Kemp, Roger L. *Economic Development in Local Government: A Handbook for Public Officials and Citizens*. Jefferson, N.C.: McFarland, 1995.

_____. *Urban Economic Development: Successful Case Studies from American Cities*. East Rockaway, N.Y.: Cummings & Hathaway, 1995.

_____. *Managing America's Cities*. Jefferson, N.C.: McFarland, 1998.

Kivell, Philip. *Land and the City: Patterns and Processes of Urban Change*. London: Routledge, 1993.

Koepke, Robert L. *Practicing Economic Development*. Rosemont, IL: American Economic Development Council, 1993.

Kolter, Philip, Donald H. Haider, and Irving Rein. *Marketing Places: Attracting Investment, Industry and Tourism to Cities, States and Nations.* New York, NY: The Free Press, 1993.

Kolzow, David R. *Strategic Planning for Economic Development.* Rosemont, IL: American Economic Development Council, 1991.

Ledebur, Larry C., and William R. Barnes. *All In It Together: Cities, Suburbs and Local Economic Regions.* Washington, D.C.: National League of Cities, February, 1993.

Luke, Jeffrey S., Curtis Ventriss, B.J. Reed, and Christine M. Reed. *Managing Economic Development: A Guide to State and Local Leadership Strategies.* San Francisco, CA: Jossey-Bass, 1988.

Lynn, Laurence E., Jr., and Michael McGeary, eds. *Inner-City Poverty in the United States.* Washington, D.C.: National Academy Press, 1990.

Marshall, Edward M. *Small Business Partnerships.* Washington, D.C.: National League of Cities, 1989.

Massey, Douglas S., and Nancy A. Denton. *American Apartheid: Segregation and the Making of the Underclass.* Cambridge, MA: Harvard University Press, 1993.

McLaughlin, Milbrey W., Merita A. Irby, and Juliet Langman. *Urban Sanctuaries: Neighborhood Organizations in the Lives and Future of Inner City Youth.* San Francisco, CA: Jossey-Bass Publishers, 1994.

McNeeley, Joseph B. *Building for the Future.* Washington, D.C.: Fannie Mae Foundation, November, 1993.

Medoff, P., and H. Sklar. *Streets of Hope: The Fall and Rise of an Urban Neighborhood.* Boston, MA: South End Press, 1994.

Milder, N. David. *Niche Strategies for Downtown Revitalization: A Hands-on Guide to Developing, Strengthening and Marketing Niches.* New York, N.Y.: Downtown Research and Development Center, 1997.

Moe, Richard, and Carter Wilkie. *Changing Places: Rebuilding Community in the Age of Sprawl.* New York, N.Y.: Henry Holt and Company, 1997.

National League of Cities. *Accepting the Challenge: The Rebirth of America's Downtowns.* Washington, D.C.: National League of Cities, 1994.

_____, and CH2MHILL. *Working Cities, Winning Ideas: James C. Howland Awards for Urban Enrichment, 1998.* Washington, D.C.: National League of Cities, 1999.

_____ and CH2MHILL. *Working Cities, Winning Ideas: James C. Howland Awards for Urban Enrichment, 1999.* Washington, D.C.: National League of Cities, 2000.

Norquist, John O. *The Wealth of Cities: Revitalizing the Centers of American Life.* Reading, MA: Addison-Wesley, 1998.

Palma, Dolores P., and Doyle G. Hyett. *Accepting the Challenge: The Rebirth of America's Downtowns.* Washington, D.C.: National League of Cities, 1994.

_____. *How to Revitalize Your Downtown.* Washington, D.C.: National League of Cities, 1999.

_____. *Local Officials Guide to Dynamic City Commercial Centers.* Washington, D.C.: National League of Cities, 1990.

Peck, Dennis, and John Murphy, eds. *Open Institutions: The Hope for Democracy.* New York, NY: Praeger, 1993.

Peterson, George E. *Confronting the Nation's Urban Crisis: From Watts (1965) to South Central Los Angeles (1992).* The Urban Institute Press, 1992.

_____, and Wayne Vroman, eds. *Urban Labor Markets and Job Opportunity.* Washington, D.C.: The Urban Institute Press, 1992.

Probst, Katherine N., Don Fullerton, Robert E. Litan, and Paul R. Portney. *Footing the Bill for Superfund Cleanups: Who Pays and How?* Washington, D.C.: Brookings Institution, 1994.

Rusk, David. *Cities Without Suburbia.* Washington, D.C.: The Woodrow Wilson Center Press, 1993.

_____. *Inside Game/Outside Game: Winning Strategies for Saving Urban America.* Washington, D.C.: The Century Foundation, Brookings Institution, 1999.

Schuman, Diane R., D. Scott Middleton, and Susan Giles. *Public/Private Housing Partnerships.* Washington, D.C.: Urban Land Institute, 1990.

Sklar, Holly. *Chaos or Community: Seeking Solutions, Not Scapegoats for Bad Economics.* Boston, MA: South End Press, 1995.

Snyder, Thomas P., and Michael A. Stegman. *Paying for Growth: Using Development Fees to Finance Infrastructure.* Washington, D.C.: The Urban Institute, 1987.

Squires, Gregory D., ed. *From Redlining to Reinvestment: Community Response to Urban Disinvestment.* Philadelphia, PA: Temple University Press, 1992.

Stone, P.A. *The Structure, Size, and Costs of*

Urban Settlements. Cambridge, U.K.: Cambridge University Press, 1973.

Struyk, Raymond, and Michael Fix, eds. *Measurement of Discrimination in America.* Washington, D.C.: The Urban Institute Press, 1992.

Sullivan, Mercer. *More Than Housing: How Community Development Corporations Go About Changing Lives and Neighborhoods.* New York, NY: New School for Social Research, 1993.

Taub, Richard P. *Community Capitalism.* Boston, MA: Harvard Business School Press, 1988.

The Urban Institute. *Special Districts: A Useful Technique for Financing Infrastructure.* Washington, D.C.: The Urban Institute, 1992.

Vidal, Avis C. *Rebuilding Communities: A National Study of Community Development Corporations.* New York, NY: New School for Social Research, 1992.

Weston, Josh S. *Rebuilding Inner-city Communities: A New Approach to the Nation's Urban Crisis.* New York, N.Y.: Committee for Economic Development, 1995.

Wilson, William Julius. *The Truly Disadvantaged.* Chicago, IL: University of Chicago Press, 1987.

Monographs

Atkinson, Maureen, Patricia Falch, and John Williams. *Marketing Your Downtown.* Management Information Service Report, vol. 28, no. 6. Washington, D.C.: International City/County Management Association, June 1996.

Austrian, Ziona, and Henning Eichler. *Urban Brownfields Site Survey: Preliminary Analysis.* Cleveland, OH: Cleveland State University, Levin College of Urban Affairs, April 28, 1994.

Bamberger, Rita J., William A. Blazar, and George E. Peterson. "Capital Planning." *Planning Advisory Service Report,* no. 390. Chicago, IL: American Planning Association, September 1985.

Bartik, Timothy J. *Who Benefits from State and Local Economic Development Policies?* Kalamazoo, MI: Upjohn Institute, 1991.

Binger, Gary, and Janet McBride. *Beyond Polemics: A Discussion of 'The Cases for Suburban Development' and 'Beyond Sprawl: New Patterns of Growth to Fit the New California.'*

Monterey, CA: Association of Bay Area Governments (ABAG), May 1996.

Black, Harry. *Achieving Economic Development Success: Tools That Work.* Washington, D.C.: International City/County Management Association, 1991.

Black, J. Thomas. *Recycling Inactive Urban Industrial Sites.* Washington, D.C.: Urban Land Institute, 1994.

Bowes, David B. "Creating Globally Competitive Communities." *Management Information Service Report,* vol. 28, no. 11. Washington, D.C.: International City/County Management Association, November 1996.

Bradley, Richard H. *Building the New Framework: A Coordinated Strategic Approach.* Washington, D.C.: International Downtown Association, 1992.

_____. *The Downtown of the 21st Century.* Washington, D.C.: International Downtown Association, 1992.

Broachway, G.P. *The End of Economic Man: Principles of Any Future Economics.* New York, NY: W.W. Norton, 1993.

Canter, Larry, et al. *Impact of Growth: A Guide for Socio-Economic Impact Assessment and Planning.* Chelsea, MI: Lewis Publishers, Inc., 1986.

Case, Anne C., and Lawrence F. Katz. *The Company You Keep: The Effects of Family and Neighborhood on Disadvantaged Youths.* Cambridge, MA: National Bureau of Economic Research, 1991.

Center for Community Change. *The HOME Program: A Brief Guide for Community Organizations.* Washington, D.C.: Center for Community Change, 1992.

Darling, David L., Jr. *Setting Community Economic Goals.* Manhattan, KS: Community Development Series (No. L-714), Kansas State University, February 1988.

_____. *Strategic Planning for Community Development.* Manhattan, KS: Community Development Series (No. L-830), Kansas State University, February 1991.

_____. *Understanding Your Community's Economy.* Manhattan, KS: Community Development Series (No. L-776), Kansas State University, October 1988.

Edelstein, M. *Contaminated Communities: The Social and Psychological Impacts of Residential Toxic Exposure.* Boulder, CO: Westview Press, 1988.

Ellis, Brinille Elaine. *Strategic Economic Development.* Management Information Service

Report, vol. 26, no. 2. Washington, D.C.: International City/County Management Association, February 1994.

Frank, James E. *The Costs of Alternative Development Patterns: A Review of the Literature.* Washington, D.C.: Urban Land Institute, 1989.

Gerry, Martin H. *A Joint Enterprise with America's Families to Ensure Student Success.* Washington, D.C.: Council of Chief State School Officers, 1991.

Kelly, Christine K., Donald C. Kelly, and Edward Marciniak. *Non-profits with Hard Hats: Building Affordable Housing.* Washington, D.C.: National Center for Urban Ethnic Affairs, 1988.

Kemp, Roger L. "Clifton's Future Vision Project." *Planners' Casebook* (No. 5). Chicago, IL: American Institute of Certified Planners, American Planning Association, Winter, 1993.

_____. "Financial Productivity: New Techniques for Hard Times." *Municipal Finance Journal*, vol. 10, no. 4, April 1990.

Kirshenberg, Seth D., and Charles Bartsch. *Brownfields: Options and Opportunities.* Management Information Service Report, vol. 29, no. 5. Washington, D.C.: International City/County Management Association, May 1977.

Kotkin, Joel. *The Future of the Center: The Core City in the New Economy.* Los Angeles, CA: Reason Foundation, 2000.

Leiterman, Mindy, and Joseph Stillman. *Building Community: A Report on Social Community Development Initiatives.* New York, NY: Local Initiatives Support Corporation, 1993.

Lichtenstein, G.A., and T.S. Lyons. *Incubating New Enterprises: A Guide to Successful Practices.* Washington, D.C.: The Aspen Institute, 1996.

Martz, Wendelyn. *Customer Service in the Planning Department.* Management Information Service Report, vol. 27, no. 5. Washington, D.C.: International City/County Management Association, May 1995.

Mayer, Virginia M., Marina Sampanes, and James Carras. *Local Officials Guide to the CRA.* Washington, D.C.: National League of Cities, 1991.

McGrath, Daniel T. *An Investigation into the Impact of Hazardous Waste Contamination Liability on Urban Industrial Land Redevelopment in the City of Chicago.* Chicago, IL:

University of Chicago, Great Cities Institute, December 5, 1995.

McLean, Mary L., and Kenneth P. Voytek. *Understanding Your Economy.* Chicago, IL: American Planning Association, Planners Press, 1992

Melaville, Atelia I., Martin J. Blank, and Gelareh Asayesh. *Together We Can: A Guide for Crafting a Pro-Family System of Education and Human Services.* Washington, D.C.: U.S. Department of Education and U.S. Department of Health and Human Services, 1993.

Meyer, Angela D., and Ronald J. Swager. *A Bibliography of Selected Topics in Economic Development Literature, 1987–1993.* Rosemont, IL: American Economic Development Council, 1994.

Moore, Mark H., and Darrel W. Stephens. *Beyond Command and Control: The Strategic Management of Police Departments.* Washington, D.C.: Police Executive Research Forum, 1991.

National Council for Urban Economic Development. *Alternative Approaches to Financing Business Development.* Washington, D.C.: NCUED, 1989.

_____. *Forces in the Economy: Implications for Local Economic Development.* Washington, D.C.: NCUED, 1993.

_____. *Industrial Development Bonds: A Resource for Financing Economic Development.* Washington, D.C.: NCUED, 1994.

_____. *Neighborhood Economic Revitalization.* Washington, D.C.: NCUED, 1994.

_____. *Urban Manufacturing: Dilemma or Opportunity?* Washington, D.C.: NCUED, 1994.

National Conference of State Legislatures. *Breaking New Ground: Community-based Development Organizations.* Denver, CO: National Conference of State Legislatures, 1991.

Nowak, Jeremy, et al. *Religious Institutions and Community Renewal.* Philadelphia, PA: The Pew Charitable Trusts, 1989.

Oakland, William H., and William A. Testa. *Does Business Development Raise Taxes: An Empirical Appraisal.* Chicago, IL: Metropolitan Council and the Federal Reserve Bank of Chicago, January 1995.

O'Connor, James, and Barbara Abell. *Successful Supermarkets in Low-Income Inner Cities.* Arlington, VA: O'Connor-Abell, 1992.

Pierce, Neil, and Carol F. Steinbach. *Corrective*

Capitalism: The Rise of America's Community Development Corporations. New York, NY: Ford Foundation, 1987.

Sampson, Robert J. *Crime and Community Social Disorganization: Implications for Social Policy.* Washington, D.C.: U.S. Department of Housing and Urban Development, 1993.

Segal, Bradley, Katherine Correll, and Robert Dubinsky. *Business Improvement Districts: Tools for Economic Development.* Management Information Service Report, vol. 29, no. 2. Washington, D.C.: International City/County Management Association, March 1997.

Schmenner, Roger W. *Energy Costs, Urban Development, and Housing.* Washington, D.C.: Brookings Institution, 1984.

Stillman, Joseph. *Making the Connection: Economic Development, Workforce Development, and Urban Poverty.* New York, NY: The Conservation Company, 1994.

Swager, Ronald J. *A Bibliography of Literature in Economic Development.* Rosemont, IL: American Economic Development Council, 1987.

_____. *Economic Development Tomorrow: A Report from the Profession.* Rosemont, IL: American Economic Development Council, 1991.

Articles

Albanese, Joe, and Scott Martinelli. "Restoration Renaissance." *Urban Land*, vol. 57, no. 12, December 1998.

Andrews, Clinton J. "Putting Industrial Ecology into Place." *Journal of the American Planning Association*, vol. 65, no. 4, Autumn 1999.

Arrandale, Tom. "Developing the Contaminated City." *Governing*, vol. 6, no. 3, December 1992.

Atkinson, Maureen, and John Williams. "Managing Downtown Revitalization by District." *Urban Land*, vol. 49, no. 9, September 1990.

Bailey, Richard. "Mall Over." *Urban Land*, vol. 57, no. 7, July 1998.

Banikowdki, J.E., K.E. Thomas, and J.L. Zegarelli. "Cleaning Up Without Getting Cleaned Out." *American City and County*, vol. 109, no. 8, July 1994.

Barnett, Jonathan. "Shaping Our Cities: It's Your Call." *Planning*, vol. 61, no. 12, December 1995.

Berger, Renee. "Building Community Partnerships." *National Civic Review*, vol. 73, no. 2, May 1984.

Black, J. Thomas. "Fort Worth: Maintaining Vitality Downtown." *Urban Land*, vol. 57, no. 2, February 1998.

_____. "People, Power, Politics." *Planning*, vol. 63, no. 2, February 1997.

Bogorad, Leonard. "Washington: A New Urbanist Frontier." *Urban Land*, vol. 58, no. 9, September 1999.

Bolan, Lewis, and Eric Smart. "Washington at the Millennium." *Urban Land*, vol. 58, no. 9, September 1999.

Bookout, Lloyd W. "Inner-City Retail Opportunities." *Urban Land*, vol. 52, no. 5, May 1993.

Bourne, L.S. "The Roepki Lecture in Economic Geography — Recycling Urban Systems and Metropolitan Areas: A Geographical Agenda for the 1990's and Beyond." *Economic Geography*, vol. 67, no. 3, July 1991.

Boyd, James, and Molly K. Macauley. "The Impact of Environmental Liability on Industrial Real Estate Development." *Resources*, no. 114, Winter 1994.

Boydell, Thomas E., and Douglas R. Porter. "Building Public/Private Collaboration in Puget Sound." *Urban Land*, vol. 56, no. 9, September 1997.

Bradley, Richard H. "Downtown Renewal: The Role of Business Improvement Districts." *Public Management*, vol. 77, no. 2, February 1995.

_____. "Vive Le Renaissance!" *Urban Land*, vol. 58, no. 9, September 1999.

Bray, Paul M. "A New Tool for Renewing the Central City: The Urban Cultural Park." *National Civic Review*, vol. 83, no. 2, Spring-Summer 1994.

_____. "The New Urbanism: Celebrating the City." *Places*, vol. 8, no. 4, Summer 1993.

Breslaw, Jon A. "Density and Urban Sprawl: Comment." *Land Economics*, vol. 66, no. 43, November 1990.

Building Association of Northern California. "Striking at the Heart of Sprawl." *BIA News*, vol. 5, no. 1, March 1996.

Carlson, David A. "Paving the Way to Economic Revitalization: 'Covenant Not to Sue' Stimulates Redevelopment in Economic Target Areas." *Massachusetts Environment*, vol. 1, no. 9, February 1996.

Clayton, David. "Las Vegas Goes for Broke." *Planning*, vol. 61, no. 9, September 1995.

Coe, Barbara A. "Public-Private Cooperation." *Western Governmental Researcher*, vol. III, no. 1, Summer 1987.

Colley, Sharon. "Housing Opens Door to Redevelopment." *American City & County*, vol. 115, no. 4, March 2000.

Cox, Robert D. "A New Approach to 'Brownfields' in Central Massachusetts." *Massachusetts Environment*, vol. 1, no. 9, February 1996.

Culbertson, Steve, and Jeff Warkins. "Rebuilding Philadelphia's Neighborhoods." *Urban Land*, vol. 56, no. 9, September 1997.

Curtis, Peter G., and Michael C. Bianchi. "Turning 'TOADS' into 'PRINCES': Financing Environmentally Impaired Properties." *Massachusetts Environment*, vol. 1, no. 3, August 1995.

Delores, Hayden. "Using Ethnic History to Understand Urban Landscapes." *Places*, vol. 7, no. 1, Fall 1990.

Dorsett, John W. "The Price Tag of Parking." *Urban Land*, vol. 57, no. 5, May 1998.

Drawas, Neal M. "Remediation Liability Management." *Massachusetts Environment*, vol. 1, no. 3, August 1995.

Ehrenhart, Alan. "The Trouble with Zoning." *Governing*, vol. 11, no. 5, February 1998.

Farrell, Christopher. "The Economics of Crime." *Business Week*, December 13, 1993.

Fernandez, Roberto M. "Space, and Job Accessibility." *Economic Geography*, vol. 70, no. 4, 1994.

Fondersmith, John. "Downtowns in the Year 2040." *The Futurist*, vol. 22, no. 2, March-April 1988.

Fosler, R. Scott. "The Future Economic Role of Local Governments." *Public Management*, vol. 70, no. 4, April 1988.

Foxen, Robert. "Approaching Brownfields: Public, Private Forces Combine to Develop Abandoned Property." *Massachusetts Environment*, vol. 1, no. 3, August 1995.

Frank, Lawrence D., and Robert T. Dunphy. "Smart Growth and Transportation." *Urban Land*, vol. 57, no. 5, May 1998.

Frieden, Bernard J., and Lynne B. Sagalyn. "Downtown Malls and the City Agenda." *Society*, vol. 27, no. 4, July-August 1990.

Froehlich, Maryann. "Smart Growth: Why Local Governments Are Taking A New Approach to Managing Growth in their Communities." *Public Management*, vol. 80, no. 5, May 1998.

Fulton, William. "Are Edge Cities Losing Their Edge?" *Planning*, vol. 62, no. 5, May 1996.

_____, and Morris Newman. "The Strange Career of Enterprise Zones." *Governing*, vol. 8, no. 3, March 1994.

Gallagher, Patrick. "Captivate and Educate." *Urban Land*, vol. 57, no. 2, February 1998.

Gihring, Thomas A. "Incentive Property Taxation: A Potential Tool for Urban Growth Management." *Journal of the American Planning Association*, vol. 65, no. 1, Winter 1999.

Glover, Glenda, and J. Paul Brownridge. "Enterprise Zones as an Instrument of Urban Policy: A Review of the Zones in South Central Los Angeles." *Government Finance Review*, vol. 9, no. 3, June 1993.

Gubala, Timothy W. "The Difference Between Economic Developers and Planners." *Economic Development Review*, vol. 10, no. 2, Summer 1993.

Gurwitt, Rob. "New Alliances." *Governing*, vol. 11, no. 9, June 1998.

_____. "The Rule of the Absentocracy." *Governing*, vol. 5, no. 9, September 1991.

Hahn, Kurt. "When and When Not to Use Incentives to Attract Business or to Retain Existing Businesses." *Government Finance Review*, vol. 12, no. 3, June 1996.

Haider, Donald. "Place Wars: New Realities of the 1990's." *Economic Development Quarterly*, vol. 6, no. 2, May 1992.

Hanan, Fran, and Patricia Vaccaro. "Design 2000." *Urban Land*, vol. 59, no. 1, January 2000.

Hardy, Ruth Ellen. "Citizen Participation." *Planning Forum*, vol. 2, 1996.

Harris, Robert R., and John H. Carman. "Battling the American Dream." *Urban Land*, vol. 58, no. 9, September 1999.

Henning, Ed. "Business Improvement Districts." *Western City*, vol. LXIX, no. 8, August 1993.

Hill, Gary G. "Paying for New Development: The Urban Structure Program of the City of Lancaster." *Government Finance Review*, vol. 13, no. 3, June 1997.

Himmel, Kenneth A. "Entertainment-Enhanced Retail Fuels New Development." *Urban Land*, vol. 57, no. 2, February 1998.

Hoeffer, William. "Using Urban Renovation Experts." *Nation's Business*, vol. 77, no. 1, January 1989.

Holden, Alfred. "Why Toronto Works." *Planning*, vol. 61, no. 3, March 1995.

Hollis, Linda E. "Baltimore: Washington's Neighbor to the North." *Urban Land*, vol. 58, no. 9, September 1999.

Hornick, Sandy. "Context Is Everything." *Planning*, vol. 56, no. 1, December 1990.

Houston, Lawrence O., Jr. "Downtown Managers," *New Jersey Municipalities*, vol. 67, no. 4, April 1990.

Howland, Libby. "Resurgence in Downtown Washington." *Urban Land*, vol. 57, no. 3, March 1998.

Huffman, Richard. "Building on Books." *Urban Land*, vol. 57, no. 5, May 1998.

Hudnut, William H. III. "Downtown: Still the Heart and the Soul of a Region." *Urban Land*, vol. 57, no. 2, February 1998.

Innes, Judith E., and David E. Booher. "Consensus Building and Complex Adaptive Systems: A Framework for Evaluating Collaborative Planning." *Journal of the American Planning Association*, vol. 65, no. 4, Autumn 1999.

Jacobson, Thomas. "Suburban Design: One Step at a Time." *Planning*, vol. 64, no. 5, May 1998.

Jensen, Peter. "San Diego's Vision Quest." *Planning*, vol. 63, no. 3, March 1997.

Jossi, Frank. "Take Me Out to the Ball Game." *Planning*, vol. 64, no. 5, May 1998.

Kay, Jane Holtz. "The Hub Is Hot." *Planning*, vol. 64, no. 3, March 1998.

Kemp, Roger L. "Economic Development: Raising Revenues Without Increasing Taxes." *The Privatization Review*, vol. 4, no. 1, January 1988.

Knack, Ruth Eckdish. "BART's Village Vision." *Planning*, vol. 61, no. 1, January 1995.

_____. "Charleston at the Crossroads." *Planning*, vol. 60, no. 9, September 1994.

_____. "Downtown Where the Living Is Easy." *Planning*, vol. 64, no. 8, August 1998.

Labich, Kenneth. "New Hopes for the Inner City." *Fortune*, September 6, 1993.

Lassar, Terry J. "Bridging a Building Boom." *Urban Land*, vol. 59, no. 2, February 2000.

_____. "On Common Ground." *Urban Land*, vol. 58, no. 10, October 1999.

_____. "Portland's On-Track Development." *Urban Land*, vol. 57, no. 3, March 1998.

_____. "Shopping in Seattle." *Urban Land*, vol. 57, no. 7, July 1998.

Lawson, Quentin R., and John N. Pannullo. "Using Marketing Strategies to Address Local Issues." *Public Management*, vol. 68, no. 6, June 1986.

Leinberger, Christopher. "The Beginning of the End of Sprawl." *Urban Land*, vol. 59, no. 1, January 2000.

_____, and Gayle Berens. "Designing for Urban Parks." *Urban Land*, vol. 56, no. 12, December 1997.

Lewis, N. Richard. "Landmark Housing." *Urban Land*, vol. 58, no. 10, October 1999.

Lockwood, Charles. "Houston's Turn." *Urban Land*, vol. 59, no. 2, February 2000.

Lowe, Marcia D. "Alternatives to Shaping Tomorrow's Cities." *The Futurist*, vol. 26, no. 4, July-August 1992.

Luce, Thomas F., Jr. "Local Taxes, Public Services, and The Intrametropolitan Location of Firms and Households." *Public Finance Quarterly*, vol. 22, no. 2, April 1994.

Mahtesian, Charles. "Showdown on E-Z Street." *Governing*, vol. 8, no. 2, October 1995.

_____. "The Stadium Trap." *Governing*, vol. 11, no. 8, May 1998.

Marshall, John T. "Rebuilding the American City: Bonds of Friendship as Bricks and Mortar." *Planning Forum*, vol. 1, Spring 1995.

McNeal, Alvin R., and Rosalyn P. Doggett. "Metro Makes Its Mark." *Urban Land*, vol. 58, no. 9, September 1999.

Meyer, Peter B., and Thomas S. Lyons. "Lessons from Private Sector Brownfield Redevelopers: Planning Public Support for Urban Regeneration." *Journal of the American Planning Association*, vol. 66, no. 1, Winter 2000.

Miara, Jim. "Residential Rebound." *Urban Land*, vol. 58, no. 9, September 1999.

Milder, N. David. "Crime and Downtown Revitalization." *Urban Land*, vol. 46, no. 9, September 1987

Miller, Robert L. "Narrative Urban Landscapes." *Urban Land*, vol. 57, no. 2, February 1998.

Miller, Terry K. "Sports Venues Bring Economic Energy Back Downtown." *Urban Land*, vol. 57, no. 2, February 1998.

Moon, J. Virgil, and Tom Majors. "An Economic Incentives Ordinance in Cobb County, Georgia, Bears Fruit in a Big Way." *Government Finance Review*, vol. 10, no. 3, June 1994.

Murphy, Linda. "The Land Market: How Is EPA Fostering Redevelopment of Abandoned Urban Properties?" *Massachusetts Environment*, vol. 1, no. 9, February 1996.

Nozick, Marcia. "Urban Issues Program Underway." *City Magazine*, vol. 14, no. 4, Fall 1993.

_____. "Urban Issues Program Underway." *City Magazine*, vol. 15, no. 1, Winter 1994.

Oliver, Gordon. "Portland Revs Up for Action." *Planning*, vol. 60, no. 8, August 1994.

Palma, Dolores P. "Downtown Revitalization." *Municipal Maryland*, vol. 23, no. 4, November 1994.

_____. "Effective Strategies for a Safe Downtown." *Municipal Maryland*, vol. 24, no. 7, February 1995.

_____. "Retaining and Strengthening Existing Downtown Businesses." *Municipal Maryland*, vol. 25, no. 3, October 1995.

_____. "Ten Myths About Downtown Revitalization." *Western City*, vol. LXX, No. 6, June 1994.

_____. "Ways to Revitalize Your Downtown." *American City & County*, vol. 107, no. 11, November 1992.

Palma, Dolores P., and Doyle Hyett. "Born Again: Downtown Revivals Offer Salvation for Cities." *American City & County*, vol. 122, no. 8, July 1997.

Peiser, Richard B. "Density and Urban Sprawl." *Land Economics*, vol. 65, no. 3, August 1989.

Pender, Robert B., and Frank C. Shaw. "Public-Private Partnerships." *Texas Town & City*, vol. 78, no. 6, June 1990.

Perlman, Ellen. "Downtown: The Live-In Solution." *Governing*, vol. 11, no. 9, June 1998.

Platt, Roger. "Recycling Brownfields." *Urban Land*, vol. 57, no. 6, June 1998.

Ressler, Thomas. "Business Incubators." *Western City*, vol. LXIX, no. 7, July 1993.

Robinson, Brian. "Curbing Urban Sprawl." *civic.com*, vol. 3, no. 5, May 1999.

Rodne, Kjell. "Diversifying the Local Economy." *Public Management*, vol. 73, no. 3, March 1991.

Roeder, David H. "Organizing for Economic Development." *Planning*, vol. 59, no. 4, April 1993.

Rosen, Martin J. "Reviving Urban Parks." *Urban Land*, vol. 56, no. 11, November 1997.

Rosenfeld, Jordan M. "Designing Urban Public Plazas." *Urban Land*, vol. 56, no. 12, December 1997.

Roy, Roger. "Orlando: Too Much of a Good Thing." *Planning*, vol. 62, no. 3, March 1996.

Rubin, Herbert J. "Community-Based Development Organizations." *Public Administration Review*, vol. 53, no. 5, September-October 1993.

Russell, Charles. "Environmental Equity: Undo-ing Environmental Wrongs to Low Income and Minority Neighborhoods." *Journal of Affordable Housing & Community Development Law*, vol. 5, no. 2, Winter 1996.

Russell, Peter. "Brownfields Redevelopment: A Developer's Nightmare or a Dream Come True?" *Massachusetts Environment*, vol. 1, no. 9, February 1996.

Rypkema, Donovan D. "Preserving for Profit." *Urban Land*, vol. 57, no. 12, December 1998.

Salvesen, David, and Craig Richardson. "Keeping Up with Growth." *Urban Land*, vol. 58, no. 9, September 1999.

Schweiger, Renate. "Seattle Revitalized." *Urban Land*, vol. 58, no. 10, October 1999.

Serrao, Gregory. "Ghost Towns or Downtowns? Saving the Cities." *Journal of Housing*, vol. 48, no. 5, September 1991.

Sink, David. "The Political Role of City Managers in Economic Development Programs: Theoretical and Practical Implications." *State and Local Government Review*, vol. 15, no. 1, Winter 1983.

Smith, Mark. "Civano: Lessons for a Region." *Urban Land*, vol. 57, no. 7, July 1998.

Starger, Steve. "Reinventing Downtown Hartford." *CT Business*, vol. 1, no. 4, November-December 1998.

Stinson, Shauna. "The Air Up There." *Urban Land*, vol. 58, no. 10, October 1999.

Stokley, Jan. "Community-based Economic Development." *Economic Development & Law Center Report*, vol. 15, no. 2/3, March-June 1985.

Sweazey, John, and Robert Schwartz. "Urban Community Housing." *Urban Land*, vol. 56, no. 11, November 1997.

Tabak, Lawrence. "Wild About Convention Centers." *Atlantic Monthly*, vol. 266, no. 2, April 1994.

Taebel, Delbert A. "Economic Development: The New Kid on the Block." *Texas Town & City*, vol. 82, no. 4, April 1994.

Taylor, Marilyn J. "Newark Turning the Corner." *Urban Land*, vol. 57, no. 2, February 1998.

Turner, Robyne S. "Growth Politics and Downtown Development: The Economic Imperative in Sunbelt Cities." *Urban Affair Quarterly*, vol. 28, no. 1, September 1992.

Ward, Janet. "Cities Engineer Train Station Revivals." *Urban Land*, vol. 114, no. 6, June 1999.

Warson, Albert. "Toronto's Waterfront Revital." *Urban Land*, vol. 57, no. 1, January 1998.

Wassmer, Robert W. "Can Local Incentives Alter a Metropolitan City's Economic Development?" *Urban Studies*, vol. 31, no. 8, August 1994.

Wiewel, Wim, Joseph Persky, and Daniel Felsenstein. "Are Subsidies Worth It?: How to Calculate the Costs and Benefits of Business." *Government Finance Review*, vol. 11, no. 5, October 1995.

Woolard, E.S., Jr. "An Industry Approach to Sustainable Development." *Issues in Science and Technology*, vol. 8, no. 3, Spring 1992.

Voith, Richard. "City and Suburban Growth: Substitutes or Complements?" *Business Review*, Federal Reserve Bank of Philadelphia, September/October 1992.

Voohis, Scott Van. "Betting on Boston." *Urban Land*, vol. 57, no. 12, December 1998.

Wolf, Virginia L. "General Planning." *Missouri Municipal Review*, vol. 51, no. 2, February 1986.

York, Jim. "Miamians at the Gate." *Urban Land*, vol. 56, no. 5, May 1997.

Other

Bendick, Marc, Jr., and David W. Rasmussen. "Enterprise Zones and Inner-City Economic Revitalization" in George Peterson and Carol Lewis, *Reagan and the Cities*. Washington, D.C.: The Urban Institute, 1985.

Bonnell, Barbara. "Inner-Harbor Development." *Lawyers Title News*. Richmond, VA: Lawyers Title Insurance Corporation, May-June 1986.

Farr, Cheryl. "Encouraging Local Economic Development: The State of the Practice." *Municipal Year Book*. Washington, D.C.: International City/County Management Association, 1990.

Gugliotta, Guy. "Rebuilding a Community from the Bottom Up." *Washington Post*, January 24, 1993, p. A1.

Lemann, Nicholas. "Four Generations in the Projects." *New York Times Magazine*, January 13, 1991, pp. 14, 16–21.

Partners for Livable Communities. *In Pursuit of Livability: A Strategic Planning Cooperative*. Washington, D.C.: Partners for Livable Communities, Preliminary Report, 1996.

Prager, Adam J., Philip Benowitz, and Robert Schein. "Trends and Practices in Local Economic Development." *Municipal Year Book*. Washington, D.C.: International City/County Management Association, 1995.

Reisch, Mark. *Brownfields Program: Clean Up Urban Industrial Sites*. Washington, D.C.: The Library of Congress, Congressional Research Service, April 3, 1995.

United States. Congress. Office of Technology Assessment. *The Technological Reshaping of Metropolitan America*. Washington, D.C.: United States Government Printing Office, September 1995.

_____. General Accounting Office. *Report to the Chair, Committee on Small Business, House of Representatives — Community Development: Reuse of Urban Industrial Sites*, Washington, D.C.: United States General Accounting Office, June 1995.

ABOUT THE CONTRIBUTORS

Affiliations are as of the times the articles were written.

Craig Amundsen, Principal of Urban Design, URS Architects, Minneapolis, Minnesota.

Richard Bailey, Director, Chattanooga News Bureau, sponsored by the Chattanooga Chamber of Commerce and the City of Chattanooga, Chattanooga, Tennessee.

Jim Constantine, Director of Planning and Research, Looney Ricks Kiss (LRK), Princeton, New Jersey.

Rosalyn P. Doggett, Senior Development Specialist, Washington Metropolitan Area Transit Authority (WMATA), Washington, D.C.

Nancy Egan, Consultant and Manager, New Voodou, New York, New York.

Alan Ehrenhalt, Executive Editor, *Governing Magazine*, Congressional Quarterly Inc., Washington, D.C.

Barbara Faga, Chairman of the Board, EDAW Inc., an international planning, urban design, and landscape architecture firm based in San Francisco, California; and Managing Partner, EDAW Inc., Atlanta, Georgia.

John Fernandez, Director of Information Services, Department of Community Planning and Development, City of Boulder, Boulder, Colorado.

Jeffrey C. Fluhr, Assistant Executive Director, Downtown Redevelopment District, City of Baton Rouge, Baton Rouge, Louisiana.

William Fulton, Contributing Editor, *Planning*, American Planning Association, Chicago, Illinois.

Hunter Gee, Architect and Planner, Looney Ricks Kiss (LRK), Nashville, Tennessee.

Robert J. Gorman, Consultant and Vice President, MRA International, Philadelphia, Pennsylvania; and President, Gorman Design, Columbia, Maryland.

Jane Hansberry, Administrator (1990–1999), Denver Scientific and Cultural Facilities District, Denver, Colorado; and Ph.D. Candidate in Public Affairs and Public Administration, Graduate School of Public and International Affairs, University of Pittsburgh, Pittsburgh, Pennsylvania.

Lawrence O. Houstoun, Principal, Atlantic Group, Philadelphia, Pennsylvania and Cranbury, New Jersey.

Libby Howland, Freelance Editor and Writer, Tacoma Park, Maryland.

Chris Jackson, Freelance Writer, Ventura, California.

Thomas Jacobson, Director of Planning, Chesterfield County, Chesterfield, Virginia.

Spencer A. Johnson, Principal and Director of Master-Planning, Callison Architecture, Seattle, Washington.

237

Anne Jordan, Managing Editor, *Governing Magazine*, Congressional Quarterly Inc., Washington, D.C.

Roger L. Kemp, Author, Editor, Futurist, and City Manager of Meriden, Connecticut.

Ruth Eckdish Knack, Executive Director, Planning, Bay Area Rapid Transit District (BART), Oakland, California (1995, 1997); and Executive Editor, *Planning*, America Planning Association, Chicago, Illinois (1999).

Terry J. Lassar, Communications Consultant and Writer about Development, Architecture, and Planning Issues, Portland, Oregon.

Charles Lockwood, Freelance Writer, Topanga, California.

Frank Edgerton Martin, Campus Planning Coordinator, Hammel, Green and Abrahamson, Inc., Minneapolis, Minnesota.

Alvin R. McNeal, Manager of Property Planning and Development, Washington Metropolitan Area Transit Authority (WMATA), Washington, D.C.

Sam Newberg, Research Analyst, Maxfield Research, Minneapolis, Minnesota.

Gordon Oliver, Writer on Transportation and Regional Land-Use Issues, *The Oregonian*, Portland, Oregon.

Zach Patton, Intern, *Governing Magazine*, Congressional Quarterly Inc., Washington, D.C.; and Student, Political Science Department, University of Tennessee, Chattanooga, Tennessee.

Martin J. Rosen, President, Trust for Public Land, a national nonprofit land conservation organization based in San Francisco, California.

Judith Rubin, Freelance journalist, Oakland, California.

Denny St. Romain, Director of Finance, CB Richard Ellis, Miami, Florida; and formerly with the Downtown Redevelopment District, City of Baton Rouge, Baton Rouge, Louisiana.

David Spillane, Senior Planner, Vanasse Hangen Brustlin, Inc., Watertown, Massachusetts.

Steve Starger, Freelance Writer, Portland, Connecticut.

Diane Suchman, Project Director, Grand Forks Panel, Urban Land Institute, Washington, D.C.

Christopher Swope, Staff Writer, *Governing Magazine*, Congressional Quarterly Inc., Washington, D.C.

Marilyn J. Taylor, Partner, Skidmore, Owings & Merrill, New York, New York.

Paul M. Twitty, Chief Executive Officer and Founding Principal, Schwab, Twitty & Hanser (STH) Architectural Group, Inc., West Palm Beach, Florida.

Patricia K. Vaccaro, Senior Associate, Dickinson Group, Chicago, Illinois.

Ernesto M. Vasquez, Vice President and Managing Partner, McLarand Vasquez Emsiek & Partners, Oakland and Irvine, California.

Albert Warson, Freelance Writer and Editor Specializing in Real Estate Development, Toronto, Canada.

INDEX